DIMENSIONS OF DEVELOPMENT

History, Community, and Change in Allpachico, Peru

Dimensions of Development traces the effects of development projects on the Andean community of Allpachico, Peru. Allpachico is a *comunidad campesina*, governed by a locally elected council of residents who manage communal property and organize collective work. Over the past twenty-five years, however, development processes have inexorably furthered capitalism in the community. Susan Vincent examines four aid projects that took place in the area between 1984 and 2008 within the context of wider state and global political and economic systems. The projects followed international trends in the field of development, aiming first to improve agricultural production and income and later to teach skills to local women. More recently, the focus has shifted to developing infrastructure in the form of a potable water distribution system and promoting participatory planning by involving community members in the decision-making process about which projects to fund. Vincent examines how these projects played out and the ways in which they reformulated the notion of community to serve the different strategic goals of both local residents and the government and development actors who implemented them.

A unique historical ethnography, *Dimensions of Development* illustrates how state and NGO projects have drawn Allpachiqueños deeper into capitalism and have brought about challenges to the local political structure. However, as Vincent reveals, the *comunidad campesina* remains the group's preferred form of representation. This book details conflicts and contradictions endemic to capitalism, as well as those that result from the incompatibility between capitalist and non-capitalist value systems and how the concept of community is altered along the way. Vincent provides a local-level analysis of the complexities of development processes on the margins of global capitalism.

(Anthropological Horizons)

SUSAN VINCENT is an associate professor in the Department of Anthropology at St Francis Xavier University.

ANTHROPOLOGICAL HORIZONS

Editor: Michael Lambek, University of Toronto

This series, begun in 1991, focuses on theoretically informed ethnographic works addressing issues of mind and body, knowledge and power, equality and inequality, the individual and the collective. Interdisciplinary in its perspective, the series makes a unique contribution in several other academic disciplines: women's studies, history, philosophy, psychology, political science, and sociology.

For a list of the books published in this series see page 223.

SUSAN VINCENT

Dimensions of Development

History, Community, and Change
in Allpachico, Peru

UNIVERSITY OF TORONTO PRESS
Toronto Buffalo London

© University of Toronto Press 2012
Toronto Buffalo London
www.utppublishing.com
Printed in Canada

ISBN 978-1-4426-4449-6 (cloth)
ISBN 978-1-4426-1271-6 (paper)

∞

Printed on acid-free, 100% post-consumer recycled paper with vegetable-based inks.

Library and Archives Canada Cataloguing in Publication

Vincent, Susan, 1960–
Dimensions of development: history, community, and change in Allpachico, Peru / Susan Vincent.

(Anthropological horizons)
Includes bibliographical references and index.
ISBN 978-1-4426-4449-6 (bound).   ISBN 978-1-4426-1271-6 (pbk.)

1. Allpachico (Peru) – Economic conditions.   2. Allpachico (Peru) – Politics and government.   3. Allpachico (Peru) – Social conditions.
I. Title.   II. Series: Anthropological horizons

HC228.A45V55 2011   306.3'098532   C2011-907289-0

This book has been published with the help of a grant from the Canadian Federation for the Humanities and Social Sciences, through the Aid to Scholarly Publications Program, using funds provided by the Social Sciences and Humanities Research Council of Canada

University of Toronto Press acknowledges the financial assistance to its publishing program of the Canada Council for the Arts and the Ontario Arts Council.

 Canada Council **Conseil des Arts**
for the Arts **du Canada**

 ONTARIO ARTS COUNCIL
CONSEIL DES ARTS DE L'ONTARIO

University of Toronto Press acknowledges the financial support of the Government of Canada through the Canada Book Fund for its publishing activities.

For the people of 'Allpachico' and for Marc

Contents

Illustrations follow page 102

Acknowledgments

This book has been a long time in the making, and builds on even longer term research. I gratefully acknowledge funding that led to this particular part of my research from the following: the Social Sciences and Humanities Research Council of Canada Standard Research Grants program, the St Francis Xavier University Council for Research, the Consorcio de Investigación Económica y Social (Peru), and the Mount Allison University Internal Research Grant program. This book has been published with the help of a grant from the Canadian Federation for the Humanities and Social Sciences, through the Aid to Scholarly Publications Program, using funds provided by the Social Sciences and Humanities Research Council of Canada. Parts of Chapter 7 originally appeared in Spanish, published by the Instituto de Estudios Peruanos (Vincent 2005b). Chapter 8 closely follows my article that appeared in *Focaal: Journal of Global and Historical Anthropology* (Vincent 2010). I am very grateful to the editors in both cases for permission to reproduce this material.

I have had the great good fortune of assistance from many of my students, as well as some from the Universidad Nacional del Centro in Huancayo, the latter co-supervised by Dr Manuel Gilvonio. In particular I would like to thank Susanne Matheson, Fabiana Li, Brianne Peters, Gabby DeLucca, Patricia Tumialán Núñez, Rosa Flores Javier, Janeth Castañeda Calderón, Tatiana Salas Bilbao, Andrea Ccahuana Belito, Gabriel Gilvonio Condeza, and Francis Obispo Romero.

In bringing this work finally to press, I must acknowledge the ongoing problem solving of Carla Haley-Baxter, and the superb map-making skills of Evelise Bourlon. Doug Hildebrand was a kind, patient, and supportive editor – just what I needed. I would also like to thank the anonymous reviewers whose critical comments helped strengthen this book.

Gavin Smith has been my intellectual guide since I was an undergraduate. Any insights that I have generated in this book are largely a result of this, while the errors are entirely my own. I also benefited from feedback from my colleagues in the Seminario permanente 'Agua, territorio y medio ambiente' with respect to material in chapters 7 and 8. Jane McMillan and María Manzano-Munguía provided very useful comments on Chapter 6. Jane Helleiner gave me much needed encouragement. The Escuela de Estudios Hispanoamericanos and the Archivo General de Indias in Seville, Spain, provided materials for Chapter 3.

I owe an overwhelming debt to the people of Allpachico who have always made my fieldwork there intellectually and emotionally rewarding, in all the best ways. I am humbled by their generosity. I would like, in particular, to honour 'Ana' and 'Jorge,' both of whom died while this book was going to press. In their different ways they were leaders in Allpachico. I will miss them.

This book could not have been written without the support of Marc Genuist, who makes all things possible.

DIMENSIONS OF DEVELOPMENT

History, Community, and Change
in Allpachico, Peru

1 Development in History in Peru

A young girl runs up the hill carrying a *manta*, a square cloth used for carrying loads on the back. She wanders along paths and fields looking for *bosta*, dried cow dung, for her mother to use as stove fuel. She comes back, herding the cattle belonging to her parents and grandparents, which had been grazing on the stubble of a harvested field all day. The faded manta on her back is full.

The girl was my god-daughter, Melia,[1] a lovely happy child. In 1998 when I watched her set off laughing after school and meander back, I thought of how this peasant image might appear to someone unacquainted with this community and its history.[2] The scene might appear bucolic to some, redolent of tradition and continuity, the strength of family, and mutual support. Another observer might decry the appearance of poverty, the use of child labour, the burning of unhygienic cow dung for cooking, the smoke polluting the Andean air.

Melia and other children her age helped their families with the myriad tasks associated with peasant life on top of their school attendance and homework. Older villagers compared what these children did with the wide range of responsibilities they had had in their youth, worrying that the rural agricultural lifestyle they had known was disappearing. To them, rather than being a typical, unchanging scene, Melia's task was an insignificant fraction of what she should be learning if she was going to continue the family farm.

Bosta could stand as an emblem of how the people of the Peruvian peasant community (*comunidad campesina*) of the place I call here Allpachico (hence, the people are Allpachiqueños) have engaged with the national economy. When I first did fieldwork in Allpachico in the

1980s, most people cooked on kerosene stoves. As inflation rose, and merchants strategized around the sales of kerosene under government price controls, the problems of dealing with quickly worthless money and the lineups involved to get staple goods pushed many women to turn to bosta and whatever twigs they could gather. Bosta became a valued product, and Melia's grandmother Tina, who had several cattle, explained to me one day that it was her 'bank,' allowing her to trade for the services of women who had no cattle of their own. Tina's husband, Jorge, worked in a mining smelter, living in a town 80 kilometres away, and she often needed help to get household and agricultural chores done. His income enabled them to buy the cattle. Bosta helped to mediate exchanges between those with wage income, however uncertain, and those with time to work and who needed money. By the 1990s inflation was under control, but government price controls had vanished and the high prices meant that kerosene and the propane that some wealthy households now preferred were out of reach for many. Bosta, the dung of an animal imported by European colonizers some 450 years earlier, perhaps itself once considered an effective and innovative replacement for the dung of the indigenous camelids, had once again become established as a common stove fuel.

History and prehistory, in more conventionally attractive forms than bosta, figure centrally in the image of the Andes. The mountains themselves look old with their worn rocks and scattered fossils of sea creatures. The ancient cultures that inhabited them in the past are constantly present in romantic configurations that inhabit the pragmatic policies for the future – tourist brochures, politicians, and rebels select from the panoply of prehistoric riches to appeal to their various audiences. In the popular rueful description of Peru as a beggar on a pile of treasure,[3] the country is presented as having been magnificent, and having the potential for a spectacular future, while in the throes of a miserable present.

In this conception, development is the process intended to join past and future. Through development, current ills are diagnosed and treated, in order that the promise embedded in the past can be fulfilled. A host of authors (e.g., Ekholm Friedman and Friedman 2008; Nash 2001; Sider 1988; G. Smith 1989; Wolf 1982) has provided excellent models for understanding how the past helps to shape the future. In Gavin Smith's words (1989: 25–6) 'culture is an engagement with the present mediated by the past.' In this approach history is not determinative but rather sets out patterns to guide possibilities and inform decision making. As Ferguson (1994) points out, history is all too often missing from development practice. In contrast, the present work firmly positions Allpachiqueños in time and place.

This study examines how processes of development have appeared in one Andean community, that of Allpachico, Peru. Allpachico is a legally recognized *comunidad campesina*, a designation that gives it rights to a specific territory, to be governed by a council elected by members of the comunidad (or *comuneros*). This council administers the territory and people, managing communal property (land as well as livestock or other comunidad enterprises) and organizing collective work on this property. Although by law all residents should be registered as comuneros, in practice in Allpachico only a fraction bother to do so. The rest, most of whom do little or no farming, judge that the benefits of membership (e.g., access to collective resources) are not worth the costs (e.g., having to participate in *faenas* – work bees). The term 'community' can also be used to refer to other forms of local collectivity apart from the comunidad. This book acknowledges these different collectivities, some of which are simply based on the self-identification of residents and migrants as Allpachiqueños, and some of which are organized by development processes, such as the groups of women who perform service for food handouts that I discuss in Chapter 6. I will refer to the legal polity as the comunidad and to the other forms as 'community,' 'collective,' or 'collectivity.'

Allpachico comes under the political jurisdiction of a small district municipality I call Piedra Blanca. In Peru's nested political structure, the next level above the municipality is the province, then the region, and finally the state. Allpachico lies at the roots of this political tree, and most of its interactions with other levels of government take place through the municipality. We will see one important instance of this in the discussion of participatory budgeting in Chapter 8.

Allpachico is situated in the Quebrada del Mantaro, or Mantaro Canyon, upriver from the flat, fertile Mantaro Valley (see maps 1 and 2). Unlike areas in the valley, Allpachico has little flat, lower altitude agricultural land; the territory lies between an altitude of 3,500 metres above sea level beside the river and 4,200 on rocky promontories, limiting what can be grown. Not only is Allpachico's land marginal, there is little of it; only slightly more than 1,000 hectares, of which perhaps 200 are arable and 600 usable for pasture. The rest is too rocky for agriculture. The population is split among the main village, also called Allpachico, located beside the river, near the highway and railway; the smaller village of Colibrí, also beside the river, highway, and railway a kilometre farther upriver; and two small highland hamlets called Trebol, a half hour's walk uphill, and Kutru, more than an hour's walk uphill. The lack of resources inside community territory has meant that Allpachiqueños have taken advantage of other features of the region, especially labour migration. The location of the community along the central highway and railway has facilitated migration employment in the regional mining and transport industries and formal and informal sector work in Lima, about 300 kilometres to the west. Over the past century, agricultural production has gradually lost importance relative to other locally based economic activities, and out-migration has increased dramatically. The population of the community has declined from about 600 in the 1980s to about 350 after 2000. Nevertheless, migrants often return to Allpachico during personal or national economic crises.

This analysis of development in Allpachico focuses on experiences between 1984 and 2008, the period over which I have carried out anthropological fieldwork there. I have made twelve trips of between one and seven months, for a total of about two years. My methods have been anthropological: I have carried out participant observation; recorded events and the appearance of the community with photographs and video; regularly carried out censuses of the households in the main village; reviewed community archives and documents; discussed life histories with older residents; and undertaken interviews among both residents and migrants to get specific comparative data. The people of Allpachico have been invariably generous with their knowledge, which is the basis of this book.

By focusing on one place, the community of Allpachico, I am countering some recent trends towards 'multi-sited' ethnography.[4] Works such as Crewe and Harrison's (1998) examination of development practice in places throughout the world have been particularly useful in uncovering some of the key assumptions of development practice. There are also excellent studies of the history of particular projects in single locations (e.g., Ferguson 1994; Gardner 1997; Mosse 2005). In contrast to these, the present work studies multiple development projects in one place over time in order to explore how past projects affect future ones and to trace the impact of these development processes on the people. In addition to allowing a glimpse of the historicity of the moulding of social life, a long-term study of one place also provides for examination of the variety of development practices and processes that have manifested themselves there. Thus, this is not an examination of one type of development practice or process across space, but of various types in their sequential appearance in a certain place.

Not all current or past trends in development practice will be represented in this study, so this is not an exhaustive critique of development practice. Further, there is insufficient space here to discuss all that has happened in the form of development in Allpachico, even if I had information about it all. Allpachico, as a poor peasant community, is a constant target of some form of development practice, if only distantly from some state or multilateral agency policy. A broad definition of development, however, has been used in tracing the history of Allpachico presented here. State projects, policies and structures, international investment, international and national non-governmental projects, along with the collective endeavours of the people themselves all make an appearance, some more briefly than others. Some of the experiences are clearly imposed from outside the community, others arose through bipartite negotiation, and yet others were engendered within the community. Despite this generality, the emphasis here is on specific community or people-oriented forms of development projects, as opposed to policies focused more generally on such goals as increasing national gross domestic product, or building large-scale infrastructure.

Because how specific projects and programs were interpreted in the community was a result of earlier experiences, the presentation is chronological. In this way, the philosophy and intentions of each innovation and intervention are examined not as abstractions, but rather in the concrete ways in which they were implemented in one place. In particular, I trace changes in both the technical and social ways in which people engage in productive processes. In this, I follow the lead of scholars such as Nash (2001), Roseberry (1989), G. Smith (1989, 2006), and Wolf (1982). These writers outline a political economy approach which acknowledges the uneven path resulting when systems of production with distinctive logics of operation are engaged in by real people with historically and culturally patterned goals and strategies, who must deal with both the advantages and the crises devolving from these systems. The plot of this history of change is thus neither inexorable nor predictable – I am interested in how and what happened, rather than in trying to model why certain events occurred (G. Smith 1989: 25).

Thus, this book applies a political economy analysis to long-term historical change in order to trace the social forms of production in

Peru – before the advent of capitalism, but mostly on its continuing advance. Over the past twenty-five years that I have known Allpachico, development processes have inexorably furthered capitalism in the community. To some extent this has happened in agricultural production, although poor land and market conditions have limited the rise of small scale capitalist farming. The people have certainly become increasingly interested in both production for capitalist markets and purchase of commodities, and we will see both of these trends through the book. Most clearly, however, the advance of capitalism has meant that Allpachiqueños have come to conceptualize their labour as a commodity in ever more contexts, including in communal faenas. This involves not simply the happenstance exchange of work for money, but planning and value calculation around the exchange. Significant differences have arisen within Allpachico in terms of property and wealth – the stuff of class. These differences are noted in the analysis below. I do not see these local class fractions as the major dynamic, however. Rather, the most obvious class configuration is the positioning of the bulk of the population as labour. At the same time, it is important to point out that none of these strands of capitalist transformation are complete. This book details conflicts and contradictions endemic to capitalism, as well as those that result from the incompatibility between capitalist and non-capitalist value systems. The book thus provides a local level analysis of the complexities of development processes on the margins of global capitalism.

Plan of the Book

This book explores development over the history of settlement in the region. In Chapter 2, I present the framework that guides the analysis of the material, by outlining a definition of development and its current intertwining with capitalism. I also reflect on the relationship between anthropology and development. Chapter 3 establishes firmly that the people of Allpachico are not without history. The region has been inhabited for about 15,000 years. Over that time different technologies were adopted, invented, dropped, adapted, and imported by the people who lived there and moved around, out of and into the area. There is no linear progression through stages of social organization and no predictable pattern. Nevertheless, both the technology and the sociopolitical structures became more complex while autochthonous or conquering elites devised ways to extract surplus from working commoners for their own consumption and to mitigate the effects of crisis. These processes changed form and direction after the Spanish Conquest, as they had under earlier Inca and Huari ones. Thus, the chapter argues that change is not recent and that an understanding of history does not mean a search for an authentic essential social form, but rather involves recognition that the transformations of the past contextualize the present. It can also give a new perspective on the meaning of development. Thus, a comparison of the dire conditions in Peru in the 1560s and 1570s and the solutions proposed by the Spanish with today's discussions of development points to some significant similarities alongside the obvious differences.

Chapter 4 picks up the historical tale with the early twentieth century legal re-establishment of the indigenous community and continues through the now-you-see-it-now-you-don't waning and waxing of community development in different forms. As Cowen and Shenton (1996) observe, community is frequently reinvoked in development policy to address the ills caused by earlier forms of development. Tracing the trail of community forms in Allpachico shows that it is not only reinvoked, but reformulated to serve different strategic goals of its members and the government or development actors who implement it.

With the discussion of community in Chapter 4 we begin our perusal of people-oriented development strategies. Chapter 5 examines an Integrated Rural Development project with the goal of improving agricultural production and income. Occurring during the worst years of economic and political upheaval at the end of the 1980s and early 1990s, the project did not, and probably could not, achieve its goals. It had effects, however, in informing how Allpachiqueños viewed future projects, as well as leaving resources that could be invested in them.

While the community as a constituted political entity, that is, as the comunidad, was the subject of the Integrated Rural Development project, in the 1990s more projects were targeted at individuals such as women and children. This form of development intervention is the focus of Chapter 6. Selecting individuals with a specific identity trait, in this case women, to receive benefits both undermined the strength of the comunidad and fed into higher levels of political networking. The contradictions of empowering the marginalized recipients of these projects are clear as the women learned to navigate ephemeral and clientelistic collectivities. The skills they learned were pragmatically valuable, if not entirely what was envisioned in the theory. The training also incited closer integration into capitalist markets.

After these two decades of experience-seeking projects, having them fail to materialize, or managing to derive what benefit they could from projects in disarray, Allpachico received an infrastructure project to build a potable water distribution system in the early 2000s. This project, led by a non-governmental organization (NGO), is the subject of Chapter 7. The emphasis on infrastructure, while around since Robert McNamara's 1970s Basic Human Needs blueprint, has been reinvigorated with the United Nations' Millennium Development Goals to be met by 2015. In the current iteration, community participation (that is, contributions of labour, materials, and money) has been identified by the World Bank as essential to reaching the goals and ensuring sustainability (Coirolo et al. 2001). The position is contradictory, however, in assuming on the one hand that there are intimate supportive bonds of community and, on the other, that people will apply capitalist economic rationality. In Allpachico the NGO's insistence on equal treatment of all participants actually called attention to inequalities among them. This project also demonstrates the growing tendency of Allpachiqueños to calculate the exchange value of their labour. Finally, it invoked a new way of understanding community – one defined geographically and infrastructurally as those who will benefit from a specific spatial service grid.

Communities were rethought once again as the post-Fujimori regime after 2001 threw Peru into the era of governance in development, manifested through structures to decentralize political decision making and finances to regional and local governments. Chapter 8 examines how this began to play out in Allpachico as budget priorities in the municipality were set through a participatory process. The interplay of possibility, the desire for political display, and new structural and practical forms of community are leading to certain kinds of projects being prioritized, others being funded, and yet others, which were recently deeply desired, being relegated to lower places on the list. In the process, we see how participatory budgeting, while theoretically promoting an accounting system that allots scarce resources to prioritized needs, is actually distorted by the varied interests of politicians and Allpachiqueños.

The conclusion will return to the theoretical foundations of Chapter 2, to which I now turn.

2 Anthropology, Development, and Capitalism

In this chapter I set out the concepts that underpin the analysis in this book. I begin by sketching the structure of capitalism, with a brief note on the unfolding of capitalism in Peru. This is followed by a discussion of definitions of development, with an emphasis on how development is linked to capitalist expansion. I then map the main development actors to show how they are linked to general historical trends. Finally, I discuss the relationship between anthropology and development, and use a famous development project in Vicos, Peru, to illustrate a history of trends in development practice.

Capitalism and Commodification

This account of development in Allpachico demonstrates how people of this region have dealt with attempts to extract their labour as well as how various political and productive risks have been addressed over millennia, more particularly focusing on the percolation of the logic of capitalism into the lives of these community members over the past twenty-five or thirty years. Capitalism constitutes a form of what Wolf (1999: 5–6) calls 'structural power.' It sets up social relations of production that impel and constrain action, and informs models of understanding. The classic Marxist industrial model (e.g., Wolf 1982: 77–9), pits two classes against each other: the capitalists who own the means of production (e.g., land, factories, machinery) and the workers who use these resources to do the actual production. The workers, without access to a means of surviving through their own property, must sell their labour power to the capitalists in return for a wage. The capitalists, in paying wages that are below the value of what the workers produce, extract surplus value, while the workers seek to retain this as part of their wages. Capitalist investors, forced by competition to lower production costs, try to lower wages and use technology to achieve ever-higher productivity.

So far this system is presented as a mechanical model set in motion by the impersonal demand for capitalist profit. However, as Roseberry (1989: 173) points out, the mechanically driven necessities of the model are implemented by humans who engage to protect what they see as their interests. It is through the struggles of capitalists to derive profits and workers to gain or improve access to livelihood that actual historical capitalist social formations – which may bear only tenuous similarity to the model – arise and are transformed. Both Wolf and Roseberry contend that, as a result, capitalist development is uneven. The focus of both is on the expansion of capitalism to other regions with distinct productive systems, for example, through European expansion. Their insistence on capitalism as a system of *production* is asserted in opposition to the dependency and world systems theory claims of Frank (1967) and Wallerstein (1974), who claimed that the poverty of the underdeveloped world was because of these countries' marginal position with respect to capitalist *trade* with the central dominant capitalist countries. Further, against Rey's outline of how capitalism articulates with non-capitalist modes of production, leading inevitably to the supremacy of capitalism, Roseberry (1989: 162–9) points out that this was only one possible result that Marx envisioned of such an encounter. The other two possibilities involved leaving the non-capitalist system in place and extracting wealth through tribute, and a new synthesis of the two. It is this last that Roseberry finds most interesting and with the most relevance for understanding the current complicated mixture of production systems in Latin America, and accords a role to historical cultural experience. The mixture is not of distinct systems that interact, but of new syntheses arising from the clash of those involved. Building on Fried's discussion of tribes as 'secondary sociopolitical phenomena,' brought into being as a result of the intervention of a state or other complex form of society, Wolf (1982: 76) declares 'I believe that all human societies of which we have record are "secondary," indeed often tertiary, quaternary, or centenary.' That is, capitalism, like other productive systems, slithers along diverted by the people who engage in it, deepening here, mixing with other forms of labour extraction there, experimenting with new forms to overcome the crises resulting from its own contradictions[1] or the vagaries of human action, all elastically governed by the rules of capital accumulation.[2]

In this view, variations of capitalist production relations not only spread, they also infiltrate as those who encounter the system re-evaluate their labour power (e.g., Chevalier 1982; Taussig 1980), various goods[3] and services[4] and their relations with others.[5] Along with class formation mentioned above, the process of commodification is a central element in capitalism. It is complex and can focus on different things in different cultural contexts. Castree (2003) provides an overview of the range of dimensions that have been identified as manifestations of a process of commodification. These are the following: privatization, alienability, individuation, abstraction, valuation, and displacement. These features are visible in the chapters to come and so merit defini-tion here. For a thing to be a commodity, it must be privately ownable, rather than a free social good. Naturally occurring goods such as water and land, for instance, have come to be privatized. This is required for a good to be sold by the person who produced it, that is, to be alienable. Individuation means that the good can be separated from its supporting context – as might happen if a religious icon, for instance, were taken from its shrine, or water from its source. Abstraction refers to the means by which one item is deemed equivalent to another similar item for purposes of replacement or valuation. For example, a mining company that contaminates one lake may create an artificial one in replacement. Valuation is a very key aspect of commodification and one that will receive much attention below. This refers to the calculation of an ex-change value for an item, rather than simply its use value as something that can be consumed. Further, this value is linked to wider capitalist processes, such as the drive to achieve profits. The valuation of labour in particular is critical to the calculation of the exchange value of other commodities. Finally, displacement hides the labour that goes into a commodity, making the value of the commodity appear as a property of the thing itself, rather than arising from the human-wrought form of its production.

Commodification and class formation are intertwined, as labour power is a basic commodity in this system. As we will see in the book, there is no general template, consistency, or inexorability to how these processes unfold. Sometimes commodification is resisted – as Taussig (1980) argued for Colombian peasant-workers; and at other times people energetically engage in transforming whatever they can find into commodities, as might happen in the informal sector[6] (Hart 1973; Mac-Ewan Scott 1979). Employers may endeavour to attract a labour force free from ties to land or other productive forces in order to control them better, as occurred during the development of capitalism in Europe. Alternatively, they may resist the conceptualization of their workers as pure workers, such as when employers of child care givers use the idiom of family to justify low wages and tight surveillance. Thus, resistance to capitalist commodification may come from either workers or employers.

The Peruvian process has been particularly uneven, fragmented, and disrupted. I focus here on the central highlands where Allpachico is located. As described by Manrique (1988: 138–9), a merchant capitalist class developed on the coast of Peru in the nineteenth century, but was checked by the War of the Pacific with Chile (1879–83). During the war's campaign in the central highlands, crosscutting interests pitted the indigenous peasantry (who fought the Chilean invaders) against the large landowners (who tended to see Chilean victory as inevitable). There is a debate about the motivations of the peasantry, reflecting, as numerous analysts have observed, that the politics of class formation have been complicated by the politics of race (Flores Galindo 2010; Mallon 1995; Manrique 1987, 1988; Thurner 1995, 1997). Geographic location is another important factor. After the war, the balance of power shifted away from the large landowners in the central (but not the southern) highlands, when many peasant communities were rewarded for their patriotism by greater political autonomy (Manrique 1988).

At the end of the nineteenth century, a new factor entered the dynamic as foreign investment in mining constituted a powerful force of capitalist expansion in the central highlands. Again, the effects were various. In one tendency, Mallon (1983) and Laite (1978) observe that peasants in some communities used wages from periodic work in the mines to support small capitalist farms and businesses, fomenting class divisions within communities, even while they resisted the pressure to proletarianize. Another pattern took hold in Allpachico, where the lack of land and resources has tended to support proletarianization rather than significant internal class divisions. Both of these tendencies were disrupted by a prolonged series of economic crises between 1975 and 1990 that negatively affected both agriculture and industry (Hopkins 1998: 89).

This book seeks to examine more closely the local level manifestation of the fraught unfolding of capitalism in Allpachico. I turn now to how development practice is embedded in this context of uneven capitalist development.

Development in Capitalism[7]

Development has, apparently, failed. Raymond Apthorpe (1972), a famed development anthropologist, was already scathingly critical of what had been accomplished by the end of the First U.N. Development Decade in the 1960s (see also Pitt 1976a), and development was again resoundingly denounced in the 1990s in works by Escobar (1995), Rahnema and Bawtree (1997) and Wolfgang Sachs (1992). Ferguson (1994) takes it as a given that development will fail and concerns himself instead with examining what its effects are. These writers understand development in the sense of an intentional intervention, through policy or project, in the lives of poor people living in poor countries. The failure is manifested, in the words of Escobar (1995: 4) in 'massive underdevelopment and impoverishment, untold exploitation and oppression. The debt crisis, the Sahelian famine, increasing poverty, malnutrition, and violence are only the most pathetic signs of the failure of forty years of development.' The cause of this failure is traced to the development industry instigated after the Second World War by the United States and Western Europe. Escobar's solution is to look for alternatives to capitalist development, locatable in societies relatively unscathed by capitalism.

Alternatively, in the view of Jeffrey Sachs (2005), development has been a success. Whereas the whole world was poor in 1800, now 'five-sixths of the world's population is at least one step above extreme poverty' (J. Sachs 2005: 51). Furthermore, all areas of the world have achieved at least some economic growth over the past two hundred years (29–30). Thus, Sachs sees development as synonymous with progress. Still, he is preoccupied by the inequalities of growth, and particularly by the one-sixth still in extreme poverty. Why did some countries not achieve the growth that others did?

> The poorest [countries] did not even begin their economic growth until decades later, and then often under tremendous obstacles. In some cases, they faced the brutal exploitation of dominant colonial powers. They faced geographical barriers (related to climate, food production, disease, energy resources, topography, proximity to world markets) that had not burdened the early industrial economies like Great Britain and the

United States. And they made disastrous choices in their own national policies, often until the last decade. (50)

His plan of action is to facilitate capitalist expansion through allowing markets to operate freely across borders. Thus, where Escobar blames the West, Sachs blames the rest for their own poverty. It is the latest version of a confrontation that Rostow (1961)[8] and Frank (1967) engaged in forty years ago.

The questions of whether world is rich or not, or whether it is not capitalist enough or too capitalist are not easily answerable. The premise outlined in the preceding section, that capitalism has spread throughout the world, albeit in extremely uneven ways, displaces the discussion from simplistic answers and solutions. Discussions about wealth and well-being and how to achieve them are the stuff of development. Definitions of development are as numerous as the debates about how to proceed.

Cowen and Shenton (1996) begin and end their powerful contribution to the debates by commenting on the range of definitions. Their work (Cowen and Shenton 1995, 1996) is a complex examination of the archaeology of the modern usage of development, noting its ambiguities, circularities, and contradictions. Development, in their view (Cowen and Shenton 1995: 28–9), has been used to refer to both an immanent process of internally generated change, and an intentional set of practices to achieve specific goals. Unlike Jeffrey Sachs, they distinguish development from progress, through a discussion of positivism. Progress, envisioned by Comte as ongoing improvement, caused chaos and disorder, and it is this disorder that intentional development was meant to address. Intentional development, therefore, is not progress, but an ameliorative set of practices to solve the ills associated with (capitalist) progress. Whereas earlier Western notions of change expected degeneration as part of a natural sequence of growth, modernism promised that growth would be linear and that degeneration could be eliminated and not merely mitigated (Cowen and Shenton 1996: 13). The measures taken to address crisis are not themselves without effects, however, and in addition to the improvements they may bring about, also carry problems which require yet more development interventions. Cowen and Shenton note recurring themes in development practice, which swing between greater and lesser roles for the state, particularly in guiding and sponsoring economic development, and between a reliance on science and a glorification of local

knowledge and community. For example, a thick network of social relations at a community level may be disaggregated through the individualization of choice, only to have community invoked again as a
cure for the social anomie that results. Further, they argue, the ultimate
goal of development is envisioned as allowing people to have power
and freedom over their own lives. The irony and contradiction is that
an enlightened external agent, in their terms a trustee, must intervene
in order to bring this about. The people have thus not chosen their
liberty to choose, but had it thrust upon them.

Cowen and Shenton reflect on current trends towards alternative development which argue that the people must choose their own future,
noting the circularity in which the people are assumed to be in a position
to choose, while the process of (alternative) development has precisely
the goal to allow them to be able to choose (see also Pieterse 1998). The
goal and the means of achieving it have been elided, and development,
in terms of an intentional trustee-led process, is still being pursued. For
Cowen and Shenton, current forms of development, including the alternatives proposed by critics such as Escobar, are inextricably linked
to capitalist ideologies and processes. For real 'free development,' we
must wait to see what the future can offer. Thus, Cowen and Shenton
(1995, 1996) refrain from prescribing a solution for current socioeconomic ills. Development as an intentional process, then, is tied to the
uneven and contradictory unfolding of capitalism. In effect, intentional
development *is* immanent capitalist development. In Chapter 3,
I continue this discussion of the difficulty of establishing a specific beginning to intentional development. We will also see how intentional
development furthers the broader infiltration of capitalism in the chapters to follow.

To sum up, Cowen and Shenton see definitions of development as
falling into two categories: one, as historical process, and the other
as intentional practice. While proponents of practice may define development as progress, achievable through strategic interventions,
Cowen and Shenton contend that they are really simply addressing
problems caused by capitalism. Chapters 5, 6, 7, and 8 analyse cases
of intentional development, focusing on practices oriented to people,
or what Brohman (1996) calls 'popular development.'[9] Because these
approaches tend to focus on individuals and communities, rather than
on macro-economic growth, they are sometimes seen as challenging
dominant models (e.g., Brohman 1996; Chambers 1997). Nevertheless,
capitalist economic patterns, especially neo-liberal policy advocating

smaller government, freer international trade, and greater individual responsibility, form an important backdrop to these strategies and can be seen to inform them (Cammack 2002; Gill 1997; Zaidi 1999). The complex outcomes of several of these people-oriented strategies outlined below demonstrate that development in Allpachico has been closely bound up with capitalism by promoting its expansion through a variety of mechanisms and addressing its crises. At the same time, the case of Allpachico shows that while some elements of capitalism are embraced, others are resisted, thwarted, and diverted.

The Implicated Positions of Development Actors

The presentation of different projects in Allpachico will highlight the roles of different actors. A common bipartite division distinguishes between government bodies and non-governmental organizations (NGOs). These categories obscure the diversity within them. A more detailed catalogue might list on the government side the following: states acting within their borders, states acting internationally or in other states, and multilateral organizations. Among the various actors that are not governments are non-governmental organizations, capitalist investors and enterprises, communities, and individuals. The diversity within each of these means that, with the exception of capitalist investors and enterprises, none of the actors map neatly onto a class structure. Specific NGOs, agencies, and individuals, however, are subject to the momentum of capitalism and thus their positions and actions are implicated in the wider political economy. I explore some of these implicated positions here.

My focus in this book is at the community level; however, like development, the concept of *community* is broad and malleable. Ways in which the community of Allpachico, and collectives within Allpachico, have been constructed are examined throughout this book, although they receive specific attention in chapters 4 and 6 below. One point that is worth making here is that the community of Allpachico planned and organized only the projects that it funded internally; it has not been able to get external funding for a project arising from the community itself. Rather, as we will see, the projects sponsored by external agencies have been opportunities that Allpachico has responded to and the people have had limited rights to change them to meet their realities or priorities. When I asked a research assistant[10] to identify funding sources in 1998, she found none that would disburse funds directly to a community; all preferred instead to work through NGOs. Thus, perforce, while the community is the subject of analysis in this book, NGO and state actors make frequent appearances because they sponsored and designed most of the projects. Their control of necessary resources accords them the power to determine the goals of development.

All of these actors, whether members of the community, NGO workers, or politicians or bureaucrats, are taken to have specific interests at specific conjunctures, tied to their political or economic positions and ambitions. Thus, rather than reifying the state or any other institutional entity (Sayer 1994), I follow Long (2001) in recognizing the politics of interfaces between people involved in the process, although I am also interested in the structures they set up and through which they operate. Most of the individuals presented in this book are Allpachiqueños, and I highlight the differences among them that lead to distinct perspectives on development projects. At the moment I will focus more on the institutional structures. The different forms of community are important here, along with the understood patterns of interaction in the political sphere. States are partly constituted by policies and practices driven by inertial exigencies, but they are implemented by people in government and bureaucracy who have their own skills and wills.

Government politics in Peru, endlessly fascinating if disheartening in themselves, have been intricately tied to capitalist development. The precise type of support for capitalist development, though, has varied greatly. Different governments have variously directly overseen policies and projects intended to improve the economy and lives of Peru's citizens, or indirectly taken a role as facilitator of national or international private capital investment which is expected to improve the economy and lives of citizens, as they pursue their ideological goals or bow to the pressure of their electorate, international lenders, national capital interests, and so on. The decisions are often designed to serve multiple purposes. Thus, as we will see in Chapter 4, policies with an *indigenista*[11] flavour passed in the 1930s were responses to lobbying by a vocal left to protect indigenous societies (through the establishment of *comunidades indígenas*) at the same time as they aimed to extract labour for public infrastructure to compensate for tight state budgets (the road conscription duty directed to indigenous men, professedly patterned on the traditional labour tribute). State policies and interests at different key points will be discussed as they relate to the projects presented in the book.

Although state presence in Allpachico continues to be spotty, it has gradually increased over the past century. The spottiness is the result of both the incapacity of state processes to infiltrate rural areas very effectively, as well as of the occasional failure of the community to submit state-required documents during periods when there were few incentives to do so. State policy and resources clearly pattern community willingness to operate within that political realm. Recently, as we will see in Chapter 8, state resources directed to municipal participatory budgeting have been the major source of development action. But while state sanctioned structures may define the rules, the communities and individual members within them continue to strategize to work in their own best interests.

Aside from outlining their own guidelines for delivering development assistance, governments also set more or less stringent rules by which NGOs operate, so that even though the latter may be 'nongovernmental,' they must work within or around these rules. Two of the major projects here, those described in chapters 5 and 7, were carried out by NGOs. The debates about the effectiveness of NGOs are covered in greater detail in Chapter 7, but a few comments are worthwhile here. The Peruvian state has regulated NGOs since the 1970s, and successive governments have adapted the form of regulation according to their own goals (Toche 2003). Toche notes an ongoing ambivalence on the part of government towards NGOs, but NGOs are also leery of this government control. Both foreign and Peruvian workers, at both foreign and Peruvian NGOs, to whom I spoke to in the early 2000s expressed the belief that the state regulates NGO activity as a way of appropriating a share of the money they bring into the country (see also Kamat 2002). Thus, many NGOs apparently did not register with the appropriate government agency, as a way of resisting possible interference. On the other hand, a census of NGOs working in the central highlands revealed a large number that *were* on a regional government registry but seemed not actually to exist.[12] This may be related to a requirement that NGOs be officially registered to be eligible for certain government funding as the directors awaited an opportunity.[13] In addition, the newspapers were full of reports in 2004 of NGOs that had political connections and had received large contracts to carry out road construction work (e.g., El Comercio 2004). Clearly there is great diversity among NGOs, and it is worthwhile to remember that their directors have their own political and economic interests (Fisher 1997; Lewis 1999, 2005; Lewis and Mosse 2006; Lewis and Opoku-Mensah 2006).[14]

In Allpachico, too, there has been a range of NGOs, including Peruvian and international agencies, as well as religious and secular ones. As we will see in Chapter 5, on occasion Peruvian agencies have taken over projects begun by foreign ones that had to leave because of the violence in Peru in the late 1980s and early 1990s. Sources of funding for NGOs are also diverse: those that have worked in Allpachico have had funding from foreign governments, international NGOs, and the Peruvian state. Each of these funders can demand conditions that influence the form of the development project.

The awkward relationship between the state and the NGOs is mirrored in that between the NGOs and the community. If there have been tensions and recriminations between NGO staff and Allpachiqueños, there have also been friendships and mutual assistance. In general, though, the relationship has tended to frame the NGO worker as a patron to client Allpachiqueños.

To a large extent, from the perspective of the people of Allpachico, whether a project came from a certain NGO, the state, or any other agency simply did not matter, except insofar as each might imply a distinct method of approach and negotiation. This, as Gill (1997, 2000) points out, can lead to people reformulating themselves to fit the requirements, rather than to projects being tailored to the needs of the recipients. The conditions of participation in a project, followed by the rewards, were the important criteria, especially during the difficult years of the 1980s and 1990s. Indeed, it became impossible to know what people might need, because their responses to questions depended on what they thought might be possible to receive (below, Chapter 8 and Vincent 2005c).

Thus, just as development practice, alternative or not, is inseparable from the dominant historical, political, and economic processes in which they take place, so too are the actors. The array of actors and interests described above will appear through the presentation of different projects in this book. A further set of actors is the anthropologists, including myself, who have researched or contributed to development processes. We now turn to this more reflexive discussion.

Anthropology and Development

Gardner and Lewis (1996) in their introduction to one of the many texts on development and anthropology (e.g., Arce and Long 2000; Cochrane 1971; Edelman and Haugerud 2005; Gardner and Lewis

1996; Grillo and Rew 1985; Grillo and Stirrat 1997; Lewis and Mosse 2006; Long 1977, 2001; Nolan 2002; Olivier de Sardan 2005; Pitt 1976b) give a historical overview of the relationship between what might be called the anthropology of development and development anthropology, the former referring to the anthropological study of processes of change and the latter to the application of anthropological skills in development (Grillo 1985: 29). As with most cultural categorizations, the distinction is not always clear. For example, while this book tends towards the anthropology of development, the critiques it contains could be used to refine some development anthropology approaches.

Some of the major lines of both anthropological development practice and its critique can be seen in discussions over the past fifty years of a well-known development project in Vicos, Peru. I review this discussion here, not to evaluate the Vicos project,[15] but rather to use it as a vehicle to examine important anthropological debates about development and to point to significant trends in development practice.[16]

Led by Allan Holmberg, this famous[17] early example of development anthropology, the Peru-Cornell Project (or PPC for its initials in Spanish), took place at the Vicos *hacienda* (large land holding) in Ancash, Peru. Holmberg was an anthropologist at Cornell University. Cornell's official sponsorship was from 1951 to 1956, although it continued to be involved over the life of the project to 1966. The problem was framed as a hacienda with an oppressed dependent peasant community, with land that had been exhausted by successive renters. The objective was to assist the community to become independent owners of the land by improving its agricultural productivity and giving the people managerial and technical training.

Holmberg (1955) described the method to be used as 'participant intervention,' a deliberate play on the standard ethnographic practice of 'participant observation.' He explicitly counterposed this approach, which he presents as taking a 'value stand' (1955: 25), to the position that it was inappropriate to meddle in another culture. In doing so, he picked up an already long-standing debate between applied and academic anthropology. Charges that applied anthropologists were complicit with colonialism by lending their services to the British policy of Indirect Rule, or shored up the apartheid system in South Africa, or informed the United States CIA about subversive politics in Project Camelot, have made many academic anthropologists see applied work as tainted. Defenders of the Vicos project, in particular Paul Doughty (e.g., 1987a, 1987b, 2005, 2010; see also Dobyns and

Doughty 1971: 18), have continually maintained that it would be un-ethical not to use anthropological skills to assist marginalized people. Doughty coordinated the PPC from 1962 to 1964. His view coincides with that of anthropologists who have, in both exasperation and self-congratulation, criticized development practice that takes place without the discipline's self-proclaimed ability to understand local culture, which would allow planned change to address real communities more appropriately and effectively (e.g., Cernea 1996; Crewe and Harrison 1998; Gardner 1997; Grillo 1985; Olivier de Sardan 2005). In rebuttal, others complain that applied work has been simplified to the point of meaninglessness because non-anthropologists rejected the detailed analyses and wider holistic vision that their reports contained (Grillo 1985).[18] Grillo (1985: 30–1) has suggested resolving the dilemma through cautious involvement: development practice can be much improved by the contribution of anthropologists, but they must be aware of the implications and prepared to deal with sceptical colleagues. Gardner and Lewis (1996), a decade later, and Edelman and Haugerud (2005a) even more recently, concur with this call for a politically aware pragmatism. Indeed, anthropologists have turned to applied anthropology in general, and development anthropology in particular, in increasing numbers.[19]

One of the deep concerns about intervention has related to the wider political significance of the planned change. I have referred above to the debate about whether poverty relates to insufficient or too much involvement in capitalism. This debate was the backdrop to the beginnings of the PPC, taking place at the height of the Cold War in the 1950s and early 1960s. The United States used international development as a tool to entice non-aligned countries of the Global South into its political sphere. Vicos clearly promoted involvement in capitalism, both in pushing industrially produced agricultural inputs and in the commercial sale of products (Mayer 2010; Ross 2010; Stein 2003).[20] However, the Vicos project was complex enough to be interpreted as both implicated in the U.S. Cold War strategy and as revolutionary in the context of 1950s Peruvian oligarchy. Ross (2010) takes the former position, focusing on the career trajectories of the personnel involved and arguing that the form of the project was essentially modernist and aimed at integrating the peasantry into a national political economy.[21] Nevertheless, Richard Adams (1964), writing during the later stages of the project, does not make this claim. His article discusses how politics affected where anthropologists did research in

Spanish America. He points to three situations: (1) national governments wanting to extend their influence in their own country or to build a national identity; (2) foreign governments wanting to extend influence in other countries, such as U.S. support for anti-communist research; and (3) other partisan groups wanting to establish a base. He gives the PPC as an example for the first and third types, but the project is conspicuously absent from the second type.

Adams' use of Vicos as an example in his third type of situation, that of partisan groups, notes the role of the *indigenista* movement in Peru.[22] Pribilsky (2010) argues that this movement had two strains: one, associated with the socialist thinker José Carlos Mariátegui, was explicitly political and communist, while the other was culturalist. This latter interpretation tended to be held by the Peruvian anthropologists associated with the project. Nevertheless, even this version was anathema to the Peruvian oligarchy, who worried about any hint of agrarian reform. In this context, the aim of transferring ownership of the hacienda to the peasants was politically volatile (Doughty 2010: 98–105). Pribilsky (2010) and Mayer (2010) describe two factors that made the transfer somewhat more palatable to a conservative government: the land was purchased by the peasants, rather than being expropriated; and they earned the money by running the hacienda like a capitalist cooperative. That the land was held by the community rather than divided into private landholdings is important to note. Mayer (2010) argues that, while there is little evidence that Vicos was the model for other peasant uprisings in the 1960s (contra Doughty 2010), it was the template for the 1969 agrarian reform carried out by the Peruvian 'revolutionary' military government.

Whether the PPC was a part of the U.S. Cold War strategy to expand capitalism or not, whether it was intended to revolutionize the Peruvian political structure or not, it certainly contributed to both. However, the political elements in the project design were whitewashed through a discourse of science. Pribilsky (2010: 185) invokes Ferguson's discussion of development as an 'anti-politics machine,' in that literature produced by development projects avoids explicit mention of even obvious political circumstances. Early writings by supporters of the project emphasize its scientific nature (Holmberg 1971a [1955]; Köhler 1981 [1963]), and one can intuit a reaction to critics alleging the subjective nature of the discipline. The emphasis on science corresponds with the prevailing notion of the time that technical knowledge could solve the problems of world poverty. U.S. President

Harry Truman's inaugural speech in 1949, for instance, makes this claim. Accordingly, Holmberg (1971a: 29) describes Vicos as a laboratory; problems are presented in scientific terms and their solutions are scientifically deduced and implemented. Indeed, the research methods and overall project were intended to act as models for social scientists and development interventions in Peru and elsewhere. The issue of the scientific character of the Vicos project continued to be debated. For example, in a recent book, Stein (2003) reviews evidence, including personal letters of project staff, disclosing rather more laxness than Köhler (1981) or Dobyns, Doughty, and Lasswell (1971a) acknowledge in their efforts to establish the scientific nature of the methodology. By the 1980s, and in contrast to the earlier writings that focused on predictive and prescriptive science, Doughty acknowledged a lack of perfection in the project and argued that no project can control what the people do with the opportunities generated through it (1987a: 150–1). Instead he positioned the Vicos project as long-term, inexpensive, and with intimate engagement by caring specialists, unlike other large-scale examples of the development 'game' (130), carrying out its emancipatory work in the face of elite and other naysayers. Instead of referring to prescriptive science, Doughty described the project in more flexible terms as 'a cybernetic loop between theory, research findings, policy and action' (133).

The focus on science and methods shows how, in addition to reflecting the broad debates about global politics and anthropological mission, the Vicos project also serves as a mirror for discussions of development practice. For example, in addressing a wide range of issues, from agriculture to managerial skills, health, education, and so on, Vicos was an early example of an integrated rural development project (Almy 1977), a type we will revisit in Chapter 5.[23] Detractors such as Glynn Cochrane[24] (1971: 17–19), in his text *Development Anthropology*, vehemently challenged these claims to science and to unusual success, and charged that it was expensive. Further, according to Cochrane, despite the range of activity, there was a lack of collaboration with experts in other fields, a point rejected by Doughty (1987a, 1987b).

Although the PPC did not explicitly address the big political questions we have just reviewed, political inequalities were discussed in terms of how they could be addressed at the local level in keeping with its goal of serving as a model for development practice. Holmberg (1971a, 1971b) presents the initial peasant situation in a timeless way as characterized by submission and powerlessness. This view has since been challenged, first by Himes (1981, largely from an earlier 1972 piece; see also Mitchell 2010). Perhaps picking up on the discipline's incipient interest in history, Himes questions the supposed complete powerlessness and poverty of the Vicos peasantry before the project began, thus contesting the claim of transformation from misery to independence. Himes emphasizes the need for historical political context in understanding peasant realities. An attention to history has been more evident in anthropological discussions of development (e.g., Li 2007) than in development agency descriptions of locales where development projects are to take place.

Even within the historical and geographical limits outlined by the PPC for political action there has been criticism of what was accomplished, raising another issue that has become a central feature of development projects, that relating to women. Babb (1985), drawing from the rich feminist discussions of the 1980s charged that, although both women and men were better off after the project than before, a lack of attention to women had led to a deterioration of their position with respect to men at Vicos. I return to the theme of gendered development in Chapter 6.

As indicated above, the method for bringing about development at Vicos was described as participant intervention. Participation has become a key word in development practice, and Vicos provides an early example, reflecting some of the issues at the centre of the current debate to which I return in Chapter 4. In the PPC, inequality was to be addressed by the active engagement of the anthropologist as facilitator – Holmberg (1971a) uses the analogy of a psychoanalyst – to encourage the downtrodden peasants to learn to manage their own property. Holmberg describes the strategies as carefully designed to blend customary accepted traditions with transformative and participatory new practices. He mentions weekly meetings with 'Indian leaders' (Holmberg 1971a: 26), but his examples show many cases in which the changes, including what types of potatoes would be sown, which pesticide to use, and who would be groomed for leadership,[25] were decided by project staff, who then tried to get the community to accept them. Himes (1981) characterized the approach as paternalistic: the first Cornell period retained the hierarchical hacienda management system, with Holmberg as patron, and project staff clearly imposed many of the decisions. In response, Doughty (1987b: 443–4; see also Dobyns, Doughty, and Lasswell 1971a: 16) has continued to

defend the protective umbrella of the project under which the oppressed peasants could become leaders, using Eric Wolf's influential
work as a shield in the process. In the 1980s, in language just beginning to be championed by other development practitioners, he asserts
the participatory (Chambers 1983) and empowering (e.g., Sen and
Grown 1987) character of the project (Doughty 1987b: 457). Indeed, in
2005 Doughty framed Vicos as having been ahead of its time in using
participatory methods which have become so popular, and lamented
the inexplicable lack of recognition of the Vicos project's early foray on
the part of the participatory development promoters.

Although much of the critique of Vicos has focused on its goal of
addressing local political equality, other themes are also apparent. For
example, Stein's (2003) treatment of the Vicos project pursues decon-
structionist trends popular in 1990s development critiques (e.g., Escobar 1995; Ferguson 1994; Pigg 1992).[26] Stein is much gentler in his
judgement on the Vicos anthropologists than, for example, Escobar
(1995) is of development practitioners. While declaring that 'no one in
the year 2002 would even consider the possibility of designing such a
project' (Stein 2003: 476), Stein concludes that the project probably did
not have much effect on Vicos: 'It did no lasting harm, and in its time I
think it did some good' (482).

I have mentioned that the Vicos project relied on community rather
than individual private land management. I have emphasized the
importance of local collectives in development practice above and
throughout this book. In his lecture on receiving the Malinowski award
from the Society for Applied Anthropology, Doughty (2005) placed
Vicos in an era when community-based work was a significant focus.
The critiques of Vicos, in his opinion, helped to displace community
in favour of large-scale trickle-down development. The current move
back to community-based development vindicated the project, which
he saw as having successfully introduced Vicosinos to the world outside their border and given them the means to deal with it.

In summary, the line traced by the defenders and critics of the Vicos
project reflects the broader trends in development debates, including
whether capitalism can provide solutions to poverty, whether projects
are pawns in larger global political battles, who the actors are and should
be, and whether local practice and technique can address big problems
of inequality. It is fascinating how this single project, chameleon-like,
has been continually reframed to represent the sequence of development
thought. The projects in Allpachico have inherited the legacy of these

debates, and we will see traces of most of these themes reflected in them. The case study of Allpachico, to which I now turn, builds on the framework outlined in this chapter. I use the concepts from political economy to analyse intentional development projects, uncovering the complex ways in which they work to further capitalism, and the contradictions that arise in the process. The actors involved in these projects are themselves caught in historical pressures.

3 Somos libres? Political Structures of Development in History in the Peruvian Central Highlands

Somos libres, seámoslo siempre.

– Peruvian national anthem

On the other hand, there is also much to suggest that world history is like a Kafkaesque nightmare of repetition compulsions, more a scenario of imprisonment in larger systems than one of self-directed and empowering evolution.

– Kajsa Ekholm Friedman and Jonathan Friedman, Historical Transformations: The Anthropology of Global Systems

The Peruvian national anthem proudly proclaims that Peruvians are free and will ever be so. Inaugurated in the heady days after independence from Spain in 1821, the anthem denounces the 'ambitious Iberian tyrant' (*el tirano ambicioso Iberino*), now overcome through the hatred and vengeance inherited from the Inca Lord (*el odio y venganza que heredara de su Inca y Señor*). The irony of a *criollo* elite invoking the empire their Spanish forebears overthrew, with the help of a significant part of the indigenous population, as they established a new political order that continued the subordinate role of the indigenous people, is emblematic of Andean history.

This chapter extends the context of current development into the distant past, examining threads of hegemonic[1] process as successive political structures spread through the region. These political orders were accompanied by economic expansion and technological impacts, the common stuff of development. Discussions of processes of development have tended to begin with the historical period after the

Second World War (e.g., Escobar 1995; Rahnema 1992). Others (e.g., Cowen and Shenton 1996) have taken issue with this short history and have extended the overview of intentional development back two hundred years to the beginnings of modernism. Still another view, discussed in the previous chapter with respect to the Vicos project, has been to shorten the historical period to the beginning of a specific intervention, ignoring the processes which have led to the current situation (see Ferguson 1994). As discussed in Chapter 2, the point at which development is believed to have begun relates to definitional perspectives about what it involves.

To impute a specific starting point to development also implies a stark contrast with earlier lifeways. The information presented in this chapter shows how difficult it is to make pat distinctions between a time before development and after, or between immanent and intentional development. Although capitalism involves distinct ways of organizing people and policies, I argue here that some of the social, political, and economic planning and problem solving that characterize intentional development has earlier precedents.[2] I point to similarities and differences between the Inca and Spanish periods, to highlight their distinct forms of political control and extraction. I will also briefly compare a period of political and economic crisis in the early Spanish period with one in the 1980s, which share superficial similarities as development problems and solutions, to delineate their important structural differences.

Rooting a discussion of contemporary processes of development in Allpachico in the distant past is not meant to imply some essential autochthonous character to present-day people. Rather, this view is intended to show how change was brought about as a result of processes, policies, events, and people. This historical overview focuses on how the elements taken to be central to current development have manifested themselves through time.

The View from Allpachico: The Local-Level Polity of Huajlas

The current community of Allpachico was founded within the last 150 years, during the last half of the nineteenth century, so we must look to wider regional studies for evidence of how forebears of current Allpachiqueños might have lived. The record of human habitation in the wider watershed of the Mantaro River goes back to around 15,000 years ago (Ravines 1972: 26). After 1500 BC, hunting and gathering started to be complemented by agriculture (Matos 1972: 35–43). By AD 200–600 herding of llamas and alpacas took over, in a largely nomadic form characterized by little socioeconomic differentiation (Browman 1974: 190; Parsons and Matos 1978: 547).

Coinciding with an ecological crisis as a result of overgrazing, the Huari culture to the south expanded between AD 600 and 900, bringing a shift in economic patterns to settled agriculture and increased trade (Browman 1974, 1976; Isbell 1972a, 1972b; Jennings 2006). When it subsided, possibly as a result of another ecological or political crisis (Jennings 2006), there was a return to regional ethnic groups (Thompson 1972).

The ethnic group occupying the Mantaro Valley, including the area that was to become Allpachico, was the Huancas (Espinoza Soriano 1969). There is disagreement about whether the Huancas, as well as the Huari before them, formed an actual state or a looser political union (D'Altroy 1987). Nevertheless, there was a major population centre, if not a capital, associated with them at Tunanmarca. Lying within 10 kilometres to the south of Tunanmarca was Huajlas, the ruins of which, in turn, are within 5 kilometres of the current community of Allpachico. Huajlas arose around AD 1200 and was a significant town with about 600 dwellings, a religious compound, and administrative offices. Orellana Valeriano (1973: 127) estimates the population of Huajlas at its height at 1,300. It was well protected at an altitude of over 4,000 metres, with cliffs overlooking the Mantaro River some 600 metres below. Access was up a steep slope with four successive stone walls. From Huajlas, one can see up the Mantaro canyon to the snow-capped peaks at the pass at Ticlio to the west, from which the current road and railroad descends to Lima on the Pacific coast. To the north, across the Mantaro River, lies the Yanamarca Valley where Tunanmarca is located. To the east and southeast is the flat fertile Mantaro Valley and the distant snow-covered peak of Huaytapallana, beyond Huancayo, is visible on a clear day. Unobserved approach would be difficult.

This strategically defensible location, which was probably the home of some forebears of the Allpachiqueños, indicates the bellicose nature of Huanca society. Huancas, even today, have a reputation for pugnacity. Archaeologists interpret the Huanca trend to move up to defended hilltops as a response to climatic change. In the wake of the Huari period and as the temperatures grew cooler, with a corresponding decline in land suitable for key crops, the Huancas withdrew from the valleys to fortified hilltops to protect themselves from marauding neighbours (Orellana Valeriano 1973; Seltzer and Hastorf 1990).

The location of Huajlas may have meant that they were rather less able than other Huanca communities to extend control over a variety of ecological zones as a way of meeting a wide range of subsistence needs. Murra's (1978) classic study of the 'vertical ecology' calls attention to the physical geography of the Andes that, with very high mountains close to the equator, provides almost the full range of climatic possibilities between desert coast or tropical jungle at sea level to arctic glaciers at the peaks. This allows for diverse products to be accessed in relatively short distances. Such a setting strongly suggests that control over different ecological zones will be highly political: control over as many key zones as possible can support political autonomy; being able to limit or permit access to the products of different zones can support political domination. We return to this in the discussion of the Inca Empire. In the case of Huajlas, the site is farther from the jungle than many other Huanca sites, and the people may have been limited to altitudes of 3,500 metres and up – too high to do much other than growing tubers or herding camelids. Accordingly, the people of Huajlas produced potatoes, quinoa (an Andean grain), oca, and olluco (both of which are tubers), and herded llamas and alpacas (Espinoza Soriano 1969: 14; Orellana Valeriano 1973: 125). This limited economic base may be part of the explanation for its name. In speculating on the meaning of the word 'Huajlas' in conjunction with its location, Espinoza Soriano (1969: 12) says the name reflects its inferior, marginal status, compared to settlements in the Mantaro Valley, and even intuits that the people were aloof and unapproachable, although he presents little evidence for this.

Huajlas, like other settlements in the Andes of the period, was occupied by an *ayllu*, a group based on real or fictive kin ties, with a hierarchy of leaders and religious specialists over dependent commoners. The Huanca *curaca*, or leader, had local political, civil, judicial, and military authority (Espinoza Soriano 1969: 17). Prior to the Inca period, curacas were chosen on the basis of their military prowess (D'Altroy 1987: 83). The curaca distributed land to newborns and took it back from those who had died (Espinoza Soriano 1969). While there were clear differences on the basis of rank, in the period before the Inca takeover of the Huancas, all households were directly involved in production (Earle et al. 1987: 102) and probably both work and resources were communally shared to some extent (Espinoza Soriano 1969).

The houses of elites did have agricultural tools, but they had fewer of them, suggesting that they undertook less direct production. On the other hand, they had more large serving and storage containers, suggesting that they were responsible for holding ceremonial feasts for all (Earle et al. 1987: 100–3). Community production led to surpluses that were locally stored, and trade also tended to be very local, between neighbouring communities rather than more widely. This evidence indicates a political system based on a hierarchical reciprocity, something about to be upscaled in the Inca Empire, wrenching it from local control.

The Inca Realm: State Development, Planting the Seeds of Rebellion

In the fifteenth century, another wave of conquest covered the Andes with the Inca expansion. Military conquest was followed by incorporation into a highly organized political economy. At the centre of Inca power was the vertical ecology, mentioned above, comprised of the control of different ecological zones: as the products of these zones circulated through a state redistributive system, it cemented the structure holding the empire together. Land from each conquered territory was apportioned to the state, the religious organization, and for the use of the local community. Goods produced on state land supported the bureaucracy as well as supplying the needs of citizens from other geoclimatic areas. Private trade continued but was limited by the amount of land people could use and restrictions on their travel, so that exchange tended to be local (Rowe 1946: 270). Instead, by inserting the state into how people got access to goods from other altitudes, the Incas made the state necessary to their lives. The goods themselves were produced through a tax or tribute in labour, engaging citizens in the functioning of the state and, thus, attempting to make them complicit in its goals. It is this organization of state officials and workers in an effective nested hierarchy based on unequal reciprocity which has most impressed analysts of the Incas.

Officials at different levels were in charge of 100, 500, 1,000, 5,000, or 10,000 tribute payers, who were married men (Rowe 1946: 262–4). Inca administration was precise enough to allow for the classification of the people on the basis of their ability to work in various capacities (Rostworowski 2005: 37–9). This allowed for a high degree of efficiency, leading not only to the production of tremendous surpluses of food and artisanal goods, but also supporting a powerful military, along with mining, road building, aqueducts, and monumental architecture (Rowe 1946: 265–9). Thus, tribute payers owed labour not only in the production of goods, but also on a rotational basis for the larger military, mining, and infrastructural projects of the state. In a description that calls to mind the workfare programs of current Western governments, Rowe (1946: 268) recounts: 'One of the greatest tributes to the efficiency of the system is that Emperors had to make unnecessary work in order to keep the MIT'A levies busy. Huayna Capac is said to have ordered a hill moved from one place to another merely for want of a more useful project ... The Emperors knew that people with excessive leisure had too much time to criticize the Government and they had trouble enough with revolts even when the people were busy.'

The system worked by implicating people in webs of reciprocity: officials were rewarded with goods, prestige, and ceremonies by those higher on the scale, and in turn rewarded their followers with goods, prestige, and ceremonies. Rostworowski (2005) argues that the framing of the relationship between the Inca and the leaders of subordinate ethnic leaders as 'pleading' and 'offering' (*ruego* and *dádiva*) gave the subordinates the right to deny Inca requests for help if they were not accompanied by appropriate gifts. The empire expanded through Inca proposals to targeted groups to enter into relations of reciprocity. If the group rejected the proposal, it was conquered through war and the spoils went to the Inca. If it accepted, it was incorporated into the reciprocal exchange of goods on more beneficial terms.

The expanding empire and the ever-increasing need to recompense loyalty meant an ongoing demand for increased production and conquest (Rostworoski 1988, 2005). Possession of goods conferred power and vast numbers of filled storehouses attested to the might of the Inca leaders (Rostworowski 1988: 257). While some deposits were sent to Cusco, most produce was kept near where it was produced and where it would be consumed. The Mantaro Valley, with its rich agricultural land, was a key area for the Inca in terms of food production and storage (D'Altroy and Hastorf 1984). There were over 2,000 Inca storehouses in the region and they held so much that the contents were still being used for years after the next conquest, that by the Spaniards.

The stores were not only used to consolidate the power structure, but to support the business of the state by feeding its permanent and temporary workers and the military, and to provide against crises, whether these were environmental, political, or economic in origin (D'Altroy and Hastorf 1984: 334; Hastorf 1990). This central planning reflects an organized attempt by the state to oversee production, regulate exchange, and address problems of local shortages of supplies or surpluses of labour.

The purpose of the system was not unlimited accumulation, as occurs in capitalist competition, but the expansion, consolidation, and augmentation of power for the Inca elite. Nevertheless, a byproduct of this quest for power did involve pressure to increase production. Power in the Inca realm was expressed through control of full storehouses and was achieved through being able to reward followers with material wealth. Although Rostworowski (1988) declares their tools to have been primitive, the transformation of the landscape through terracing and irrigation systems reflects an investment in technology that, along with the careful organization of labour power, was intended to maximize productivity. Livestock, too, had been bred to provide animals with specific characteristics, such as llamas for carrying loads and for meat, and alpacas for wool (Rowe 1946: 219). Thus, the Incas, although they may not have invented any technology that had not earlier been in use (Espinoza Soriano 1990: 415), did work to apply it and to organize labour in production in order to achieve maximum results, in a state-led precursor to a kind of Taylorism.

The Huancas, like other conquered groups, were integrated into the Inca political economy. They were added to the population of the realm, their products increased the economy, and they were drafted into the military in order to maintain and expand the size of the state. They were not simply subjects, since their leaders were coopted into the Inca bureaucracy in cases where their ability and compliance made this possible. Clearly the Incas combined force and incentives in their hegemonic project. These local leaders ceded their independence in exchange for playing key roles in a powerful empire. The pay-off was significant. Thus, the curaca of Huajlas was given a wife, the daughter of a noble, by the Inca leader Huayna Capac[3] (Espinoza Soriano 1969: 24), indicating his participation in the reciprocal state system. This made him honour bound to respond to requests for support by the Inca (Rostworowski 2005). The followers also perceived advantages in better diets and fewer conflicts (Earle et al. 1987).

The incorporation into a large political organization led to greater consolidation of Huanca territory, eliminating the internal bickering that had characterized the people earlier (D'Altroy 1987). However, the Inca economy, productive as it may have been, faced an unsustainable upward spiral of demand (Rostworowski 1988, 2005). Officials at every level were pressured for goods from above and below in order to maintain control in the reciprocity-based hierarchy. Ongoing conquest and, after 1527, the civil war between Atahualpa and Huascar for the empire, required huge numbers of soldiers to be drawn from the citizenry. With these demands and despite the advantages of membership in the Inca Empire, the Huancas retained their desire for independence, demonstrating the contingency of their acceptance of Inca domination. When the Spaniards arrived in 1532 the Huancas offered their new cohesion and skills to the European invaders to help overthrow the Inca overlords. Thus, ironically, the Incan hegemonic project gave the Huancas the tools that led to the downfall of the Inca Empire (D'Altroy 1987). The impressive military and economic machine fell, not so much to a few men with guns and horses, but because its pattern of economic production and accumulation was politically unstable, undermining its legitimacy to its citizens but not obliterating the transformations it had achieved (Rostworowski 1988, 2005; see also Espinoza Soriano 1973, 1986).

Early Colonial Peru: From Reciprocal Hierarchy to Unidirectional Extraction

The Spanish Conquest took four decades of fighting, accompanied by the spread of disease and the disruption of prior production systems. The effect on the political landscape was extensive, although it is important to note that indigenous systems were not completely dismantled.[4] Curacas lost subjects to death and to military or labour service to the Spanish. The Spanish also reorganized local polities, displacing some traditional leaders and establishing new leaders who took advantage of the new opportunities (Ramirez 1996: 29). There had been some scope for ambitious individuals to advance in the Inca Empire, for example through *yanacuracas* (lower level indigenous leaders) who replaced their rebellious superior curacas (Rostworowski 1988: 68), but this paled beside the possibilities – for a select few – arising from the chaos after the arrival of the Spaniards.[5]

   An example of this indigenous individual opportunism can be seen in the person of Felipe Guacrapáucar, son of one of the three top Huanca curacas, each of whom was in charge of a region of Huanca territory (Espinoza Soriano 1973: 170–5). His case demonstrates the re-working, rather than the replacement, of indigenous systems within the Spanish hegemonic project. In 1563, Guacrapáucar travelled to Spain, ostensibly to seek redress for the sacrifices the Huancas had made on behalf of the Spanish. He carried letters from each curaca outlining the contributions they had made in people and goods, and listing their demands. In the event, he pressed his own case, suppress-ing the letters of the curacas of the other two regions, and even the claims of his own father. The concessions Don Felipe requested went beyond the honours the Spanish Crown was prepared to give to indig-enous leaders. While certain Spanish privileges were granted – such as a coat of arms – others were denied, including his request to be named *encomendero* of his region. *Encomiendas*, which we will discuss further below, were accorded to Spanish conquistadores as a reward for their services (Stern 1993: 27–8). The encomendero had the obligation to represent the interests of the Crown and Church to the subjects, and in exchange could exact tribute and labour from them.

One concession Felipe Guacrapáucar received, however, had im-plications far beyond his personal ambitions: the Crown agreed to prohibit the establishment of haciendas on the floor of the Mantaro Valley, leaving this rich fertile area in the hands of indigenous people (Espinoza Soriano 1973: 173). The area of Allpachico, although not in the valley, belonged to one of the indigenous communities estab-lished there, Huaripampa. Thus, the historical trajectory of the people of Huajlas, and eventually of Allpachico, ended up relating more to the ways in which indigenous people directly created their place in the colonial system and, after independence in 1824, in the Repub-lic of Peru, than to how they served local Spanish landowners. Dif-ferences between the indigenous and Spanish realms of control were marked in the colonial era, leading to 'two [racially distinct] republics' which gave way to 'one divided' on racist grounds after independence (Thurner 1997).

Certainly the relationship of the Spanish conquerors of Peru to the Andean people differed from that of the Incas. While the Incas may not have been successful in imposing a single vision of the state to which all of its citizens subscribed,[6] they did establish a political system incorpo-rating citizens and leaders, both of whom had rights through reciproc-ity, as well as responsibilities. The Spanish were much less interested in developing a citizenry than in extracting wealth. Thus, the conces-sion Felipe Guacrapáucar received prohibiting Spanish haciendas in the Mantaro Valley was not challenged by the Spanish because their focus was on the mineral wealth to the south rather than on farming (Arguedas n.d.: 13).

The institution of the encomienda reveals much about the logic of the Spanish colony in comparison to the Inca Empire. While Ramirez (1996: 61) notes that there was a superficial similarity between the Inca system of trusteeship and the Spanish encomienda, there were also significant differences. In the Inca system, wealth and feasting were physical manifestations of the power of leaders, to such an extent, as we have seen above, that the escalation of reciprocal demands became unwieldy (Rostworowski 1988). For the Spanish, wealth was important, but at least as important were honours, such as titles or Felipe Guacrapáucar's coat of arms. The latter were so important, in fact, that the Peruvian colonial elite had more titles but less wealth than that of Spain's other colonies (Flores Galindo 1987: 125). In this system, wealth moved up the hierarchy while honours came down. This was a significant difference in the extraction of wealth from the Inca system. Remember that leaders under the Incas were a conduit for goods going both up and down the hierarchy, and based their legitimacy among followers on the ever-increasing volume of stores under their command. For indigenous leaders, required to collect and hand over tribute from their followers to the Spanish without receiving resources to redistribute back down and buttress their status, the squeeze became oppressive (Ramirez 1996: 34). Rights to tribute and labour, and how the levels of taxation were calculated became critical. Hence, Guacrapáucar made these a central part of the concessions he demanded (Espinoza Soriano 1973: 172–3).

The amount of tribute, used to provide labour to extract wealth from the mines, as well as in goods or money, was based on the number of adult male citizens in an encomienda. War and illness decimated the population but the Spaniards had no efficient continuous census reporting as the Incas had. Indeed, encomenderos resisted more accurate population counts by the Crown so they could limit the amount of tribute they had to pass on (Stern 1993: 121–5). Thus, lower numbers were reported up, thus trying to reduce the outgoing wealth, and higher numbers demanded from those lower on the ladder, in an attempt to increase incoming wealth from tribute (Mayer 1972: 353–4). Further, while the Incas had strictly controlled mobility, ensuring that citizens were either at home under the authority of their local leaders or on approved state business in other locations, again the

Spaniards – and the local curacas in their charge – lacked the Inca ability to control people. Subjects failed to return home after participating in armies or performing encomienda labour elsewhere, or ran away to avoid the demand to pay tribute. As *forasteros*, or outsiders, they would not have had the rights of citizens, for example to land, but they would also not have had the tributary burden. Don Felipe had some success with his petitions to demand regular tribute from the forasteros in his territory and to require that his citizens living elsewhere be forced to return (Espinoza Soriano 1973: 172–3).

Crisis in the Sixteenth Century: Governance I

By the 1560s, Peru was in crisis, reeling from tensions over tribute, shortages of labour, and the ongoing Inca resistance. At one level, the crisis manifested itself in a moral and economic debate over the encomienda system in Spain and among the Spanish in Peru, while at another the indigenous people, even those who had proven their loyalty like the Huancas, planned rebellion. The economic, moral, and ideological dimensions of the situation, woven through local and global levels, call to mind the straits in which Peru found itself four centuries later at the end of the twentieth century, as we will see in chapters 5 to 8. The precise forms and reasons differ, but both periods were characterized by economic stagnation, external demands for tribute or debt payments, inconsistent and ineffectively administered policies, and uprisings with a millennarian[7] air.

The debt crisis faced by Peru in the 1980s and 1990s, with international lenders demanding repayment,[8] had its sixteenth-century counterpart in Spanish King Felipe II's (Philip II's) economic demands. Felipe II, trying to maintain what he had inherited of the Hapsburg Empire, was engaged in putting down internal insurrections and the Dutch uprising, along with repelling Turkish invaders. He needed money. Because the Crown's share of New World wealth came largely from the tribute that trickled up from the indigenous people, to their curacas, on to the encomenderos and so on, he looked for a way to eliminate some of the middle people who took a share along the way (Stern 1993: 97). Could the encomienda system be abolished to turn the indigenous people into direct subjects of the Crown? Until the 1550s there had been no rigorous method of ensuring that a share went to the Crown. Facing the threat of losing access to crucial labour power, the encomenderos offered a huge sum in exchange for exclusive hereditary rights to the people. The indigenous leaders did likewise, in an attempt to arrest the outflow of their people. As we have seen, the Spanish had left indigenous political structures in place, reorienting them to serve Spanish goals of domination as well as to extract labour, tribute, and goods. By creating new local territories through the encomiendas and redrawing the lines of the old ones, however, the Spanish had caused the number of curacas to increase as minor leaders were freed from allegiance to their former ayllu chiefs and instead dealt directly with Spanish encomenderos (Sempat Assadourian 1994: 209–92).

Liberal priests such as the Dominican Bartolomé de las Casas and Domingo de Santo Tomás, horrified by Spanish abuses, agreed that the encomiendas should disappear (Bauer 2001).[9] They cited the global moral force of the papacy to argue that the Pope had ceded Peruvian souls to Spain so that they could be protected and saved. While de las Casas and Santo Tomás wanted the king to maintain guardianship of the souls, allowing priests access to them, they also radically argued that the indigenous people themselves should be accorded more political authority over their affairs.

This global-level political, economic, and moral battle had a local parallel in the discontent of the indigenous people. As noted above, they had borne the brunt of the Conquest and its ongoing struggle, giving their lives in combat, their goods and labour in tribute, and dying from new diseases. They were being pressured to give up their spiritual beliefs for those of the European priests. We have seen one way that they could avoid some of these burdens by escaping and becoming forasteros. By the 1560s there were organized collective forms of resistance. Most significantly, the continuing resistance of the Incas constituted one pole of dissent to Spanish rule. Hidden in the jungle east of Cusco, successive Inca kings launched attacks against the Spanish and their indigenous allies, with short respites, until 1572 (Stern 1993). But there were also other options for indigenous people who did not yearn for the return of the Inca system.[10] One of these was the Taqi Onqoy.

The Taqi Onqoy is described by several analysts (Millones 1973a, 1973b; Stern 1993; Wachtel 1973) as a millennarian movement, offering a spiritual Andean revivalist solution to problems resulting from the invasion of foreigners. It arose in 1564 in Parinacochas (Stern 1993: 51), in the current department of Ayacucho, a region known in the 1980s as the epicentre of Sendero Luminoso (Shining Path).[11]

Sendero Luminoso is the revolutionary movement whose actions and repression led to the deaths of up to 69,000 people between 1980 and 1990 (Comisión de la Verdad y Reconciliación, Perú 2004: 9).

Sendero Luminoso's sixteenth-century precursor, Taki Onqoy, was described as more spiritually driven and less militaristic, but it still worried the Spanish colonial authorities. Followers were enjoined to give up Spanish beliefs and practices and return to an Andean world view. They would sing and dance uncontrollably in spirit possession (Stern 1993: 52). Women were apparently particularly prone to joining the movement. Recent reinterpretations of Taki Onqoy suggest that the movement itself was insignificant. Rather, it was manipulated by an ambitious Spanish priest to further his own career and to discredit the Dominicans, who advocated greater autonomy for indigenous people (Mumford 1998).[12]

Taki Onqoy may have been a minor localized form of expression of indigenous resistance to the new situation, but there is evidence that indigenous unrest was widespread: closer to our area of study there was another example. In 1565 a store of arms manufactured by the Huancas was discovered in Jauja, apparently in preparation for an armed uprising (García de Castro 1921; Espinoza Soriano 1973: 175–8). The preparations were discovered before coming to fruition and the acting viceroy responded by sending one of the encomenderos of the area to investigate. Those arms that had not been destroyed by the Huancas were confiscated.

The significance of Taki Onqoy and other forms of local rebellion, however, is not simply that they involved resisting Spanish authority: the other side of the struggle, as it was in the case of Sendero Luminoso, was how authorities reacted. In both cases, the outcome extended and strengthened the political reach of the state. In the late sixteenth century, the Spanish were deeply worried by the situation and a flurry of reports flew about to analyse the problems. Clearly, government initiated studies and proposed solutions are not the invention of modern democratic states. The most wide-ranging and detailed study was carried out by Juan de Matienzo in 1567. Matienzo was appointed in the late 1550s to the post of *oidor*, or magistrate, in what is now Bolivia (Lohmann Villena 1967: xxvi).

Matienzo not only heard cases relating to local justice matters, but also researched the history of the Andean region to propose solutions to the problems. He had arrived during the debate over the future of the encomiendas and had taken the side of the encomenderos against that of the liberal Dominican priests. Thus, in his view, the Incas had been cruel despots, and their subjects were rescued by honourable Spaniards (Matienzo 1967: 6–14). The first part of Matienzo's *Gobierno del Perú* minutely deals with issues concerning the indigenous people with respect to governance, tribute, morality, economy, work relations, religion, and relations with the Spanish. The second part analyses the governance structure of the Spanish and the infrastructure and tribute obligations, religious bureaucracy, and comportment of the European population.

Matienzo's vision was for a system of indigenous labourers, farmers, and craftspeople, under the direction of Spanish encomenderos, mine owners, and factory owners. In an early episode of anti-collectivist policy, he attacked the abuses by the curacas of their people and recommended the institution of private property for indigenous people to replace the collective administration of land by local leaders (Matienzo 1967: 19–24, 57–9). On this point, he cites Aristotle, claiming that private property will lead to greater care of resources. Payment for obligatory and voluntary labour in mines or other work should be made to the individual rather than to the curaca, as had been the practice in the past when the curaca was responsible for raising the money to pay tribute. This would allow individuals to invest in livestock and other goods, leading to their improvement and incorporating them into the economy.

Further, Matienzo argued, the people should be moved to towns, where they could be administered by Spanish officials (1967: 48–56). He even provides a model layout for the central plaza, with its church, hospital, and jail. His attention extends to concerns that feature prominently now in development trends, involving health and environmental sustainability. Thus, he indicates where human waste should be disposed of in order to protect people from illness (53), and urges reforestation and conservation practices so that there is a future supply of firewood (273–4).[13]

Many of Matienzo's recommendations were shortly to be put in place by Viceroy Francisco de Toledo. His arrival in 1569 ended several years of provisional, ineffectual, or corrupt viceroys (Hemming 1983: 389; Stern 1993: 76). Toledo himself went on an extensive tour of the Andes to study the situation. Among the most significant changes for indigenous people, he implemented Matienzo's suggestion to resettle them from rural areas to towns (*reducciones*) more accessible to the Spanish, and rearranged the productive relations and techniques to revive mining in Potosí (Stern 1993: 76–7). He also captured the remaining Inca king, Túpac Amaru, in 1572 and executed him.[14]

Viceroy Toledo is perceived as a strong political leader who reorganized the political and economic structure of Peru. This restructuring wrenched local political ties, replacing them with a greater reliance on the state. He seems to have done this, not for personal gain, but to bolster the colonial system.[15] Indeed, Stern is quite impressed at Toledo's ability to carry out such transformatory reforms, attributing his success in part to the demoralized state of both indigenous people and elites (1993: 77). Toledo adopted Matienzo's suggestion of moving indigenous people to Spanish-style towns and restructuring their relationship to the state. Huajlas was abandoned at this time (Espinoza Soriano 1969: 16–17), although not everybody moved to the appointed centre of Huaripampa (Adams 1959: 51; see also Silverblatt 1987).

The line of authority also changed. The Toledan reforms of 1570 changed the form of local political representation, explicitly forbidding curacas from serving on cabildos, or councils. Instead, those in charge of governing the affairs of the indigenous people were elected each year. This was intended to limit the power of the traditional curacas (Thurner 1997: 37), while still maintaining separate, although hierarchically linked governance systems for Indians and Spaniards. As Thurner points out, while separate, these ethnically based 'republics' developed integrally linked to one another.

A third area in which Toledo oversaw change was technology. Production in the mines in Potosí had fallen because of continuing labour problems and having reached the limits of exploitation given in an earlier mining system. Along with restructuring the labour system, with more effective forced labour, Toledo implemented the new amalgamation method, using mercury from mines in Huancavelica, to revive silver production (Stern 1993: 76; Hemming 1983: 371, 407).[16]

There are features of this sixteenth-century crisis that recurred in the twentieth century as the backdrop to the projects discussed in this book: economic stagnation, external pressure for tribute or debt payments, social and political unrest, and global debates about morality and profitability leading to the revitalization of production organization and technology, all being addressed through the transformation of governance structures. The attempt to revitalize the sixteenth-century Peruvian economy was repeated with Fujimori's neo-liberal reforms of the 1990s, which, among other measures, privatized the mining sector in the hope of attracting investment to improve its efficiency.

I do not wish to overstate the similarities, however. Wolf (1999) reminds us to pay attention to the overarching structural power relations that guide the specific goals pursued and how those goals are pursued by politically positioned actors. The logic underpinning the sixteenth-century crisis and its resolution was that corresponding to feudal extraction, although there is also the foreshadowing of investments in technology and more secure access to labour, if not exactly the creation of a proletariat. Elite players, or those ambitious Spaniards attracted to the New World out of the promise of becoming elite players, had their eye on the privileges and honours accorded after the Conquest. The labour force was, in large part, literally forced to work, and the drive to produce was based on the elite's desire for wealth and honour and the Crown's demand for tribute.

In contrast, the structure underpinning the crises of the 1980s to the present in Peru is capitalist. Comparing Matienzo's report with a 2005 World Bank poverty assessment (Sánchez-Páramo et al. 2005), we see similar concerns for poverty, education of the poor ('poor' is used rather than 'indigenous'), and a recommendation to promote individual land titles, seen as a way to improve access to credit. Like Matienzo, the report sees collective landholding as a brake on rural development: 'At the same time efforts to increase land titling should continue. Provisions should also be made to account for the high prevalence of communal property of land among the indigenous population, and the negative impact that this may have on the capacity of the individuals in these communities to access credit' (Sánchez-Páramo et al. 2005: 9). These prescriptions are thus explicitly related to the capitalist economic growth of Peru, rather than to the moral justification of the domination of the indigenous people and of the extraction of tribute from them.

The pattern established by Toledo structured the colony through the seventeenth century, in which the indigenous people slowly reformulated their culture and lives to this new reality (Silverblatt 1995). This does not mean there was no resistance: the most obvious is the 1780s indigenous uprisings by Túpac Amaru II and Túpac Katari. In the event, the greater danger to the Spanish empire lay in the ambitions of the colonial criollo elite, comprised of people with European roots born in the colonies, who spearheaded the fight for independence from Spain in 1821. I now turn to a discussion of some of the political implications of the republic for the people of Allpachico.

Republican Peru: Continuing to Seek Freedom, or Upscaling Subjection

While the criollo elites may have reveled in their new independence from Spain, the indigenous peoples were still bound to service in haciendas or to local regional elites. Because there were no large landholdings in the area of Allpachico, thanks to Guacrapáucar's concession from the Spanish king, it was to the local centres of power, some indigenous and some mestizo, that the people were subject. Thurner (1997) argues that, although in theory the republic created a single polity in which all were citizens, in practice the indigenous people were kept out of full citizenship by the criollo rulers. This did not keep them from endeavouring to exercise their legal rights as they tried to negotiate their place in the nation, wending through the different interests and concerns of the indigenous elites, criollo landholders, the church, and the state.

In the central highlands, a mining-merchant-landholding elite slowly and unevenly promoted a process of incipient regional capitalist development, according to Manrique (1987). Contreras (1988) sees this as articulated with the peasant economy, rather than transforming the latter. Remember that access to land had remained largely in indigenous hands in the Mantaro Valley in the colonial era because of Guacrapáucar's deal with Spain. After Peru became independent, in a revival of Matienzo's anti-collectivist sentiment, Bolívar abolished indigenous communities and ordered their land to be distributed among the families (Piel 1970: 117–18). The result in many cases was the appropriation of land by indigenous and non-indigenous elites. There is evidence that this occurred to some extent in the Mantaro Valley (e.g., Grondín 1978a), but it seems to have been less acute than in other areas. Thus, Mallon (1995) observes that peasant subsistence production strengthened until about 1850. Because the people of Allpachico bought their land from the indigenous community of Huaripampa in 1929, I assume that this area remained in the hands of the indigenous peasantry.

Although subsistence agriculture was their mainstay, the regional peasantry also participated in the regional mining and commercial economy. Contreras (1988) reviews work patterns in the Cerro de Pasco mines to discover that the labour-intensive mining extraction relied on temporary workers during the agricultural off-season. Only the much less labour-intensive mineral refining stage required a permanent labour force. Further development of this economy would have required technological innovation and the establishment of a proletariat. Any move in this direction, however, was interrupted by the War of the Pacific, and when it was resumed in the early part of the twentieth century, the reins were in the hands of foreign capital and the Lima-based bourgeoisie (Manrique 1987).

The War of the Pacific was thus an important event in the history of the regional economy, and, as we will now see, was also pivotal in how assertions of local independence affected the establishment of the community of Allpachico.

According to local oral history, the community of Allpachico was formed at some point in the mid-nineteenth century, as a result of a dispute between senior and junior members of an extended family which comprised the then common community of Allpa. Up to the time of the dispute, Allpa was a herding satellite of a Mantaro Valley community, Huaripampa, which had been established as a reducción under the Toledo reforms of 1570. Those living in the satellite would have been engaged in hierarchical reciprocal ties with those living in the town, who held the legal title. Thus, the satellite dwellers were in a position of dependence, herding livestock for the town dwellers.

This relationship reflects the colonial tributary form, rather than the liberal individualism promised by the republic. Satellites were responsible for carrying out various public works in administrative centres (Alberti and Sanchez 1974). In the case of Allpachico, this may have been the regional dominant city of Jauja or Huaripampa or both. The distance from these centres (between about 15 and 20 kilometres) may have offered some protection, but when they did have to go to fulfill their obligations it was an added burden. Many of the political border disputes in the region centred on the struggle of the satellites to achieve independence from these centres. Adams (1959: 31) describes how Muquiyauyo, a larger satellite of Huaripampa, long resisted the domination of the latter and gained independence to become its own district capital in 1886.

The reason for the dispute within the satellite family in Allpa is not clear, but because the story is phrased in terms of senior and junior branches of the family, it may have had to do with access to resources or power within the group. In any case, the junior branch moved away to establish themselves along the banks of the Mantaro River, a place closer to better agricultural land and farther from the pasture. The date of the move is unknown, but it had certainly taken place by the War of the Pacific, between 1879 and 1884.

Despite the fact that Peru lost the War of the Pacific to Chile, it is widely celebrated in the central highlands, where successful skirmishes or acts of bravery highlight local involvement (Manrique 1981, 1987, 1988; Tullis 1970). After Peru lost the sea campaign, the Chileans invaded the central highlands in 1881. Indigenous peoples' participation has been extensively analysed in a debate over whether it was an ethnic battle arising from local tensions with white elites (Bonilla 1978; Favre 1973), or a patriotic move as the peasantry built their position within the state (Mallon 1983; Manrique 1988; Thurner 1997). The evidence from the region of Allpachico tends towards the latter explanation, although it is also shot through with struggles for local autonomy of satellites and annexes from administrative centres.

The key event commemorated in this region involved the ambush of a detachment of Chilean troops, who were either on patrol or foraging up the Mantaro River from Jauja where they were stationed (Mendoza Melendez n.d.). A leading member of the community of Piedra Blanca, five kilometres farther upriver from present day Allpachico, organized peasants from the area to attack the Chileans at a narrowing of the river canyon.[17] The Chileans were forced to retreat, but the suspension bridge crossing the river back to Jauja had been cut.

The event is one of many in the region, and its significance in terms of the war is unremarkable. In the postwar period, however, Piedra Blanca managed to leverage it to great advantage. Specifically, Piedra Blanca was granted district capital status (Concha Posadas 1971: n.p.), freeing it from various obligations to its centre, also Huaripampa.[18] This sort of independence was often accorded as a reward for service in the War of the Pacific (Mallon 1983: 105; cf. Adams 1959; Grondín 1978b; Manrique 1987: 172). Allpachico became an annex of Piedra Blanca, helping to break its dependence on the Mantaro Valley town that still held title to the land. Within a few decades, that, too, would subside. Slowly, the tributary dependency that subjected the people of Allpachico to traditional Mantaro Valley centres was being replaced by the more contractual rights of local and national citizenship.

Conclusion

This historical survey has focused on how the people of Allpachico have engaged in wider political projects. The Huancas, Incas, Spanish, and republicans all instituted structures which conceptualized the people as resources, from whom wealth, goods, labour, or political support could be extracted through different mechanisms in each period. Each dominant system reformed the economic base and people's role in it, and tried to deal with the inevitable crisis through technological innovation and political reorganization. Because planning to achieve specific economic goals, along with technological innovation and social reorganization, are taken to be hallmarks of intentional development, it is hard to pinpoint when such development started. Nevertheless, while the tools of crisis resolution may be similar in different periods, the overarching structure is distinct. Thus, the Incas reformed the Huancas as a united ethnic group bound to the state through rights of reciprocity, while subject to obligations of support. The Spanish replaced this with a unidirectional tributary system, which extracted labour and wealth while leaving significant control in the hands of local indigenous leaders. The tributary system was slow to change in the Republic of Peru, but ambitious indigenous peoples gradually worked to achieve autonomy through insisting on rights of citizenship. The struggle in each period was embedded in the possibilities allowed by the political and economic structure (Wolf 1999). As we move forward in time to examine the twentieth and early twenty-first centuries, the structure gradually becomes more capitalist. In the next chapter, we turn from the larger dimension of the polity to the local community to see how it has become a vehicle of development for many actors, from the people to the state and beyond.

4 Community Development: Definition, Context, and History in Allpachico

> The complexity of *community* thus relates to the difficult interaction between the tendencies originally distinguished in the historical development: on the one hand the sense of direct common concern; on the other hand the materialization of various forms of common organization, which may or may not adequately express this. *Community* can be the warmly persuasive word to describe an existing set of relationships, or the warmly persuasive word to describe an alternative set of relationships. What is most important, perhaps, is that unlike all other terms of social organization (*state, nation, society,* etc.) it seems never to be used unfavourably, and never to be given any positive opposing or distinguishing term.
> – Raymond Williams, *Keywords: A Vocabulary of Culture and Society*

Community is an important keyword in development practice. How it is defined and what the implications are for its mode of implementation in practice are thus central issues. Williams' observation that community can refer to both existing and alternative groups is very relevant in development practice, as we will see. In this chapter I review conceptual and instrumental framings of community and place Allpachico in the context of a specific Peruvian understanding of the term. I begin by reviewing briefly some of the ways in which community is invoked in development and then turn to focus on how the relationship between the community and the state has been analysed. I also outline some important differences among households in Allpachico. This framing of the issue provides the basis for a discussion of the particular significance of the peasant community in Peru, before turning to a history of Allpachico as a community in the twentieth century.

The Community in Development

In Chapter 2 I discussed the Peru-Cornell Project (PPC) in Vicos, Peru. This project took a community as its subject of intervention, building on a strong anthropological interest in the community as a focus of study (e.g., Arguedas 1968; Redfield 1956; Wolf 1955, 1957, 1986). This was not the first time that communities had received attention in development policy and practice (Cowen and Shenton 1996), but it was important in constituting local-level action as a major theme in the wave of development after the Second World War, with its multifarious multilateral, bilateral, national policy, and NGO-led strands.

A wide variety of development trends explicitly focuses on some articulation of the local. Hickey and Mohan (2004b) review a range of participatory approaches from the 1940s to the early 2000s, including community development, liberation theology, alternative development, participation in development, social capital, and participatory governance. The number of different approaches and their constant reformulation to deal with criticisms of prior versions attest to the importance that some iteration of 'community' has in current development practice. Although there were important earlier cases of participatory development, including Vicos (also Khan 1997)[1], Chambers' work (e.g., 1983, 1994a, 1994b, 1994c, 1997, 2008) is probably the best known, so I will focus on it here.

The emphasis in Chambers' discussion is on the participation of the people in articulating their concerns, analysing their resources and needs, and carrying out solutions. His insistence that 'the people can do it' provided an important check to outside expert authority. Early forms of participatory rural appraisal (PRA) assumed a particularly romantic and homogeneous notion of community, but Chambers (2008) and other PRA proponents (e.g., Guijt and Shah 1998) more recently acknowledge internal divisions based on such elements as wealth and gender.[2] Although Chambers insists that development workers should use their best judgment rather than apply rote practice, techniques are central to participatory approaches, using facilitators to generate information and ideas from participants, often organized in groups or assemblies.

Much of the criticism of participatory approaches charges that they are 'tyrannical' (Cooke and Kothari 2001; Hickey and Mohan 2004a), applying rote methods with an incomplete and naive understanding of power, or allowing the power of group dynamics to swamp minority interests.[3] While PRA may warn about project capture by male elites within communities (e.g., Chambers 2008: 35–6), there is little attention paid to the wider political economic dynamics that create poverty. Further, Chambers is extremely vague about how the subject population is to be defined. Despite frequent invocations to pay attention to the 'who' of development (e.g., *Whose Reality Counts?*, the title of his 1997 book, and the 'Who Counts?' and 'Whose Space?' chapters in his 2008 book) there is little discussion of how these people are to be determined, beyond references to 'lowers,' as opposed to 'uppers,' and women rather than men. He also mentions 'the poor' or 'the people.'

This vagueness ostensibly allows for flexibility and self-identification. Thus, for example, in a World Bank publication, Coirolo et al. (2001) refuse to define the community in their Community-Based Rural Development approach. They argue there are too many possible forms for local organizations to take. Nevertheless, their presentation makes it clear that the successful ones are formally organized with clear membership structures and rules, and have partnerships with government, NGOs, and other agencies. They are thus envisioned as part of the larger society and interacting with it. However, this position demonstrates a paradox: while the people are lauded as capable of undertaking the direction of their futures themselves, facilitators are the ones responsible for deciding which of the people are the legitimate representatives – presumably the poorest and most marginal (Cowen and Shenton 1996). The process both assumes an existing autonomously capable community, and strives to achieve an ideal community, something only possible through the help of outside facilitators. As Pieterse (1998: 348) observes of participatory types of development: 'Running the risk of flippancy, one might say that the kind of world in which alternative development works is a world that does not need it.'

In addition to the paradox over the identification of community boundaries, the lack of attention to the external context is a major problem in these approaches. Chambers repeatedly warns about authoritarian interference by facilitators, government officials, development agents, and so on, but there is no analysis of the relationship between such major sectors as the state or the market. Let us now turn to the dynamic between the community and these broader forces.

The Community and the State

Analysts writing from a wide range of theoretical positions have examined the relationship between the community and the state. For example, from a Marxist viewpoint, Cowen and Shenton (1996) study state policy about communities, viewing it as part of the state's trusteeship role in trying to mitigate the negative effects of capitalist crisis. They observe that policy may see communities as a barrier to growth in some periods, and as the central mechanism to be used in, as well as being the goal of, interventions in others. Here, community is formed by state processes, themselves the product of specific historical circumstances. State economic management and political negotiation are the major forces, while community agency is given short shrift in this analysis.

Alternatively, in a Foucauldian account, Rose (1999) focuses on identity-based communities as nodes in the implementation of governmentality. He traces the transformation from a system in which governments discipline citizens through institutions and rule enforcement towards ever more decentralized and informal mechanisms of managing behaviours in a society. With the multiplication of ways in which individuals identify themselves – through neighbourhood, ethnicity, sexuality, interests, and so on – they come to see themselves as members of various communities. Rose argues that this sense of community membership induces self-regulation, thus minimizing the need for disciplinary force. Identity rather than economic processes is central to this view. As with Cowen and Shenton, again there is a limited role for community or individual agency, since everything is understood to be part of the same power system in Foucauldian analyses.

Li (2007: 17–19) addresses the problem of agency, noting that Foucault's insistence that subjects cannot be external to power is limiting. For this, she turns to Gramsci, who recognizes the coexistence of competing hegemonic projects. For Gramsci, while one set of ideas may be dominant, alternatives await means and opportunities to challenge it. Hardt (1995: 37) offers a way to reconcile some of the differences between Marx and Foucault, maintaining a focus on economic relations: 'Straining their periodizations a bit, we could say that Foucault's societies of sovereignty correspond to feudal relations of production; disciplinary regimes rely on what Marx calls the formal subsumption of labor under capital; and the societies of control point to the real subsumption of labor under capital.' We can use this framing to see how disciplinary means and extensions of control are used to induce people to acquiesce to their own exploitation, either directly through the exchange of their labour power, or indirectly through the exchange of the products of their labour. This places production relations at the centre of the dynamic, and allows the researcher to examine both the disciplinary instrumental policy that Cowen and Shenton emphasize, while also trying to uncover the historical agency through which capitalist citizens are formed subjectively.

I now turn to a discussion of how the institution of the community has been formulated by different strategists at the state and local level. This is followed by a history of the community of Allpachico in the twentieth century to show how the various actors negotiate around community as practice and as project.

The *Comunidad* in Peruvian Policy

The community has been a central actor in the Peruvian sociopolitical realm, albeit with different structures, uses, and content in different historical periods. Here I focus on the provision established in the 1920 Constitution setting up the legal status of *comunidad indígena* (indigenous community), and its later transformations. After 1969, the comunidad indígena became the *comunidad campesina* (peasant community). These legal forms of community were layered on top of earlier experience. We have seen in Chapter 3 how in the development of both the Inca and Spanish states the local community was an organizational means by which resources could be produced and extracted. However, at the same time that the local community could be used as a tool for extracting wealth, the necessary coordination this involved among the people allowed them to resist such extraction and domination. While the Incas are described as having ways to minimize this resistance through hierarchical reciprocity and state surveillance, the Spanish colonial authorities, both before and after the Toledan reforms, were ineffective in infiltrating local life. Current projects to decentralize the government so that regional and municipal levels have more power might be seen as the latest drive to incorporate local communities into the larger political economy, a process begun some few thousand years earlier. The success of this initiative will depend on such elements as effective coercion by the state or community response to incentives offered in the process. Thus, one focus here is the increasing density of the relationship between local populations and the larger polity.

As we saw in the last chapter, separate indigenous communities were officially abolished after the Wars of Independence in 1824, although this did not mean their actual disappearance (Piel 1970: 117). With the collection of tribute still in the charge of the community leaders, and with the desire in the communities to make their own place in the nation, there were more forces in place to maintain the groups than to destroy them. In 1895 when Nicolas de Piérola took over the government, he announced, among other modernization programs, that there would be a project for the 'civilization and incorporation' of Indians (Mallon 1983: 133). These attempts to deal with the 'Indians' came at a time when the peasantry was called on to provide more intensive labour than ever before for national development and to serve foreign capital investment. That is, their labour was needed for the mines, the railways, and the fledgling industrial growth in Lima. Later, in the 1920s and 1930s, they would also be required to build roads. Economic growth had advanced beyond the stage when public works service duty, the importation of black slaves, or indentured Chinese labourers could provide the necessary labour.

The project of incorporating this labour force squarely addressed their indigenous identity, alongside an apparently opposing movement that had the goal of protecting indigenous people.[4] The indigenista movement, discussed in Chapter 2, tended to idealize 'traditional' Andean culture,[5] while incorporating a paternalistic attitude to Indians (Piel 1967: 396), considering them to be 'noble savages' (Flores Galindo 1983: 24).[6] The government of Augusto Leguía coopted indigenist language, along with its paternalism, through the creation of an agency for the 'Guardianship of the Indian Race' (Davies 1974: 77). At the same time as this interest in indigenismo was taking place at the intellectual and bureaucratic levels, the vocabulary was becoming a rhetorical medium for the indigenous people themselves, who began to agitate for land (e.g., Piel 1967: 397). In response, in 1920 Leguía recognized indigenous communities in the Constitution (Pike 1967: 222). I use the Spanish term, *comunidad*, to refer to the legal entity, while community will be taken to cover the wide range of more informal collectivities that have practical existence.[7]

The 1920 Constitution did little more than recognize the comunidades' existence and declare that the law would address their rights. Although the article passed with only two votes against it nothing was done to promote it throughout the 1920s (Basadre 1970, vol. 13: 45). Communities were not required to register, and only 321 of them did so before 1930 (Davies 1974: 90).

The legal recognition of the comunidad indígena was reiterated in the 1933 Constitution, and in 1936 registration was required in order to benefit from the provisions of the law (Davies 1974: 124). There were potential advantages to official registration: the 1933 Constitution declared comunidad lands to be inalienable and undertook to give land to those which had insufficient. However, there was also the obligation to work some land communally. From 1933 to 1939, 700 communities were granted recognition, including Allpachico. President Benavides sent agents to modernize production techniques and settle land disputes (Pike 1967: 275; Mallon 1983: 270–1; Trivelli 1992).

Mallon sees the recognition of the comunidad as an integrating pressure to bring the indigenous people under the control of the government:

> Perhaps most important for the peasant sector in general, the 1920 constitution made the state the key intermediary in political and property relations between Indian communities and the larger society. Because it also made peasants dependent on the government to settle internal disputes over politics and resources, the legal recognition of Indian communities would in the long run accomplish more than any other law to integrate the peasantry into the developing capitalist economy. (Mallon 1983: 232; see also Long and Roberts 1978: 4)

Legal comunidad status provided a means for the state to instigate development by using local labour and resources to build roads, schools, irrigation channels, and so on, and was thus framed as the 'embryo of a new society' (Urrutia 1992: 3–4; see also Long and Roberts 1978: 314). Legal status constituted one means by which the state could access comuneros and allowed the comunidad to petition for (but not always receive) state resources. It could also, as Grondín (1978a) pointed out, facilitate the internal exploitation of some comuneros by others.

In 1969, the comunidad got a policy makeover by the 'revolutionary' military government of General Juan Velasco Alvarado. Velasco had taken power in a coup in 1968 and set about implementing reforms that the previous Belaúnde government had been unable to achieve (Cotler 1983).[8] Agrarian reform and repatriating the economy from foreign ownership were top priorities in an agenda described as neither communist nor capitalist.[9] Thus, the agrarian reform was intended to dislodge land from the grip of a traditional oligarchy, while nationalization of mining and petroleum, along with new industrial and labour policies, addressed foreign domination. The emphasis in the agrarian reform was on collective production: cooperatives were set up on the former sugar estates of the coast; Social Agrarian Interest Societies were instituted in former haciendas in the highlands; and the statute on the comunidad indígena was rewritten, now calling it a comunidad campesina. The military government's experiment is largely considered a failure, although Lowenthal (1983) argues that it did achieve necessary structural transformation of the Peruvian elite. The agrarian reform is one of the failures: although vaunted as a centrepiece of the overall reform, there were few resources to ensure that production could compete with cheap food imports. The latter was a priority, because support for industry and the urban proletariat resulted in food price controls that hurt farming incomes (Thorp 1983). Indeed, Trivelli (1992: 24) notes that the number of comunidades recognized over Velasco's seven years in power (431) was lower than in the five years of the previous Belaúnde government (624). Further, 1970 was the only year in which no comunidades were recognized since 1919.[10] Thus, despite apparent government support for the comunidad, little changed except for the statute.

Researchers also lost interest in the comunidad per se. Urrutia (1992) notes that after the 'golden age' of comunidad studies in the 1950s and 1960s, Peruvian anthropologists changed their focus from the institution to examine processes of integration into capitalism, peasant economy, stratification, and migration, among other themes. While they may have retained the community as their subject, foreign anthropologists were also incorporating more complexity in their research. For example, Gavin Smith's (1989) case study of Huasicancha combines attention to economic processes with an analysis of the role of the community as an institution and as a set of practices and discourse. The study is based on Huasicancha's long-fought struggle for land with a neighbouring hacienda. From the mid-twentieth century, Huasicanchino households became intensively engaged in a variety of activites, including peasant agriculture and informal-sector work in Lima and other cities. People invoked community as the vehicle through which they could make claims on others, thus avoiding monetarily costly market prices, as they negotiated multiple activities. In this way, commodified and non-commodified factors were entangled in simple commodity production. In turn, this entrenchment of the idiom of community provided village leaders with a tool around which to mobilize for the land, a struggle linked to their own livelihood strategies. 'Community,' then, had many meanings, and these changed at different moments in the political fight and through economic practices. Thus, Smith insists on the continued significance of community for Huasicanchinos, while recognizing that this significance was dynamic, heterogenous, and entwined with their engagement in the wider political economy.

Peasant uprisings over land and the response by the state in the 1960s and early 1970s gave way to a period of policy neglect. This lifted slightly in the late 1980s, when Alan García's first government (1986–90) showed support for the comunidades and even allocated funds to them.[11] In the context of severe crisis in the capitalist economy, along with deteriorating political security because of the rise of Sendero Luminoso (Shining Path) and associated military repression, the comunidad came to be a fairly safe place – at least those outside of the zones of terrorist activities. However, frequent poor management and high inflation detracted from the effectiveness of García's funding (Robles Mendoza 2002: 112–14).[12]

With the 1990s and the neo-liberal government of Alberto Fujimori, both government and researchers[13] (e.g., del Castillo 1992; Diez 1999; Golte 1992; Mayer 1996; Mossbrucker 1990; Pajuelo 2000; Urrutia 1992, 2001) contemplated the future of the comunidad campesina. Consistent with his accommodation of neo-liberalism, Fujimori did not view collective endeavours kindly, and he implemented legislation that would allow for comunidad land to be privatized and for comunidades to be dissolved (Robles Mendoza 2002: 114–16). Both of these new policies aimed at undermining the comunidad were put in place as part of a plan to instigate capitalist agricultural production. Private land titles would permit individuals to use their land as collateral for bank loans to invest in production. In theory, although not always in practice, land in comunidades is owned in common and distributed to households on the basis of need. Even where land was effectively privately controlled, people did not always have valid titles. Privately owned land was subject to land taxes, so there was a disincentive for people to apply for titles except in exceptionally productive areas. In the end, Fujimori's policies had little impact (Robles Mendoza 2002: 116). The economic stability brought about by his reforms did little to address the gap between rich and poor in the country.

This avoidance of the comunidad political structure continues in the 2000s. As we will see in chapters 7 and 8, projects and municipal participatory budgeting both attempt to sideline the comunidad by courting or creating other civil society groups. The second government of Alan García, beginning in 2006, in stark contrast to his first presidency, has attacked the comunidad, proposing legislation to facilitate privatization of the land, although some of the key elements were repealed (Eguren, Castillo, and del Castillo 2008). Again, capitalist production is taken as the preferred engine of growth, as García explicitly targetted producers who do not use all of their land. Nevertheless, comunidad status continues to be important to their members. There are now over 6,000 comunidades campesinas, with about half of Peru's rural population, controlling 40 per cent of the agricultural land (Eguren, del Castillo and Burneo 2009: 29).

This overview of the history of the comunidad in Peru in the past century demonstrates a cycle of greater to lesser government support, linked to wider economic conditions and policy. From having been seen as the basic cell for fomenting local development in the 1920s and 1930s, a notion reiterated after Velasco's 1969 agrarian reform, then picked up again by García in the late 1980s, now, again, the comunidad is being presented as a barrier to growth. Comunidades and comuneros have adapted to these circumstances, seeking legal status and government support when this offered opportunities (even, at times, counter to government attempts to eliminate them), and undertaking other activities as they arose (see also Mayer 1996; Nugent 1994). While different governments have attempted to undermine the comunidad, so far comuneros may neglect it at times, but they do not abandon it. Experience shows that it can be a helpful institution in times of crisis, and Peru's peasantry is all too familiar with crisis. Experience of the comunidad also provides the template for the new collective endeavours – while the comunidad may not be in style, this does not mean that governments or NGOs have abandoned collective forms. As we will see, while the comunidad was the normal organizing structure for development projects until the end of the 1980s, in the 1990s other local organizations were used or created to deliver projects, especially in the construction of infrastructure, such as electricity and water and sewage systems. Let us now see how one comunidad, Allpachico, negotiated its way through the twentieth century.

The Comunidad of Allpachico

Legislation about communities is only a part of what goes into the particular formation of a specific collective. Allpachico's experiences are also the product of a variety of other factors. Geography and resources are among the most important. As I have already described, Allpachico has few agricultural or other resources, and the people have relied on income from informal- and formal-sector work in the region for over a century. As the community's dependence on farming decreased, its political affiliation also changed from indigenous farming elites in the Mantaro Valley in the nineteenth century to the municipality of Piedra Blanca after the War of the Pacific. Their economic and political independence from Mantaro Valley elites was purchased at the cost of greater integration into the regional and national political economy, such as through labour migration.

By the early twentieth century the people were working in the mines of the region. An American company, the Cerro de Pasco Copper Corporation, won exploitation rights to rich copper deposits in the area, lucrative in the age of electrification (Laite 1981: 57). The corporation needed workers, who were initially reluctant to leave agriculture. The need for money to pay taxes, buy land, or fund fiestas, however, as well as coercive recruitment techniques, slowly convinced peasants to enter the mines (Alberti and Sanchez 1974; Contreras 1984; Flores Galindo 1983). Cerro de Pasco's smelter began operation in 1922 at La Oroya at the top of the Mantaro Canyon, emitting toxic fumes that destroyed agricultural land down to the valley 80 kilometres away, further forcing peasants to seek wages to replace their lost crops (Laite 1981). Allpachico's land was affected by the smoke, although no compensation was ever paid.

Apart from mining, Allpachiqueños worked on the railway that linked the Mantaro Valley to Lima, carrying ore as it went. With their wages, in 1929 they purchased the land in a sale-purchase agreement with their mother community, Huaripampa, from which they had achieved political independence a few decades earlier, replacing it with Piedra Blanca as their district capital. They purchased 652 hectares of pasture land in common, and 108 people bought individual plots. The plots of land purchased varied in size and value, indicating that there was already some differentiation, although there is little evidence that those who bought more passed on consolidated wealth to future generations. Some people who purchased land actually lived elsewhere.

In 1936, Allpachico was recognized as a comunidad indígena in the first major wave of communities seeking such status. Long and Roberts (1978) point out that it was the communities that were most engaged in the national economy that tended to apply for the status. The census taken of the community as a requirement for the application shows that this was true of Allpachico. Of the 120 men on it, five are listed as miners. This is lower than the reality; my research indicates that at least nineteen men worked in the mines in the 1920s and 1930s. The discrepancy could be a result of the wish to present the community as agricultural in the official application, or it could reflect the fact that the men tended to work in the mines for short periods at this time. Further, only eleven of the men were illiterate and, with the exception of the illiterate men, those between the ages of 22 and 74 had electoral and military service documents, indicating their participation in national state processes. In addition, two of the sixty-one women listed as heads of families (they are mostly single mothers or widows) have occupations other than *hiladora*, literally 'spinner.'[14] One of these women is listed as being an *empleada*, a designation which commonly refers to domestic service (perhaps for one of the American families associated with the Cerro de Pasco Copper Corporation, or to some other white or pink collar work), and the other woman is a cook. These are the only two literate women, so that while the application describes the school existing in the community as mixed, few women had had the opportunity to study there. Apart from earning money through wage labour, the people of Allpachico also grew grain which they sold in the market in Jauja: many older residents told me of how they would walk to Jauja, carrying the grain to sell in the market there. Thus, although the data are scanty, they do indicate that the people of Allpachico were actively engaged in the wider political economy.

Comunidad status offered the promise of government support for internal development and economic growth. In effect, almost immediately on receiving recognition, the comunidad of Allpachico began a suit to get more land. Adjudication by the state eventually allotted a small amount to the comunidad in 1941, but another attempt to increase the land base is still unsettled, although currently not active. They also attempted to get compensation for the damage caused by the Cerro de Pasco Copper Corporation smelter at La Oroya, but, as I have already indicated, received nothing, nor did the comunidad receive much else in the way of state assistance.

While they may have hoped for more support from the state when they became a comunidad indígena, they also adopted a local political structure that fostered autonomous projects. At the time that Allpachico applied for legal status, they had already built a school for both boys and girls. They subsequently got state recognition of the school, with state support for teachers and materials.[15] Older residents describe how the bell for the church was brought from La Oroya by the community and of how they built a bridge across the Mantaro River to replace an earlier rope and basket system. The tone, as people talk of the past, is nostalgic. One man remembered how authorities, who were named by turn rather than elected, were whipped with nettles to symbolize the burdensome responsibility of the office. The memories laud the willingness of community members in the past to attend meetings and faenas, in sharp contrast to the present *dejadez*, or laxity.

Conflicts and Complementarities in Households and Hamlets

Despite these romanticized memories and its success in carrying out autonomous projects, Allpachico's life as a comunidad indígena has not been completely harmonious. In 1954 the *barrio* of Colibrí undertook an attempt to achieve independence from Allpachico by applying to become a separate comunidad. This did not succeed, but there continues to be resentment on the part of the residents of Colibrí towards the main settlement of Allpachico, particularly when the latter requests their labour for projects from which they will not benefit. The fight for independence on the part of Colibrí, as it was earlier for Allpachico, and continues to be the case for comunidad annexes (see Laos 2004), was and is clearly linked to the desire to attain outside resources and keep labour for barrio projects. Colibrí has developed much of its own infrastructure, including a bridge across the Mantaro River, a chapel, a cemetery, a water system, and a meeting room, thus allowing it significant autonomy as an annex of the comunidad. The highland hamlets of Trebol and Kutru, with much smaller populations, have been less organized in their resistance, although their residents certainly express resentment when they are asked to support projects from which they will derive little benefit.

Another source of internal tension relates to the primary economic activity, and is most clearly in evidence between farmers and migrant workers.[16] Table 4.1 shows the distribution of households by main sources of income in 1987, while Table 4.2 shows the same for 2007. Both are based on a majority of the people who lived in the comunidad at the time.[17] The tables show a decline in the role of agriculture as a mainstay for households over these twenty years. The 1987 figures underrepresent full-time farmers because they do not include nine households situated in the upper altitudes. It takes about an hour to walk from Kutru to Allpachico, from which one can get transportation to a job, so it is unlikely that anyone who lived there also engaged in waged work. The households from the more distant hamlets are included in the 2007 information.

The 1987 figures also show a more even age distribution. Of the sixty-four households listed in 1987, by 2007 twenty-four had moved away. There were two main reasons for this: elderly villagers with migrant children moved to live with them, and some of those present during the national economic crisis of the 1980s later left to seek better opportunities when the economy stabilized. To offset this, others returned to Allpachico after retiring from long-term employment. The other forty either still lived in Allpachico or had died there.

The demographic shift is also related to the transformation of the local wage market. In 1987 there were still quite a few men employed by the railway or the big mining companies in the region. These were comparatively good jobs, although the inflation of the period undermined wages. Still, men kept their employment since there were few other options, and they were supporting their children who were unable to get such jobs. By 2007, the older men were all retired and the young men who stayed in Allpachico tended to work in the small rock quarries of the region – jobs with lower wages, poorer benefits, and less stability than those of their fathers' generation. Polluted and crime-ridden Lima was not an attraction for them, although there was a greater variety of jobs available there and many of their peers had migrated. This means that the category of 'wage, usually with agriculture' among Allpachico residents has changed significantly from the 1980s to the present period, referring to households with a far more precarious income.

Men's livelihood patterns show more variety than women's. For women, the major opportunities in the highlands have been through

Table 4.1
Information from 1987 interviews concerning economic activities by age group

Economic Activity	Age Group				Totals
	20–39	40–59	60–79	80+	
Primarily agriculture with other supportive activities	4	18	14	1	37
Non-agricultural informal or temporary work	1	2		1	4
Wage labour, usually with some agriculture	3	10			13
Business		2	2		4
Pension and agriculture		1	5		6
Totals	8	33	21	2	64

informal, self-employed sales. At no time has there been a female employment sector similar to the mining and transport one for men. Thus, women who stay in Allpachico – and often those who leave – tend to be pluriactive, engaging in farming, sales, and myriad small opportunities. The differences among them are not in the activities per se, but in whether they carry these out for themselves or for others. We revisit women's activities in Chapter 6.

A few sketches of households in the major categories of primarily farming, wage with farming, and pension with farming will give a better idea of what each involves. We will meet most of these people in later chapters. Because men's activities are more diverse, more influential in determining household status, and more easily characterized than women's, the presentation tends to focus on them.

Pascal and Judith were born in the late 1940s and have spent most of their adult lives farming in Allpachico. Pascal is actually somewhat unusual in that he studied veterinary medicine at the national university in Huancayo, but was expelled for his radical political activities. They are better off than most of those who have spent their lives farming, having benefited from Pascal's father's investments in land. His father was a long-time railway worker. Pascal has also been able to use the knowledge, self-confidence, and connections he got from his truncated studies and political activism. Judith has played a large role in the farming, as well as being deeply engaged in a plethora of informal activities. Pascal has served as president of the comunidad, as well as

Table 4.2
Information from 2007 informal census concerning economic activities by age group

Economic Activity	Age Group				Totals
	20–39	40–59	60–79	80+	
Primarily agriculture with other supportive activities	7	13	8	2	30
Non-agricultural informal or temporary work	3	2	2	1	8
Wage labour, usually with some agriculture	10	3	1		14
Business					0
Pension and agriculture		2	8	4	14
Totals	20	20	19	7	66

in several executive positions. Most of the comunidad presidents have been men from among the wealthier of the farming or wage-pension with farming households.

Mimi and Pancho are more similar to the norm of the farming households. Born in the early 1950s, both were illegitimate children, and they inherited very little land. They earn income through share-cropping, working as agricultural labourers (*peones*), and undertaking odd jobs whenever they come up. They are involved in a dense network of exchanges with others. They now receive assistance from their children, all of whom have migrated away. Somewhat surprisingly, given his low economic status, Pancho became president of the comunidad in 2008.

Laura provides another version of the farming and other activities household. She was born around 1940 and has six children. She is separated from their father, from whom she gets no support. Laura inherited a bit of land – less than her brothers as she says men are favoured – but no house. In 1987 she was living in the house of an Allpachiqueño who had migrated to farm in the jungle near Satipo. In the 1980s, she scrambled to make ends meet by picking up odd jobs, managing to be present whenever a richer household might have need of an extra hand. Her children also helped out, and by 1995 she was living with one of them in Lima. This daughter and her husband had a stable income, and Laura's economic situation improved significantly.

Gisela is in a similar position, but is twenty years younger and has stayed in Allpachico. She is a single mother with several children by two different fathers. The fathers have provided little support. She has a small bit of land and has had some help from members of her family, now including her older children. She also works for others and sells food and drinks at fiestas in the area. Poor single women like Gisela and Laura are particularly active in the comunidad, as they cannot afford the fines for non-attendance at faenas and may hear of an opportunity for a job or some other benefit.

Jorge and Tina have gone from the 'wage and agriculture' category in 1987 to the 'pension and agriculture' category in 2007. They are among the richer residents. Jorge worked for upwards of forty years, mostly at the smelter in La Oroya. That he was born around 1940 meant that he was able to enter a large mining company in the 1960s when wages were relatively better. His generation of male workers was concentrated in two places of employment: the railway (Enafer), and the huge mining/agriculture complex of the American-owned Cerro de Pasco Corporation. The mining operations of this company were nationalized in the 1970s to become Centromin. Jorge worked for both the Cerro de Pasco Corporation and Centromin. This allowed him to accumulate capital and enjoy some workplace benefits. Many in his cohort moved away permanently from Allpachico, but Jorge invested in land and agriculture there. Tina oversaw the farming operations on a day-to-day basis while he was working, and reared their seven children. Tomasa, whom we will see again in Chapter 6, is one of them. Tina also used her resources creatively to help the family during the hard years of economic crisis. They also have a small cocoa farm in the jungle near Satipo and a house in Lima, both of which serve to help their children and grandchildren. Jorge has served as president of the comunidad since retiring, and Tina has been active in many of the local women's committees.

Among the younger generation, as I indicated above, those in the category of wage and farming are not so fortunate as Jorge and Tina. Few of these households have much land, and growing distaste for farming, especially among young women, has meant that there is little interest in agricultural production. In any case, local conditions limit productivity. For young men and women with little training, there are few local employment options. Thus, born in the 1980s, Yolanda helps in her mother's small shop. She has also become a municipal councillor, as we will see in Chapter 8. She and her husband Antonio have a daughter.[18] Antonio, like most other men his age who have stayed in Allpachico, works in one of the rock quarries of the region. It is hard work, and the young men complain that they cannot physically continue long enough to qualify for a pension, even if they work for one of the few companies that offer such a benefit. Medical insurance constitutes a more immediate and much appreciated benefit that keeps the men working despite the poor pay and conditions. Unlike the earlier generation of men for whom there were two major employers, Antonio's cohort is split among several small quarries, limiting their ability to help one another out. Most of these quarries are 20 kilometres away, and the men must get up very early and return home late at night. They work six and a half days a week. Antonio works at a quarry too far away for daily commuting, so he only spends from late Saturday to late Sunday in Allpachico. The wages pay for daily expenses, but long periods of layoffs eat into any savings.

The sketches I have presented above demonstrate the kinds of wealth and activities that households depend on, and that condition their reactions to the different projects to be discussed later. The above examples are not definitive, and there is variety in each category. Stage in life cycle, historical period in which the heads came of age, economic status of the parents, and so on, all play a role in the resources available to each household. A daughter's lucky marriage could raise a poor single mother to an ease of life she otherwise could only dream of, as happened for Laura. Thus, many of the opportunities that arise for individuals and households come from chance opportunities, from someone in their social network, or from the general national context. Although I have not included them in the descriptions above, migrants play an important role in Allpachico, through leaving land to be sharecropped (although increasingly the land is simply abandoned through a general lack of interest), sponsoring fiestas, and supporting kin in the community. People like Laura, Gisela, Mimi, and Pancho are particularly likely to develop reciprocal relationships with migrants. These reciprocal ties are the other side of the tensions that can arise between households in different economic circumstances.

I have mentioned internal conflicts between households, especially between residents and migrants, as well as among the different hamlets in the territory of Allpachico. These conflicts are linked: the larger population centres of Allpachico and Colibrí both have hybrid economies, mixing peasant agriculture, small-scale commodity production, and wage income. These centres have tended to want improvements that will facilitate inclusion in the wider economy, such as education, bridges, support for market-oriented production, and residential services. There are some overlapping interests here between residents and migrants, but also tensions over how to organize and evaluate contributions of labour and inputs. Trebol and Kutru, both more intensely focused on subsistence production, have wanted support for herding and agriculture and have had much less interest in projects that link with wider markets and processes.

Although differences in resources are the basis for both reciprocity and conflict, the socioeconomic differentiation leads to limited class development within the community. There is too much volatility in how households relate to one another, and in class position from one generation to the next, as well as great overlap in their general interests. As we will see in Chapter 8, these general interests are coming to be more related to the fact that they share a residential territory than that they are all involved in common economic pursuits. This has led to prioritizing the construction of service infrastructure over local economic development. From the 1980s to the present there has been a gradual increase in the commodification of social relations within Allpachico, although this is very partial and uneven. We will see this in the chapters that follow, along with the attendant tensions. Rather than significant internal class development, the trend is for Allpachiqueños to join the Peruvian working class. The slow abandonment of arable land is a result. The voices calling for resources to be put into developing agriculture are getting older and fewer. Despite this, I do want to insist that these processes are complex. Poverty and crisis, conditions with which Allpachiqueños are all too familiar, disrupt prevailing tendencies. Further, the historical patterns demonstrate cyclical waves of both community retrenchment and forays into the wider political economy according to the situation.

Comunidad Development

Since Allpachico received official status as a comunidad, this insitution has been one of the resources available to its people. As I have noted above, from the 1930s on, the comunidad has sought state support, although rarely was any received. Until the 1980s, though, the original idea for what a project would accomplish arose from the comunidad itself. The school pre-existed legal recognition of the comunidad, and the church and bridges were autonomously constructed. A water supply project in the 1960s illustrates the roles of comunidad and state as they were balanced then. This will stand as a comparison for the recent water project discussed in Chapter 7 and the state funded projects that are the focus of Chapter 8.

Community informants are vague about the dates and details of the projects they claim to have been responsible for, but around the mid-1960s, a major water supply project took place, in which reservoir tanks were built and pipes brought water to several public taps. This replaced an earlier system in which some water was brought via an open aqueduct from the highlands, while springs supplied the rest. Older villagers remember how an earthquake in 1947 cut the flow of water from one of the springs. When Don Federico tried to excavate around the spring to get better access to water, it just went farther underground. In any case, the water from the springs escaped through its natural flow, and got muddied from washing and livestock. In addition, migrants who had enjoyed public water infrastructure in work centres wished to recreate it in their community. Thus, the people of Allpachico built a cement reservoir from which pipes carried water to six or seven public taps at different points in the streets.

Allpachiqueños insist that this project was entirely their own idea, and most also claimed that they had funded it themselves.[19] They raised money among those living in the community and those with jobs elsewhere. Many of the inputs were local materials, such as the stone that formed the reservoir, but they would have needed to buy cement, as well as pipes and valves to take the water to taps in the streets. Most people I talked to insisted that no resources from government or other outside sources were contributed.[20] The community itself designed the system and did the work through community faenas. They hired a villager who worked as a mason for the mining company in La Oroya. He completed the cement parts during one of his vacations. Once the system was completed, the comunidad maintained it and ensured that people did not abuse the infrastructure or resource.

The project was carried out for a specific practical purpose: to provide a clean, constant water supply for the people of the village of Allpachico, both residents and migrants who expected to return to the community to live. A separate project took place at another time in Colibrí. As we will see, more recent projects are not so focused on immediate practical results. In addition to its pragmatic purpose, there was some local political strategizing as comunidad leaders strove to be able to point to an important project during their time in office in order to gain prestige. One of the retired comuneros, Don Máximo, claims the 1960s water project as his contribution, as do the rest of the executive of the time.

Despite their efficacy at carrying out some projects on their own, the people of Allpalumuchico did not lose their interest in gaining support from the government. After 1968, the apparent support of the military government for peasant agriculture sparked some renewed activity. A comunidad census was carried out in 1971, listing qualified and lapsed comuneros (those who lived elsewhere and did not maintain comunidad responsibilities) seemingly in the hope of receiving some government help, again without luck. Allpachico was not included in any of the reorganization brought about by the agrarian reform. Later in the decade Allpachico hosted the annual conference of the national peasant confederation (Confederación Campesina del Perú or CCP), an umbrella group critical of the national government. This was a major event for a small peasant community, although by the time of the Allpachico conference the CCP had lost some of its earlier energy. Many Allpachiqueños who were teens or young adults at this time recount that they organized themselves into a political force, painting murals and publishing news on public billboards. The momentum continued into the early 1980s with a project directed by a Peruvian NGO.[21] A new civic building was constructed, a comunidad-run store at which to buy agricultural supplies was instituted, and agricultural techniques were taught. This project interacted with the comunidad campesina, and membership was high as people sought to benefit from it. My first period of fieldwork, in 1984, followed the completion of this project. The comunidad held regular meetings, cultivated fields, and owned a communal flock of sheep.

The comunidad initiative continued, and by the time of my return in 1987 Allpachico had another project underway, this time directed by a foreign NGO. I describe this in greater detail in Chapter 5. Again the local organization worked through the comunidad leadership and membership continued fairly high. However, this was also a period of increasing political and economic instability. Further, the difficulty associated with earning a living elsewhere revived migrants' interest in Allpachico.

After 1990 the economy stabilized, although agricultural prices continued to be low and costs of manufactured goods were high. In

Allpachico, where more lucrative crops cannot be grown, the amount of land cultivated decreased rather than increased, and people gradually took to labour migration again, especially as the political unrest eased. Comunidad membership declined as it became clear that agriculture could not provide much of a living. In the late 1990s, attendance at the very irregularly called meetings plummeted and comunidad leaders found it extremely difficult to convince members to help harvest communal fields, even though they would receive some of the harvest in exchange for their work. Further, given the lack of natural resources in the area, there seemed to be no other reasons to join the comunidad campesina. Throughout much of the 1990s the comunidad did not submit audits and paperwork required to keep it in good standing with various government bodies. This meant that Allpachico was not eligible for some government programs and projects. Further, after the 1990s much state and NGO funding was allocated according to a poverty map prepared by the government. Because one of the other comunidades in the municipality of Piedra Blanca had various resources, the average income in the area was higher than the ironically coveted 'extreme poverty' designation necessary to be a high priority for development. The people of Allpachico bitterly resented that they were shut out of assistance while other nearby communities in different municipalities were eligible.

This complex set of issues means that many of those who live in Allpachico have not become members. In any case, development projects now tend to avoid the comunidad, as we will see in chapters 6, 7, and 8 below. These reasons make it essential to distinguish between the comunidad and community. Despite the decline in interest, however, the comunidad is not dead: it informs and supports a variety of communal patterns of work and celebration and remains a shadowy figure in all development processes, providing logistics and experience.

Conclusion

We have explored different conceptualizations of community in this chapter, observing how it is cast as both actor and goal in much development, paradoxically viewed as autonomously capable and, at the same time, in need of an outside facilitator or resources. Rather than being a bounded social grouping, the community is more usually inherently mixed up in wider political and economic processes (see also Nugent 1994). This is certainly the case with the Peruvian comunidad campesina, at once a product of state policy and of peasant strategies for livelihood and political status. Thus, Allpachico's history exhibits a cycle of interest and neglect in the comunidad, according to the possibilities the institution offers at any moment. Allpachico is not necessarily typical: it is quite different from Huasicancha, for example, where the concept of community was central to identity, livelihood, and political mobilization (G. Smith 1989). Nevertheless, in both Allpachico and Huasicancha, 'community' is dynamic and heterogeneous. For both, too, the state plays a major role in their constitution and their strategies; in particular, Allpachiqueños have hoped for resources from their legal status, although they have rarely been successful.[22] I have endeavoured here to establish a framework that acknowledges the important role the state plays, in conjunction with capitalist investment, while also recognizing that the negotiation of different players dealing with various events and conditions is what creates history.

Allpachico has been and continues to be a variety of communities, based on legal, residential, or other grounds of common interest, but this does not mean that it is essentially cohesive. There are ties that bind Allpachiqueños, but there are also tensions. I have argued that these have not turned into strong internal class divisions, although economic differences do fuel some of the conflict. Rather, just as interest in the comunidad is currently waning, so is the relevance of social ties with other Allpachiqueños. Instead, the people's livelihood goals have become oriented towards employment in the region or in Lima. I wish to emphasize, however, how volatile these trends have been over time. Allpachiqueños are well acquainted with crisis, and have returned to the community in times of economic or other stress. Because, as Cowen and Shenton (1996) argue, intentional development is aimed at crises in capitalism, let us now turn to an examination of projects in Allpachico.

5 Teach a Man to Fish (and a Woman to Sew) . . . Integrated Rural Development and Basic Human Needs

Give a man a fish and you feed him for a day; teach a man to fish and you feed him for a life time.

– Proverb

This proverb is so well known it has become the name of a non-governmental development organization (see www.teachamantofish.org.uk). Its philosophy underwrites a couple of development assumptions: that poverty is the problem, to be resolved by supporting income generation; and that this support may involve a variety of ancillary elements such as education. At the same time, it assumes the problem is with the 'man' and his failure to know how to make use of available resources. This chapter shows the flaws of this view.

In the late 1980s, Allpachico was the beneficiary of a community-based Integrated Rural Development project, led by a foreign NGO I will call here Multi-Need. As we will see, the project reflected some common shortcomings: it was overly technical; there were charges that some villagers were favoured over others; and the income-producing elements were insufficiently planned in terms of providing training, carrying out market surveys, and providing incentives for villagers to make the changes necessary to benefit from improvements. Apart from these problems, and more importantly, the historical context of economic and political crisis would have damaged the prospects of success of any project, however well planned.

Even though the late 1980s Peru was an extreme case, there is always a broader context. I begin with an overview of Integrated Rural Development and Basic Human Needs approaches. The great overlap between them justifies presenting them together. As we will see, they have yo-yoed between local and wider areas of action as each framing was undermined by its attendant difficulties. These approaches are selective in the ways they assume interaction with broader processes, usually relying on greater integration into capitalist markets by promoting production for sale. At the same time they often ignore the problems associated with market dependence. A description of the Multi-Need project in Allpachico illustrates one example.

Integrated Rural Development, Community-Based Integrated Rural Development, and Basic Needs

While development after the Second World War in Western-aligned poor countries was initially more focused on promoting large-scale capitalist growth, critics charged that the benefits did not 'trickle down' to the population in general, as had been promised. Calculations of numbers of people living in poverty were startling in spite of overall growth (Streeten et al. 1981: 10–11). We have already seen that the development focus on communities has a long history. In the 1960s, one form of this arose that argued that a range of different needs had to be addressed at once, rather than focussing only on one need. Vicos, discussed in the introduction, provides an early example.[1] Rondinelli (1979: 389–80) describes Integrated Rural Development approaches:

> They attempt to coordinate a 'package' of investments and services that will accomplish the following: 1. Increase agricultural output and productivity, thereby transforming rural regions from subsistence to commercial agricultural economies in order to meet the basic food needs and raise the incomes of the rural poor. 2. Stimulate agro-processing, agribusiness, and related rural industries in order to diversify local economies, provide greater employment opportunities, and generate internal demand for domestically produced goods. 3. Increase access of the rural poor to the social services, facilities, technologies, and infrastructure needed to improve health, nutrition, literacy, and family planning – thereby increasing the productivity of individual workers, raising the overall standard of living in rural areas, and stemming the tide of rapid rural-to-urban migration. The intended beneficiaries are small-scale farmers, rural entrepreneurs, migrant workers, shifting cultivators, and landless laborers, as well as squatters and low-income workers on the fringes of the urban economy.

Integrated Rural Development was thus complex in terms of its focus, combining support for commercial production with a range of social, health, and education programs, and also often in terms of scale. Whole regions and countries came to be the field of action as projects were scaled up. The enthusiasm spread quickly. Cohen (1987: 15) recounts that: 'during the 1970s large amounts of government and donor funds were expended to promote them [i.e. Integrated Rural Development projects]. For example, between 1975 and 1980, major international donors working in Latin America alone expended 20 percent of their allocations, or US \$2 to 2.5 billion, a figure that would be greatly increased if nationally financed contributions were included.'

Not surprisingly, Cohen says, the frequent consequence of such rapid implementation of large and complex projects was failure.[2]

In his well-known study, Ferguson (1994) critically examines an ambitious Integrated Rural Development project in Lesotho. Rather than evaluating the project on the basis of its own goals, he examines what the real impact on people was. While in terms of increasing agricultural income the project was a failure, it implanted state institutions and mechanisms for control. This happened in an apparently apolitical way, in which the problem of poverty was presented as a technical one, addressed through the concern of foreign donors and the Lesotho government. He argues that the framing of the situation as one of marginalization and isolation from markets disregarded both historical commercial production dating back at least to the mid-nineteenth century as well as the current heavy involvement of both male and female migrant labourers in South Africa. In effect, the project depoliticized the way in which Lesotho was tied into the regional economy.

Closely associated with the Integrated Rural Development trend was the Basic Human Needs approach. Ruttan (1984) compares the two approaches, suggesting that Integrated Rural Development included both agricultural and non-agricultural project activities, while Basic Human Needs tended to focus on the latter. These include rural industries, public works, health services, schools, local government, and so on. Webster (1992: 34) summarizes Basic Human Needs this way:

> The basic needs strategy seeks to do two things:
> (a) to relieve as quickly as possible absolute poverty through intensive direct assistance to those in desperate circumstances: [sic]

(b) to meet the 'basic needs' of all in terms of material wants such as food, clothing, shelter and fuel, and also, as some argue, social needs such as education, human rights and what is called 'participation' in social life through employment and political involvement. At the heart of this approach lies a desire for social justice and welfare based on a concern that the material resources of a society should be distributed more evenly throughout the population.

Basic Human Needs was a major interest of the World Bank, which was joined by other multilateral organizations such as the International Labour Organization (ILO) and the United Nations. The idea was to outline programs relating to the quality of human capital (health, education, and other social elements) to address poverty rather than focusing solely on income enhancement (Brohman 1996: 201–25; McNamara 1973; Ruttan 1984; Streeten et al. 1981). In the end, Kamat (2002: 6–7) tells us, a debate within the World Bank ended with a conservative faction successfully arguing for 'redistribution with growth' over the supporters of more resources for Basic Human Needs, with the result that the latter was severely restricted. Webster (1992: 35; also Streeten 1995: 19) observes that 'there has been little real attempt to implement the basic needs policy properly.' Governments and international aid organizations tended to avoid redistribution of resources and the thorny problem of how to identify and deliver social needs. More acceptable were the elements concerning charitable donations of food and technical and material support for agriculture and cottage industries.

The idea that small businesses are a good way to boost poor people's income continues to be a staple in development projects, most obviously in the rising popularity of micro-credit.[3] Projects that incorporate an element to improve income through increased agricultural production oriented to sales or through the production of goods and services obviously push participants into capitalist markets. Critics charge that this 'bourgeois orthodoxy' (Mohan 1997) encourages project participants to be exploited in the capitalist system (Escobar 1995: 160–3; Leys 1996). Through the provision of limited forms of income in rural areas, a reserve army of labour is kept pacified and ready should capitalist investment need labourers at some point. The generally low level of production of their businesses ensures that paid employment would be attractive to project recipients. When the problem is framed as insufficient local production, rather than of wider systems of economic and political marginalization, the economic and political structures that disadvantage the poor remain unchanged along with the potential for more just transformation.

While both Integrated Rural Development and Basic Human Needs were designed to provide broad ranging policy, infrastructure, and social service support to poor citizens, implying a redistributive transformation of national wealth, the actual change was minimal. Instead, there was a return to more localized projects with more limited goals (e.g., Ruttan 1984: 398–9). The project that took place in Allpachico was an example of this, as a community-based Integrated Rural Development Project. It had a range of activities, mostly focused on agricultural production and small-scale industry. We now turn to a description of the Multi-Need project.

Multi-Need in Allpachico: Phase One

In the late 1980s Allpachico was the recipient of a broad ranging project generously funded and carried out by a foreign NGO I will call Multi-Need. This project was community based, simultaneously working on several different activities to improve agriculture and livestock through training sessions and donations of resources, provide opportunities for income earning, and reinforce the comunidad governance structure.

The Multi-Need project, through its various areas of action, helped people survive in Allpachico in a time of national political and economic crisis. The project came about as a result of contacts between an organizer for Multi-Need and workers for a Peruvian NGO that had carried out an earlier project in Allpachico. This organizer was looking for a community in which to sponsor an integrated rural development project, and Allpachico was chosen. In contrast to more recent projects in Allpachico (see chapters 6, 7, and 8), this project worked explicitly through and provided resources to the comunidad campesina.

The project took some time to get started. During my fieldwork in 1987 the project staff would show up only occasionally, but by 1988 they had a very regular presence and activities were being carried out with some urgency. As I will outline in a moment, the political violence was getting worse and the foreign staff was starting to think about leaving the country. They wanted to get the project firmly established by 1989 when they left. In 1992 the project was contractually turned over to a Peruvian NGO I will refer to as Peru-Need.

This sequence of events meant that there were distinct stages to the project, and, as we will see, the priorities of Multi-Need were different from those of Peru-Need.[4] The political and economic situation in Peru was the major factor driving this transformation, so we begin with a description of the context.

Context

Negotiations for the Multi-Need project began in about 1986. As I have already indicated, Peru was in difficult circumstances politically and economically. After twelve years of military rule, the country had returned to democracy in 1980, but at the same time a maoist indigenist group, *Sendero Luminoso* (or Shining Path, officially the *Partido Comunista Peruano*, the Peruvian Communist Party, or PCP), initiated its attempt to achieve a revolution.[5] Political violence increased and exacerbated the economic problems that inconsistent government policies engendered (Pastor 1992; Thorp 1991).

Over the years of the Multi-Need project, from the late 1980s to early 1990s, the political violence steadily worsened. Each time I returned to Peru during the 1980s, the situation had deteriorated since my previous visit, with no improvement in sight. While Ayacucho, to the south of the region in which Allpachico is located, and Lima, to the west, were the main foci of violence, Allpachico is on the road between the two.

Although Allpachico was not an epicentre of violence, the people could not count on escaping it either. Both Sendero Luminoso and the special army units charged with fighting the guerrillas committed acts engendering terror. It is important to note that attacks on local community leaders and development workers were frequent.[6] Senderistas tried to organize Allpachiqueños living in the more isolated hamlets, and painted slogans throughout the community. The foreign development staff left in 1989 after receiving warnings from Sendero. Indeed, my own fieldwork in 1988 was cut short when an American aid worker was killed in an ambush not far away. The violence also explains why people were reluctant to take on political roles in the comunidad of Allpachico, thus impacting on the administration of the project. Twice the military rousted people from their beds in the night and searched houses, focusing in particular on Don Pascal, who worked closely with the Multi-Need staff. In Chapter 4 I noted that Pascal had some training in veterinary medicine at university, although his studies were truncated when his leftist political activities led to his expulsion in the 1970s.

If it were not enough that the army and Sendero Luminoso engaged in violence, others also took advantage of the climate of violence to destroy property or kill enemies. Thus, when the train bridge a few kilometres from Allpachico was blown up in 1986, some blamed construction companies who wished to generate work for themselves. Stories were told of killings made to look like political assassinations, but which were actually the result of personal feuds. Some of the men worked for mining companies, which were targets of raids as the guerrillas sought dynamite or other materials. Others, who had moved to the jungle near Satipo or in the Huallaga Valley, were caught up in actions carried out not only by the military and Sendero, but also by drug traffickers. The environment was saturated with the possibility of the violence that no one discussed, to avoid arousing interest of either the army or the guerrillas.

The economic situation grew worse alongside the violence. In 1985 newly elected President Alan García announced restrictions on payments of the external debt. This led to international lenders refusing to lend any more money to Peru, and investors were uninterested in risking capital given the internal conflict. High government spending and continued policy inconsistency further contributed to enormous instability in the economy and in personal safety in the country. The economic crisis was severe – inflation over the period of García's presidency is estimated at 2.2 million per cent (Boloña cited in Cameron 1997: 61). High inflation; few employment opportunities; recurrent labour strikes; and guerrilla attacks on means of transportation, infrastructure, and political figures of all levels of government combined to produce horrendous living conditions. People returned to Allpachico as a relatively safe environment, or as their possibilities for earning income elsewhere vanished, although they also left when an opportunity appeared somewhere. It was hard to make long-term plans in this volatile environment, and people learned to grasp at whatever was being offered.

At the same time, the climate of violence and economic instability led to an attenuation of social relations. Unemployment, strikes, inflation, high prices for purchases and low prices for sales of agricultural produce, and long lines for government subsidized goods such as kerosene affected all forms of livelihood. Farmers found it hard to purchase inputs and consumer goods with what they received for their crops; workers saw their income shrink with inflation or disappear completely when they were on strike. Allpachiqueños had long experienced personal and household economic crises, but they could mitigate them through their networks built with their families and neighbours. In the 1980s, though, with the whole country in severe straits, the immediate cost of helping someone else usually outweighed the potential future benefit of being helped in turn. While family bonds continued to be strong to try to ensure mutual survival, links outside of the family became very brittle, even as they multiplied as everyone sought a trade that would offer some benefit, however minimal (Vincent 1992). A casual observer might have been misled by the constant interconnections between people into thinking that communal life was stable and vibrant and there were few obvious ruptures between people. Instead, villagers would avoid contact with those to whom they owed debts or with whom they had established some kind of trading relationship. Thus, Clara, owner of a small shop, hid one day from her usual supplier after she had bought from someone else offering cheaper goods. This was a period when a shopkeeper might require customers to buy packets of cheap shampoo to be able to buy a subsidized staple product like powdered milk. With prices of some goods regulated by the government, shopkeepers would withdraw goods from circulation just before rumoured price hikes. Otherwise the amount for which they sold a good would not cover the cost of replacing it. Profit margins were so small that they charged for fragile plastic bags to carry purchases in if the shopper did not have a carrying bag. One way to deal with the problems of access to goods was to create a *casera* relationship between shopkeeper and customer. The customer would be morally committed to buying from a specific shop and the shop would be morally committed to trying to meet the customer's needs. These relationships, however, were volatile because no one could afford to maintain them if a better offer arose. Everyone complained that while he or she had fulfilled a duty to others, those others never reciprocated, thus justifying a future refusal of help.

In this era of hyperinflation, money was avoided in exchanges of both labour and goods. Women, as those less associated with money, whose labour was seen as less valuable, and who were viewed as suitable objects of charity, could be asked to 'help out' villagers with more land or livestock. They could be given food, a share of the crop, or cast-off clothing in return. Laura, one of the single mother farmers we met in Chapter 4, was extremely diligent in being available to do odd jobs for people, such as cleaning the courtyard after the cattle had left for pasture, or helping to cook at large gatherings during fiestas or the harvest. One day when Laura's daughter went to buy sugar from a local shopkeeper, to have this put on her mother's tab, the shopkeeper asked for a load of a wild herb used to store with potatoes instead. An elderly woman sitting nearby took advantage of the opening to make a similar deal, giving a package of pasta noodles for soup for the promise of the herb.

Although this sort of barter could provide opportunities for those without access to monetary income, especially single mothers such as Laura who usually found it difficult to buy goods, it could also restrict production. Tomasa found herself having to trade chicks she had hoped to raise for meat and eggs for shoes for her children when an itinerant trader came through with used shoes.

Men, more associated with wage-earning, looked in vain for jobs outside of Allpachico. Many households were uncertain how long they would be in the community. No one made long-term plans. Government attempts to stabilize the economy, such as through García's 'sincering of prices' in 1988, or Fujimori's 'Fujishock' in 1990, when subsidies were lifted and the price of staple goods skyrocketed overnight, caused further hardship. Even with the gradual curbing of inflation after 1990, the high prices for the goods they had to buy and the low prices for the agricultural produce they sold meant that Allpachique-ños were not any further ahead.

In this context, a project that built for the future without providing an immediate solution to livelihood needs, as the Multi-Need project did, could not be received with universal enthusiasm, although it also would not be soundly rejected. Three types of households had clearly distinct perspectives on the project: those with a long-term commitment to farming; those with migrant waged workers who hoped that the situation would stabilize and allow their wages once again to provide them with a preferential position; and those with neither jobs nor much land or livestock, whose living was the most precarious. The project tended to appeal most to a subsector of the first group: full-time farmers with significant amounts of land and livestock. They had invested in a future in the community and had the time to put into the faenas associated with the project. They were able to influence the direction of the project because they had the clearest ideas about how it could benefit them and their interests largely matched those of the agricultural technicians who staffed the foreign NGO.

The Best-Laid Plans of the Two NGOs . . .

Multi-Need proposed to carry out an Integrated Rural Development-Basic Human Needs project with an emphasis on environmentally sustainable agriculture and small industry production. This project involved a generous donation of expertise and resources from the foreign NGO to the comunidad campesina of Allpachico. As I show in this section, many of the intended goals of the project addressed the concerns of development critics by attending to locally appropriate technology and environmental sustainability. We will see below how the implementation of the project diverged from these goals.

Multi-Need carried out a diagnostic study of Allpachico before beginning its project (Di Domizio et al. 1987). The foreigners who worked for Multi-Need were agricultural technicians, and the evaluation and recommendations are largely technical in content, concentrating on agriculture and livestock. The project in Allpachico was intended as a pilot for an eventual broader intervention. Thus, although there are specific details in the diagnostic study that pertain to Allpachico, the general framing of the problem was more abstract. The document begins with a reference to 'uncontrolled demographic increase' (Di Domizio et al.: 1, my translation), leading to an increased demand for agricultural products. 'Market pressure' is accompanied by farmers trying to achieve high yields by putting more land into cultivation and soil exhaustion, while this abandonment of traditional land conservation methods degrades the soil. The use of chemical fertilizers and pesticides is seen as having contributed to the impoverishment of the soil while, because it increases costs of production, also leading to economic instability. Deforestation, the document charges, constitutes a further debilitating factor. Apart from these human-caused ills, the Andean environment itself is seen as requiring special methods, because most of the fields are on slopes rather than flat land and there is a scarcity of water for irrigation. The study blames these physical and human-caused conditions for the unprofitability of agriculture, which leads to migration to the city.

These factors are not overly relevant in Allpachico, where agricultural production would seem to have declined since the 1930s, but not because of impoverishment of the soil resulting from overproduction. Rather, as we saw in Chapter 4, agricultural production was affected by pollution from the smelter in La Oroya, at a time when it also became apparent that waged work offered better returns than the already marginal land in Allpachico.

Despite the technical background of its authors, the study positions itself against a pure science solution to the problems, which they say does not take into consideration the needs of the physical environment. While agriculture was the major focus of the document, the challenge, as they frame it, is to develop a solution that will be environmentally sustainable. Bill Adams (1993: 207) has referred to the 1980s as 'the decade of "sustainable development,"' and the authors of the report show a dedication to the concept. Thus, the proposals reflect a concern for environmentally sensitive solutions to problems of erosion, over-grazing, poor soil fertility, and lack of forestation. Organic mulches, use of green manure, cultivation perpendicular to slopes instead of the existing parallel system, crop rotation, hilling potatoes, and reforestation are among the recommendations. Nevertheless, they see that improvements will not lead to major commercial production given the generally poor conditions and they seek merely to 'qualitatively and quantitatively improve production in order to ensure better nutrition and quality of life for the population, guaranteeing at the same time their real cultural autonomy' (Di Domizio et al. 1987: 4, my translation). It is both a modest and a very ambitious goal.

The authors show concern for ensuring that the project was culturally appropriate. Part of this involved the promotion of indigenous plants and technology, consistent with another international trend, indigenous knowledge, which was gaining strength at that time (Fairhead 1993; Purcell 1998; Salas 1994; Sillitoe 1998). Interspersing crops with different root systems in order to maximize use of soil nutrients is noted to be 'in common use among the farmers in the Department of Cajamarca'[7] (Di Domizio et al. 1987: 69, my translation). Various plants are suggested for different purposes, such as hedging or green manure, because they are locally available. Further, along with decreasing the number of livestock, they recommend replacing sheep, with their sharp hooves which damage the pasture, with 'more profitable and less destructive Andean camelids' (77, my translation). Alpacas and llamas are indigenous to the Andes.

The document addresses local social structure in a reference to 'historical anthropological' sciences and to the need to take into account socioeconomic factors which lead to soil degradation, although how the project intended to do this is contradictory. For example, at one point the authors say that there is a good availability of labour in Allpachico in order to produce compost, although the increased work involved in creating horizontal furrows is suggested to justify a rototiller (Di Domizio et al. 1987: 72). I have described above how return migration increased the population of Allpachico at this time, but this did not necessarily mean that people could access labour when they wanted. A household's own labour might be tied up in opportunities or obligations that presented themselves, and the costs of accessing a replacement could be great (see also Collins 1984). The document does not demonstrate an awareness of the complexities of these social realities. The authors are, however, determined to develop a low-cost model that would allow the community to develop itself, thus avoiding paternalistic relations with outside financiers (Di Domizio et al. 1987: 79). Still, in the event, the NGO gave in to comunidad pressure to get a tractor and other farm machinery.

While the initial diagnostic study focused on agriculture and land, the Multi-Need project also incorporated small-scale industry. To complement subsistence agricultural production, they planned activities that could generate income, including a clothing workshop, a carpentry workshop, and honey production among other small initiatives. They also carried out some improvements to comunidad buildings, such as installing a small bathroom in the quarters where they stayed when in Allpachico, the first such facility and the only one for many years.

Thus, this initial stage took poverty, resulting from poor agricultural practices and conditions, to be the problem, to be solved through increased subsistence production in environmentally sustainable agriculture with a faint flavour of 'indigenous knowledge.' It also attempted to provide for people to earn some money from the workshops. The technical framing of the problems and solutions ignored other reasons for the poverty of the people of Allpachico, such as artificially low prices for agricultural goods because of government controls or market inequalities, unstable employment and wages in the regional economy, or inadequate government attention to rural issues (Hunefeldt 1997). There is no mention of the national economic crisis, and no market survey was carried out to see if clothing, wood products, or honey could be profitable.

Multi-Need: Phase Two, Peru-Need

Multi-Need's foreign staff left Peru at the end of the 1980s, and the project was gradually transferred to a Peruvian NGO I call Peru-Need. This second phase of the project was quite different from the first. As I have discussed above, the original study demonstrates a concern for environmental sustainability through conservationist agricultural methods. Further, all of the donations of resources (the tractor, livestock, workshops, etc.) occurred in the first phase. Thus, the second phase was to oversee the final stages of implementation, although Peru-Need also developed parallel activities not covered by the contract among Multi-Need, Peru-Need, and Allpachico. An undated document written by members of the community (including Don Pascal) and a worker for Peru-Need outlines a plan clearly related to what were perceived as areas where the Multi-Need project had not fulfilled its goals (Ramos et al. n.d). Alongside this plan was an agreement to implement it. A final report by the NGO sums up one version of what happened (Equipo Peru-Need, Programa Sierra 1996). I was absent between 1988 and 1995 and rely on these documents along with information I collected from Allpachiqueños several years later to discuss this phase.

The Multi-Need diagnostic study was situated firmly in the sustainable environment philosophy and promoted income-generating activities, but the Peru-Need/Allpachico proposal (Ramos et al. n.d.) shifts into governance and capacity building through strengthening institutions. It is signed by four comunidad members and one representative of Peru-Need, designated as a consultant. Two of the comunidad authors (both men, one of them Don Pascal) have dedicated most of their productive activity to farming, while the other two (one man and one woman) have returned to Allpachico between bouts of work in Lima or smaller regional cities. The proposal emphasizes the participatory nature of the process through which it was developed. It mentions the comunidad's 'ancestral culture' and the importance of collectivity, both features that underwrote the turn to the comunidad campesina, as we saw in Chapter 4. Finally, it presents members of the community as poor and in very difficult circumstances. The community is described as politically and economically vulnerable, while seeking, through solidarity, to forge its own autonomous destiny. Thus, in contrast to the largely technical framing of the Multi-Need study, with its minor nod to culture and politics, this study emphasizes the latter, and replaces technical language with bureaucratic organizing and scheduling.

In outlining the problems to be faced, the Peru-Need/Allpachico proposal first refers to the Multi-Need document. Lack of arable and pasture land, exhausted by overuse, along with twin market problems of costly inputs and low agricultural prices, in addition to competition from imported foods, led to restricting farming for subsistence only. Unemployment, low wages, and the fact that the textile and carpentry workshops provided by Multi-Need were not functioning are all mentioned. Then follows a list of sociopolitical problems: inequality among comuneros, increasing individualism at the expense of collective interests, reluctance of comuneros to participate in the communal organization, illiteracy among women, lack of technical knowledge in communal and artisanal development, and lack of awareness of issues such as health.

The proposal's objectives were based on improving the communal structure to take advantage of existing resources. If the first phase of the Multi-Need project hoped to address poverty though sustainable agriculture, this proposal sought to do so through strengthening the institutional infrastructure. In order to do this, it outlined a series of committees to be formed, educational seminars to be held, and plans to get equipment repaired and put to productive activity. Thus, where Multi-Need's seminars had been on technical skills, such as crop rotation or terracing, Peru-Need's were more managerial, including how to do market analysis, accounting, pricing, marketing, market analysis, along with health, legal, and administrative training (Ramos et al. nd; Equipo Programa Sierra 1996). Technical skills were left to 'self-training' (*autocapacitación*) of the participants according to their area of specialization. Because a lack of technical knowledge had been recognized as a problem, not arranging for external assistance in this area would appear to be a major shortcoming of the project. The plan includes an organigram of the new comunidad campesina with its subcommittees and detailed schedules showing the days of the months over a seven-month period when each event was to take place and which committee or agency was responsible.

As with the Multi-Need study, these documents rarely refer to the broader political and economic conditions. The final report explains that Peru-Need came to be involved when the Multi-Need staff left because of the increase in political violence. The violence is not, however, used to justify the paralysis of the project in Allpachico: 'no activities were undertaken due to the lack of interest of comunidad authorities' (Equipo Programa Sierra 1996: 1, my translation). In fact, as I have indicated above, the lack of interest was a result of people's unwillingness to take comunidad leadership positions as this made them a target in the political conflict.

Similarly, descriptions of the problems in Allpachico are largely confined to internal rather than external conditions. The undated plan discusses poor and scarce agricultural land, the appropriation by individuals of productive machinery, internal inequality, and comunidad disorganization (Ramos et al. n.d.). Low prices for agricultural goods, high prices for basic consumer goods, and a lack of jobs are mentioned, but only the last of these is addressed in the document, through the hope of generating employment.

Where Multi-Need had promoted what it saw as traditional methods to support environmental sustainability, Peru-Need's agricultural support was solidly mainstream. The NGO provided medicines and two purebred sheep for reproduction for livestock, and seeds, fertilizers, and insecticides for comunidad fields. There is nothing to indicate that the agricultural methods being proposed involved anything other than the usual industrial chemical inputs, in contrast to Multi-Need's interest in indigenous knowledge.

We can see by this overview that the plans of Multi-Need and Peru-Need overlap in those activities related to agriculture and small industry, but that the overall perspectives of the two NGOs were quite distinct. Let us now turn to a description of the implementation of these plans.

What Happened

The initial Multi-Need project intended to improve the local economy in a sustainable way by addressing agriculture and local small-scale production. This meant that the projected benefits were more long term than short term, and would help those dedicated to staying in Allpachico over those less optimistic about the future in farming. Thus, households which owned significant land or livestock were enthusiastic about the assistance offered to improve production. It was well worth their while to participate, and they could pressure for machinery and other elements that helped them build their economic base and avoid some of their labour costs. They had agricultural knowledge and skills that allowed them to interact with the staff with greater ease. All households, however, hoped to gain something from the project. Some of the aspects of the initial Multi-Need project addressed the comunidad in general while others provided training or resources to its members. Comunidad membership was high at this time, because it was required for participation in the project. The comunidad also retained ownership of most of the resources donated by Multi-Need and was to receive a share of the payments or profits for the rental of tools and machines and from the workshops.

In keeping with the training of the foreign NGO staff and the 'peasant' label of the comunidad campesina, the largest part of the project focused on farming techniques, presumed to be of use to all. The activities aimed to increase yields while trying to conserve the fertility of the soil as well as improving livestock and pasture (Di Domizio et al. 1987). This was done through encouraging the planting of certain types of crops and rotations as well as teaching methods to prevent erosion. Trees, both eucalyptus (an introduced species) and native species, were planted in various areas. Although the project tended to promote labour-intensive methods such as terracing, a tractor with a full set of attachments and other machines were also donated to the comunidad. On the livestock side, a sheep bath was constructed, a veterinary post established, and high-quality rams and ewes purchased, along with a flock of ten white alpacas, white alpaca wool being worth more than brown or black.

Again deriving from the presumed communal character of the comunidad, most of the work was done through faenas that were obligatory for comuneros. The sheep bath was built and the trees planted through this mechanism. Although the process assumed a collective interest in agriculture, as we have seen in Chapter 4 Allpachiqueños actually have diverse interests. Efforts to build a sheep bath and to undertake reforestation encountered this. Households with livestock, for example, sent members to the faenas to build the sheep bath and help in vaccinations; those without animals ignored this part of the project. Households with a strong farming interest but in which the adult man was away working could not always participate even though they might benefit in the long term, because their current labour supply was limited.

Similarly, the forestation part of the project clearly illustrates the differential interest of those certain of long-term residence in the community and those in more unstable circumstances. Several tree planting faenas were held, but not all of the seedlings got planted and those that were did not receive the care needed to ensure their survival. Even now, more than twenty years later, the eucalyptus trees planted on one slope are the size this species usually reaches in five years. The trees could provide firewood or construction material for the future, but all of the wealthier households had kerosene stoves and did not use firewood at that time.[8] Others used bosta, or cow dung, which they either had direct access to through their cattle or picked up in the countryside. Some of the poorer households could not count on still living in the community when the trees were large enough to harvest.

Apart from resources and activities that were implemented through the comunidad, much of the project was directed to individual members. Thus, the information sessions on agricultural methods such as soil conservation, dealing with livestock and small farm animals (rabbits, guinea pigs, chickens, etc.) were to help individuals get greater yields, as well as to improve production on the comunidad's fields and flocks. Vaccination campaigns likewise helped both communal and individual livestock. To provide an incentive to herd owners to reduce overgrazing, twenty of the high-quality sheep were to be given to owners of the largest flocks if they agreed to cut the size of their herds. In this way only the wealthiest comuneros would benefit. Certain households were chosen to experiment with certain crops or techniques. The seminars were directed at men, rather than women, despite the fact that women, especially those whose husbands were away working, did a major share of the agricultural work. While women did not seem to resent this preference for men, there was some resentment towards those chosen to carry out the experiments by those who were not.

Don Pascal's household in particular was on good terms with the Multi-Need staff and was the target of whispered complaints. Pascal's university studies made him the obvious choice to run the comunidad veterinary clinic, and he was in the way to receive many of the benefits of the project. His wife, Judith, was chosen by the Multi-Need staff to prepare their meals, for which they paid, causing further bitterness.

Individualization was also evident in the few elements carried out with hired workers rather than through faenas. These were of interest to people as they could earn a bit of money through the project. As we will see in chapters 6, 7, and 8, projects offering immediate benefits such as wages or food came to be of great importance through the 1990s, affecting Allpachiqueño attitudes towards subsequent projects. In the 1980s, though, this practice was unusual.

There were only a couple of days of work for which people were hired, but the textile and carpentry workshops very clearly directed benefits to individuals. The workshop tools, while owned by the comunidad, could only be used by a certain number of people who would get training. This caused resentment among those not involved.

By 1988 sewing and knitting machines and a loom were in place and classes began to instruct women in their use. The women had not been encouraged to become involved in the agricultural side of the project, and the textile workshop was an obvious Women in Development (WID) component, corresponding to the trend in development practice of the period.[9] The Multi-Need project provided training in the use of the machines and there was some jockeying for position among women to be chosen as the director (the successful candidate was from one of the wealthy farming families), as well as to be one of the women chosen to attend the classes. The goal was to allow women to make clothing to sell locally, but no market study was done to examine whether this would be profitable. This part of the project reflects a trend among many development projects to teach women to perform jobs that constitute low-paid female ghettoes in developed countries.[10] The women eventually produced some aprons which they sold during fiestas. However, this artisanal clothing production had to compete with an industrial textile sector, and the women involved say they earned no money from this work. It did not operate for long, and in the early 1990s the best of the sewing and knitting machines were stolen. The workshop shut down completely, and the remaining materials and machines were left to gather dust.

The carpentry workshop had not been fully set up by the time the Multi-Need staff left, and training never got underway. Don Pascal told me some years later that men only had time to go in the evenings, and that was when supporters of Sendero Luminoso were out painting graffiti on village walls. The men were reluctant to expose themselves to possible danger and soon left the workshop alone. There was an impressive collection of saws, planers, routers, a lathe, and so on, but the motors were stolen and what remained was locked away, unused and unuseable. Thus, this workshop was less divisive if also less beneficial than the textile workshop.

The rest of the project similarly dissipated, fell apart, or vanished. The tractor was run without oil within a couple of years and for most of the time has not been in working condition. Its implements were lent to the comunidad of Piedra Blanca where they were damaged. Without the tractor, the road that had been built to the higher altitude fields was not necessary and has not been maintained. The Multi-Need staff had left two pickup trucks to the comunidad when they left. These were sold in the early 1990s to fund an autonomously generated electricity project (see Chapter 7). However, there were rumours that the generator they purchased cost the equivalent of the sale price of one truck and that someone must have pocketed the rest of the money. The alpacas did not adapt to the pasture in Allpachico and were sent to another community, which has since refused to acknowledge Allpachico's ownership of the animals. The improved variety of sheep interbred with the local sheep and the offspring have gradually declined in quality. Thus, in terms of the material contributions of the project, there was little long-term success.

Peru-Need's final evaluation (Equipo Programa Sierra 1996) comments on the social and organizational impact of the project, again a depressing conclusion of failure. The document is a litany of incomplete actions, lost resources, and failed objectives. A series of bureaucratic and administrative activities are listed as having been accomplished. One of these gets particular emphasis: the creation of a new comunidad statute in fulfilment of Ministry of Agriculture requirements for comunidad recognition. This allowed Allpachico to receive a donation of books from the national library, proclaims the report. Comuneros tell me that these books were old and useless and they are certainly not in circulation as resources.

In addition to the new statute, new committees were formed and given training in proper procedure (Equipo Programa Sierra 1996: 3). However, the report notes that several were short lived: the carpentry and metalwork committee, the forestry committee, and the women's committee had all ceased to function. Further, the report complains of comuneros not paying for livestock services or goods at a comunidad store Peru-Need had set up, of pilfering and theft of resources, of misused funds, and generally poor management. Certainly, in light of the focus on strengthening the comunidad institutional structure that corresponded to this phase, it was a resounding failure.

Conclusion

If the agency report was condemnatory about community participants, they have had a similar view of Peru-Need, levelling the same accusations of pilfering and lack of interest at the project workers. They remember the foreign Multi-Need staff much more positively, although at the time there were complaints of ineffective advice, rare appearances, and favoritism towards some comuneros. Most of all, now, there is regret that so much of what Multi-Need left behind has vanished or is unused. The political and economic crisis that made the foreign staff leave the country caused hesitation about participating in leadership positions in the comunidad as well as in some parts of the project, and pressured people to seek short-term help over long-term solutions; this was clearly a major factor in the failure of the project. However, the description of the project goals and implementation suggests that there would have been some major problems anyway.

The actual or potential problems cover a broad range, as we have seen. The project enforced a division of labour that pushed women away from agriculture and towards domestic-related activities, especially through the textile workshop. The production of clothing was unlikely to generate a profit, given the existence of a highly competitive national clothing industry and the low wages associated with it. Internal conflict accompanied not only the workshops, but also resulted from the distinct ways comuneros could benefit from the different activities. As I have pointed out, the project's focus on agriculture, along with reforestation, tended to be of most use to dedicated farmers, who had the time and resources to take advantage of this. The poorest villagers, landless labourers and single mothers, were less well placed to profit. There was also the potential for labour-saving machines, such as the tractor, to take jobs away from the agricultural labourers. Nevertheless, the chequered outcome of the project limited the entrenchment of class differences.

Under the conditions in which it was operating, the Multi-Need project probably did as well as could have been expected. Perhaps the thefts were perceived by various project participants (maybe including the NGO staff) as the most effective way in which people could benefit. Resources did, apparently, make their way to beneficiaries, whoever they were. There may also have been some long-term advantage resulting from the skills learned throughout the project. Thus, a woman who ran the community store for a time later opened her own store. Several women were working in the textile industry in Lima in the decade following the conclusion of the project, although most of these seem to have learned their skills in technical schools rather than in the short-lived textile workshop. Still, awareness of it might have sparked their interest. Another woman got her father to buy her a knitting machine like those she had learned to use in the workshop and used it to make sweaters for sale until it, in turn, was stolen. Any changes in land use seem to be more the result of recent reforestation projects, and the furrows continue to run up and down the slopes rather than across them. While people do use some compost and manure in their fields – they always did to some extent – they complain that the land no longer responds to organic fertilizers as in the distant past. Thus, it appears as though the educational benefits, 'teaching a man to fish,' were even more tenuous than the material benefits from the donated resources.

Maybe the most important legacy of the Multi-Need project is as part of the accumulated experience on which Allpachiqueños drew to make future decisions. Thus, the failure to improve the local economy taught the people to be leery of future promises and to be careful of devoting too much energy to them. Further, that even the Multi-Need agricultural technicians believed that farming in Allpachico was unlikely to be productive added to the growing prejudice against it. Out-migration picked up again, as soon as national conditions stabilized. Suspicion of others increased, and Allpachiqueños were hesitant to allow any more community resources to be used by only a few villagers. After the sale of the trucks, they also became reluctant to allow the sale of any of the unused machines left by the project, something that could have generated capital to invest in some productive possibility. Allpachiqueño understandings of the Multi-Need project thus continue to inform their reactions to subsequent projects, as we will see in the chapters below.

6 Developing People: Gender and the Turn to Individuals as Foci of Development

In this chapter we turn from development processes that focus on communities to those that work with people selected for a specific characteristic, such as gender, age, or parenthood. Although 'community' retains an irresistible attraction as a forum of development, by the 1970s it was recognized that communities were not harmonious homogeneous wholes. The trend towards disaggregating societies had begun much earlier – Foucault (1973) asserts that it was a mark of modernism to analyse and categorize the constituent parts of the social world as well as the physical one. Attention to addressing the needs and rights of individuals in societies, selected for a specific identity characteristic is at least as old. Thus, self-organized European and Euro-North American women fought for suffrage in the nineteenth century, and individuals such as unwed mothers and orphans were suitable objects of charity in externally generated projects.

The rights being fought for in these examples were for individuals, but other battles, such as those by or for indigenous peoples, had community rights as their goal. These latter often entail limits to the individual choices of their members, justified as necessary to ensure cultural survival. Philosophical debates have addressed the impasse between liberal individualism and communitarianism (e.g., Bauman 1996; Fraser 2005; Kymlicka 2007; Lash 1996). These debates have echoes in the development literature. Here I concentrate on those dealing with women, the most common identity group addressed by development projects in Allpachico.[1]

I begin with an outline of how development theory and practice have addressed women's concerns, then turn to Allpachico. Gendered development in Allpachico shows a reordering of local community along gender lines. Although empowering women is a central goal of this approach, Tomasa's story shows how complex the results can be. Gendered development, like the project discussed in Chapter 5, has furthered the transformation of the community away from subsistence and into capitalist markets.

WID and GAD

Although various kinds of assistance had been directed to women before then, Ester Boserup's (1970) classic work on agriculture and development illustrated that the distinct contributions made by women had not been taken into account in the design of development up to that point, with devastating consequences for the rights of the women. This study called attention to heterogeneity within communities and to the differing needs of women in particular. Thus, in development theory, the groundwork was laid to ensure that women were involved in development projects. The early form of this strategy, Women in Development, or WID, took the position that women had been left out of development and now had to be added in activities that directly involved them. Picking up on the Basic Human Needs trend of the time, they attempted to improve women's position by providing them with income earning that would allow them to be independent of their husbands and families (Rathgeber 1990: 496). There has been much criticism of this approach, calling attention to the way it added to women's already heavy burden, limited its focus to the economy, and did not address the wider political relations which prevented women from full societal participation.[2]

The intellectual successor to WID, Gender and Development (GAD) made two important changes in response to the criticism: one was to expand the concept of the target population from women to gender roles in general, and the other was to politicize the strategy in order to focus on empowerment rather than on the income producing/basic needs focus of WID (e.g., Kabeer 1994; C. Moser 1993; Sen and Grown 1987). Thus, going beyond gender, all of the poor, marginal, and vulnerable members of a community were to be assisted in improving their positions. These changes were largely confined to the theory, however, rather than carried out in practice. 'Gender' tended to continue to mean 'women' (see also Marchand 2009: 921), and often the elision was even more precise to refer to 'mothers,' if not 'mothers of young children' (Vincent 1999). Further, 'empowerment' often took

the form of training sessions alongside income-generating or charitable activities.

Development projects aimed at women may take either individualiz-
ing or collective forms of organization. Sardenberg (2008) distinguishes
between liberal empowerment, which focuses on the individual, and
liberating empowerment, which involves collective self-organization.
While she concludes that some liberal projects may have the effect of
raising women's consciousness, Sardenberg (2008: 23) agrees with Kabeer that 'in order to bring transformative changes, women's empowerment is dependent on collective solidarity and action.' This emphasis
on collective action is widespread (e.g., Cleaver 1999; Parpart, Rai, and
Staudt 2002), although there is also a sophisticated discussion of differences within groups, and recognition of various sorts of power (e.g.,
'power to,' 'power over,' as well as 'power with').[3] These discussions
give rise to a very different form of individual-collective tension from
that emanating from multicultural contexts: their goal is for individual
women to enjoy freedom, and the power of the collective is believed
to further that goal. There may be differences between whether the individual (C. Moser 1993) and the collective (Kabeer 1994; Parpart, Rai,
and Staudt 2002: 12) is the focus of attention, but all have the goal of
working towards women's ability to participate fully in society. In Allpachico, as we will see, the tendency has been to collectivize women.
The goals and strategies surrounding these collectives based on identity are distinct from those of communities based on ethnicity or other
presumed primordial ties: while there may be some discussion of
essentialist ties among women, strategic or otherwise (Sardenberg
2008: 24), there are no arguments that a collectivity of women should
have powers over its members in a parallel way to how some communitarians argue for cultural rights over their members. Rather, cultural
communities are more often seen as oppressive for women or other
constituent groups, while, with some exceptions (e.g., A. Moser 2004),
the identity-based collectives are assumed to be empowering for their
members.

Individuals, identity-based collectives, and communities constitute
distinct ways of organizing the subjects of development and have distinct implications for the lives of the people involved. Are communities weakened as collectives of members challenge traditional norms
or as individuals gain greater choice in how they manage their lives?
Do individuals find their lives circumscribed by projects that focus
on the community? In what follows, I analyse a variety of projects in

Allpachico to demonstrate the complex and sometimes unexpected ways individuals and communities lose and benefit from development projects focused on women.

Gendered Development in Allpachico

Groups organized on the basis of a specific identity trait are not new in Allpachico: there have been both self and externally organized groups on the basis of gender, age, and migration for at least fifty years.[4] Among them are the long-standing self-organized religious committee, government sponsored programs that require women to form a collective (e.g., Vaso de Leche, described further below), and shorter-term work for welfare projects which are either government or NGO sponsored. The externally generated groups reflect common themes. First, most projects involving women assume and impart the idea that women are domestic and family-oriented in ways that obscure the real range of·women's roles. They also work through collectivities that are fairly tightly controlled with respect to the activities involved, membership, and behaviour of the members, and that can be manipulated by politicians seeking votes. This control largely belies the message of any empowerment or leadership training that might be involved. Nevertheless, women do use the collective organizational skills and power to achieve various goals. What happens in these projects is very much tied up with other events and processes at the local and wider societal level. For example, membership in a project collective may need to work around personal conflicts between women. Further, despite the philosophical arguments about the need for women's groups to challenge community oppression, the community political leadership may actively seek projects for them. Male leaders can see advantages in their wives and daughters gaining the benefits (usually food or income) offered by these projects. The rise in popularity of women-oriented development projects coincided with declining emphasis on projects organized through local political leadership, and with the gradually increased presence of state services, including support for women victims of domestic abuse. These services are inadequate, not permitting women to exercise complete independence. At the same time, all of these new forms of association contribute to a pattern of contingent networks, flexible, and breakable when they no longer serve. These forms of networks provide a medium in which power can be exercised, but which also becomes very vulnerable to the larger power conduits in Peruvian society.

I will explore these themes through recurrent reference to the life experience of Tomasa, a woman born in the early 1960s and who has been caught up in the patterns of change both within and beyond All-pachico. Tomasa is the daughter of Jorge and Tina. Remember that Jorge had a stable job in the mining smelter 60 kilometres away in La Oroya until his retirement in 1995. This permitted him to invest in a cocoa farm in the jungle near Satipo and in a house in Lima, as well as building up his farm in Allpachico, managed by his wife until his retirement in 1995. Their wealth provides their children with support and resources beyond that which most Allpachiqueños can enjoy. To-masa married Rómulo in the early 1980s and went with him when he worked in the regional mines. His work was a short-lived contract, since at this time the companies avoided hiring long-term proletar-ians like Jorge. The couple moved to various locations, finally settling in Allpachico in the late 1980s where both became very active in the community. Rómulo served on the comunidad executive, including as president, and Tomasa took leadership roles in the various women's groups. In the 1990s they had five children to provide for. Rómulo was a self-employed tradesperson. He is also from Allpachico, but his father and uncles had never formally divided the small amount of land they inherited and Rómulo has never insisted on his own rights. Tomasa was the one who had fields and engaged in agriculture, while Rómulo tended to look for money plying his trade. Such work was not easy to come by at this time, especially given increasing state pressure to have registered papers and pay the goods and services tax. Without proper papers he could not bid or work on larger construction projects in cit-ies, while his informal status allowed those who did employ him to underpay him. Tomasa's contribution was essential to the household in this context. In the early 2000s their marriage fell apart and both ended up living outside Allpachico, although they also both retain ties there and visit regularly. I will expand on various events and experiences of their lives below.

Domestic Women

WID and GAD interventions in Peru built on earlier projects to change women's lives. For example, the twentieth-century attempt to estab-lish a proletarianized workforce, something that had been a problem for large-scale employers since the Spanish Conquest, took the form of trying to create a specific kind of family culture. The American-owned Cerro de Pasco Copper Corporation, which carried out operations in the central highlands and was the employer of many Allpachiqueños, built company towns along the lines of those in the United States. The mines and smelter tended to be in isolated places at high altitudes, with such a harsh climate that workers had to be enticed to live there, and their needs had to be supplied while they were there. Thus, arrangements were made for housing, medical services, provision of food, primary education for children, and so on (Goodsell 1974: 169–89; Laite 1981: 66–7). The cost of providing these services was high, and the corporation set about trying to decrease its role, as Goodsell (1974: 178) explains: 'Being responsible for all aspects of workers' lives is thus not only expensive to management but a giant headache. As a result the trend has been towards the so-called "clean wage," payment in cash only rather than noncash benefits such as free housing and food. Experiments have been conducted in "self-help" and community-development type projects designed to create a positive substitute for paternalism.' Among these 'self-help' and community development projects were 'housewifization' projects directed at women. Dewind (1975) describes how social workers were hired to teach workers' wives to become more like North American housewives. They promoted North American middle-class values including limiting the use of company housing to nuclear families of workers, teaching women how to decorate their homes, and the benefits of refrigerators for storing foods:

> Rather than make the women happy, the social work program humiliated them by making them feel as though their rural way of life was inferior. Then it frustrated them by teaching them to want and need more than they could afford to buy. Anger was directed at the company because it set wages at levels which would not support the standard of living it taught the women to aspire to. Added to this indignity and frustration was the knowledge that the company was pressing them to change their lives out of its own self-interest. (Dewind 1975: 66)

That is, the programs were meant to keep the women happy so they would not harass their husbands, so the husbands would not in turn blame problems on the company. As a result, Dewind says, the women formed *comités de damas* (women's committees) which actively supported their husbands' job actions. These projects thus had two effects: they presented a strong association of women with domestic work and family; and they gave impetus to political organization and mobilization skills that the women could use for their own ends or that could be manipulated by the outside. I return to the second set of effects below, but first I want to explore how current projects continue to revolve around women's presumed domesticity.

The projects Tomasa has been involved in are related to motherhood, focus on domestic activities, or build on women as supplemental rather than primary income providers (see also Boesten 2003). The Vaso de Leche (literally 'Glass of Milk') program is a good example. This program is run by the municipal government, with support from the state, and has the objective to provide food for children younger than seven and to undernourished children under age 12. If there is sufficient food, the local organizer may also sign up elderly villagers who do not have regular support from family members. Alongside the food distribution, those whose children are registered must commit to undertaking public works, and may do activities such as knitting or cake baking. In Allpachico this has usually entailed cleaning the plaza and track to the bridge – very much in keeping with the image of women as responsible for domestic cleanliness, here translated into public housekeeping. One father has been involved in Vaso de Leche while he was unemployed and his wife worked, but he was not pressured to do the cleaning. He and the elderly recipients did attend the training sessions, however, as these took place just before food distribution. The training sessions had to do with topics such as female hygiene, health during pregnancy and childbirth, and the importance of breastfeeding.[5] The assumption that public health messages for women can be spread through this mechanism makes it less likely that men will feel comfortable taking more responsibility for their children.

The association between women and food is also obvious in a project from the 1990s to set up a *comedor popular*, a type of restaurant that has become famous in Lima as a 'soup kitchen' which provides cheap meals to the popular classes, and free ones to the women who work there. In Allpachico it was more a mechanism to get the state food support for the meals, with extra food and ingredients to take home.

Other programs aimed at women also incorporate domestic activities and crafts, just as in the company sponsored women's projects (in which Tomasa had learned to stick pins in a bar of soap, winding ribbon around the pins to make a decoration), mentioned by DeWind. Thus, Tomasa and her cohort have crocheted bedspreads, learned to sew with sewing machines, baked cakes, knit, glued pasta on cans, sewn backpacks, and made tablecloths out of old produce sacks in their different women-oriented programs. What is striking about these products, apart from their domestic craft quality, is how unlikely most of them are to be commercially viable. The first three have the most potential to permit women to exchange beyond the household, but, as we saw for the textile workshop in Chapter 5, competition from the commercial textile industry means that crocheting, knitting, and sewing are not very profitable. Further, few women have ovens to bake with, let alone compete with industrial baking.[6] Instead, these activities seem to be a way of underlining women's proper concern with the home, and providing something to do while they are together.

Another set of activities aimed at women is less obviously domestic, however. Tomasa has also learned to raise worms to produce compost, plant trees and shrubs, and carry out manual road repair. Other projects in the region, but not in Allpachico, taught people to raise chickens and guinea pigs. Worms, chickens, and guinea pigs are all kept in or near home, and so still reflect the assumption that women's activities must be compatible with the domestic sphere. The planting of trees and shrubs is part of erosion prevention projects, arguably part of agricultural housekeeping. The road repair project – for which the women, led by Tomasa, had to fight to be eligible – is the clearest exception to the domestic rule. That the women did argue to participate in road construction hints that they saw no inconsistency between this work and their gender roles. Indeed, women regularly herded large livestock, such as cattle and donkeys, from girlhood to old age, and were actively involved in planting, cultivating, and harvesting crops.[7] They frequently glossed this as domestic work – in the 1980s, women would tell me that they only worked in the home, even while they were harvesting potatoes or bringing the cattle home. The majority of the projects, though, ignored this actual range of women's roles, assuming a definition of domestic encapsulated by housework, cooking, and child rearing.

These projects relate to women's presumed family responsibilities in another way: the incentive for participation was usually a food handout or, less often, a small wage as in the road repair project. This incentive built from earlier organized charity and programs for poor women, and escalated after the first self-organized comedores populares began 1978 in the poor Lima neighbourhood of Comas (Blondet and Montero 1995: 55–6). Both the comedores and Vaso de Leche originated in the economic crisis of the 1970s and 1980s. While the first comedores came from the grassroots, Vaso de Leche was an initiative of Lima mayor Alfonso Barrantes in 1984. It was so popular because of the effects of the crisis on the poor that women successfully convinced the president to make it nationally available. NGOs, the government, and feminist organizations all took note and vied for a share of action in both programs. Despite the support of some feminist groups, other commentators observed that building on women's responsibility for food provision and organizing distribution through women-only programs were unlikely to improve gender equality (Jelin and Pereyra 1990: 10–14). Further, the right of a citizen to demand basic access to food was undermined when the comedores were administered by NGOs and framed as charity.

Work for welfare – workfare – programs directed to women started in the same period: Laurie (1997) traces it to the García government of 1985–1990. She argues that the unexpected popularity of government-sponsored work programs among women led to their being conceptualised as welfare rather than as productive work. Women's contribution has always been important to their households, but until the 1980s male migrant work in the mining and related sector overshadowed it. At this time hyperinflation and high unemployment among men led to widespread hardship. In the 1990s, with a stabilized structurally adjusted economy, peasants still faced low prices for their products while having to pay high prices for other goods. A crackdown on the informal economy by the state took away these accessible and flexible (if not very profitable) forms of livelihood while not providing good jobs in the formal sector that would allow people a steady sufficient income. Over these two decades of economic crisis (the 1980s and 1990s), women's contributions became proportionally greater and more visible, both to household members and in the official world of government and non-governmental support programs. As we will see in a moment, President Alberto Fujimori in particular exploited this situation as a way of earning support.

If politicians, NGOs, and the organized women's movement were enthusiastic about the grassroots women's collectives that arose through these programs, poor women were also clearly thrilled about the new forms of assistance.[8] All of the projects were temporary, and many required participants only one or two days a week at different times of day. This timing fit in with women's greater control over how they spent their day (although I want it to be clear that women did not really have 'extra' time to spend on these projects and usually other chores had to give way or get done at other times). Further, the reward for participation was often in food, something women saw a direct need for because they did the cooking. A close association between wages and masculinity often deterred men from engaging in these projects. Tomasa, like other women, was an enthusiastic participant in every project she could register for.

This emphasis on domesticity sits awkwardly alongside project goals of empowering women. Rather than building from the entire range of women's responsibilities, these projects marginalize women's contributions in farming and promote commercial production. In their emphasis on organizing women under local leaders, they also suggest that women aspire to more managerial roles. We turn now to how the collectives work to explore this latter theme of forms of management.

Controlled Collectivities

All of the projects that have taken place in Allpachico for women have involved collective mechanisms, usually through specially formed groups and with minimal formal connection to the comunidad. We have observed above some of the activities the women undertook – gluing pasta on empty tins, for example – the purpose of which seems only to be to occupy women while they spend time together. I have noted above a strong theme in the feminist development literature towards collective forms as having more potential to empower women. We examine below ways in which this can happen, but first we focus on how women are controlled. One way, of course, is in the presentation of models of femininity that we have just discussed.

Another is through the manipulation of groups by political parties. Starting at least with Belaúnde in the 1980s, followed by García (Laurie 1997; Radcliffe 1993), political parties have mobilized women supporters by offering them material incentives. Fujimori was particularly famous in this regard in the 1990s (Blondet 2002; Crabtree 1998; Rousseau 2006). By the time Peru implemented a Structural Adjustment Program during his presidency, the negative effects on the poor were well known. Because of this, the International Monetary Fund permitted governments to establish programs to mitigate the problems for vulnerable populations. Fujimori exploited the opportunity

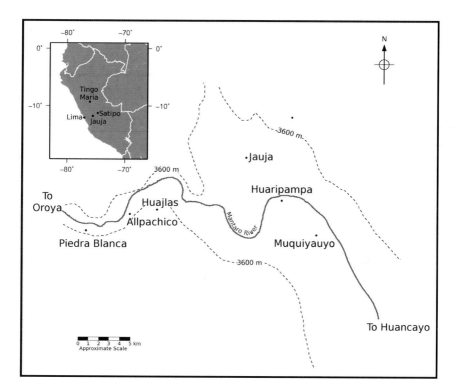

Map showing the location of Allpachico.

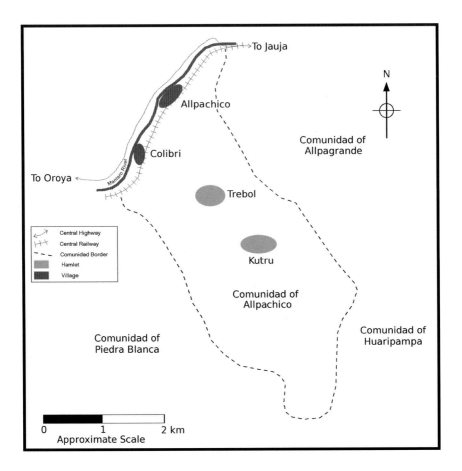

Map of the *comunidad campesina* of Allpachico.

Two members of the religious committee work in a faena to move rocks for the construction of the new church.

The ruins of Huajlas, looking towards the Mantaro Valley to the east.

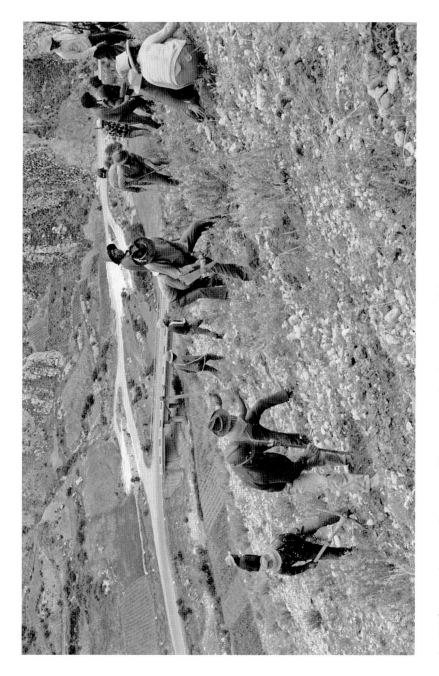

A 1987 *faena* to plant eucalyptus seedlings on a rocky slope as part of the Multi-Need project.

The women of the *comedor popular* cooking lunch in 1995.

A *faena* to harvest the comunidad potato crop in 2007.

A *faena* in 2008 to clean up material from the destruction of the old school and the construction of the new one.

to get political support. Thus, at the end of the decade, Tomasa was involved in campaigning for President Fujimori's party, which, in the 2000 election, either offered food to supporters or managed to get them registered in programs for which they were otherwise not eligible. She commented cynically that she had to get what she could during the campaign because politicians tended to ignore the electorate after-wards. Judith, Pascal's wife, compared two meetings. In one, in the post-Fujimori era, she went to a day of speeches by women politicians about women's rights. They did not get lunch or even water, and she finally left at mid-afternoon. They just wanted votes for nothing, she said. She contrasted this to one sponsored by Fujimori, when women from a hundred communities were fed, housed, and told to get votes for Fujimori, which she said they all did. Clearly, at least some women felt more satisfied with the material benefits of clientelism than with talk of empowerment.

The collective organization of women is used to carry out public edu-cation on topics such as health, as we have seen. These training sessions can be highly coercive as women are required to attend or risk losing their right to food distribution.[9] While some of the messages may be useful, others are not. Thus, Jacinta was furious when, as a member of the Vaso de Leche, she was required to attend a talk by a French nutri-tionist in the municipal capital, Piedra Blanca, in 2007. This woman, she said, had characterized the local menu as deficient and directed them to buy olive oil (at 25 soles a litre, compared to about 5 soles a litre for the usual oil), to serve just a light soup and fruit for supper and to eat rice only once a week. How, Jacinta fumed, was she to afford these things? How was she to get her children to eat their porridge without sugar, or her husband to manage on a light soup after a day doing hard work in the rock quarry? How would raw vegetables help them deal with the cold climate in Allpachico? What was wrong with bread, rice and potatoes – especially potatoes, a quintessential Andean crop and some-thing she could provide from her own land? In truth, though, Jacinta's fury was unusual. Another young woman, Maita, thought the talk was *muy bonito* – 'lovely,' although she admitted she was unlikely to follow the advice.

There is certainly a pro-capitalist message in promoting participa-tion in markets as sellers and consumers in some projects, but this does not necessarily imply an emphasis on pure individualism and there is little tolerance for women to pursue their own agendas. Thus, on various occasions women (and sometimes men in community projects) have been designated as 'problems.' These are women who express out loud in public settings the complaints that are more generally expressed within the group. Jacinta, for example, would be at risk of being labelled a problem if she expressed her opinion too widely. Also, the Vaso de Leche women complain bitterly about having to attend parades and clean the plaza as well as about the quality of the food. However, when some acted on these complaints by refusing to participate or by complaining directly to the mayor of Piedra Blanca, who administers the program, they were denounced as causing problems by both the mayor and other women.

The collectives are thus controlled not only by external rules and agencies, but also by the women themselves. Recipients may not appreciate the difference between the two, as when mandated rules of membership are read by women as the work of the local organizers. Thus, the Vaso de Leche program is supposed to be aimed at children under seven years of age, but the local organizer in 2002 extended it to poor elderly residents. She was extremely reluctant to remove them because of the problems it would cause. Elderly Serena had complained to me in 1999 that she was kept out of the program for no reason, and was happily collecting a share in 2002. She would have been outraged at being denied once again, and would have interpreted it as a personal affront.

The ties developed among women in these collectives seem less horizontal and supportive than vertical and clientelistic. Various women in Allpachico complained that they were kept out of various projects by Tomasa or other local women leaders. Interpersonal conflict can also keep women out of projects, as Tomasa herself became aware. When the woman she accused of having an affair with her husband was registered in a project, Tomasa was denied the right to join. Other women explain that they have not joined certain programs because they perceive conflicts with other members. Many, like Maita, try to keep a low profile and not put themselves forward or express their opinions. While some analysts of the comedores populares have read the solidarity of a group united behind a single leader as demonstrating collective power (e.g., Andreas 1989), or see the goal of mitigating the negative effects of structural adjustment as resistance (e.g., Hays-Mitchell 2002), in Allpachico women not included argued that these collective projects were exclusionary and hierarchical. Differences in access to strategic resources, such as acquaintance with a government official, have a material effect on the networks women negotiate with each other. Those not invited to join a project are understandably alert to the lack of power derived from being outside of a collective.

Powerful Collectivities

The collectives of women organized by projects are not always rife with conflict and exploited by powerful outsiders, however. They have also used their collective power to put pressure on other community members and on the comunidad to achieve specific goals. Many of these have to do with the domestic and family nurturing part of their lives, which, as we have seen, have tended to be themes in the development projects offered to them. Thus, several of the women tell of invading a parcel of land in the 1980s to claim it for the construction of a health post. They remember this as an expression of strength, although in the end nothing happened. In another example, when a man won a lantern in a draw during a fiesta in 1987, a group of women shamed him into donating it to the medical post. This was before the community had electricity. More recently, in 2008, the mothers of women in the preschool program proactively took a small piece of land for a green space, in defiance of the comunidad president's complaint that they should have asked for it with a properly written request. There was also a group of women belonging to the school parents association that successfully lobbied for the reinstatement of the complement of teachers, after low enrolment had caused the regional authority to cut a teaching position. This was in 2004, but by 2008 the teacher complement was back down to two.

While there is currently little acknowledgement of solidarity among women who face family problems, a couple of women have told me that they collectively confronted an abusive husband to protect his wife in the 1990s.

Although not as spectacular as land invasions or confrontations in domestic violence, women's collectives are also very effective organizers of fundraisers, dances, parades, faenas, and so on. I have seen a community feast organized on a day's notice because of well-practiced knowledge of how much food and fuel each person needs to provide, who should be in charge of which dish, and so on. This is a long-standing and very impressive logistical ability.

In addition, two self-organized women's groups have existed in recent years. One, of young women who were the counterparts to a group of young men, was shortlived because of interpersonal conflicts. The young men had the primary goal of playing soccer, but also undertook several public projects, such as carrying out minor repairs to the bridge.

The other group of women is the religious committee (*comité religioso*). This has involved the same four or five women for years, all of them over 60 now. Occasionally a younger woman joins. They learned their organizational abilities from the comunidad and mining company projects. This is the most dynamic self-organized group[10] in Allpachico, having spearheaded the replacement of the old church in a campaign of over ten years. The old church had metre-thick adobe walls that left little room for congregants and was replaced with a new one of cement and brick. Ana, the leader of the group, has an extraordinary charisma and energy that allows her to browbeat community members and the diocesan bishop alike into supporting the project. She is unique in Allpachico in leading through the force of her personality, rather than using control of key resources to influence her followers.

Rather than fostering abilities like Ana's among a wider range of women, empowerment training sessions have had a limited effect. In 1997 I took ten students to Peru for a field study course on gender and development. We spent several days in Allpachico. While there we had a meeting with women participating in the Vaso de Leche program, to hear from them of their experiences with this government sponsored program aimed at women. Given the theme of the course, I asked the women to elaborate for my students on what they had learned in a leadership workshop they told us they had experienced. The women were hard-pressed to come up with anything, and finally the male president of the comunidad who had organized our session – Tomasa's husband Rómulo, as it happens – prompted them with a very clear outline of some of the basic principles of rural women's empowerment. He, at least, had learned what needed to be presented as goals in applications for projects available to women's groups.

The incident reflects a tendency we have seen above for projects to enact activities rather mechanically. None of the health education, domestic activity training, or the empowerment sessions was requested by the women. Rather, external NGOs and government programs planned them, with a view to assist rural women, or at least to be seen to do so. As with all educational programs, some women greeted them enthusiastically and learned assiduously (even if it was sometimes impractical to implement the new ideas), while others put in their obligatory attendance until they could receive the handouts and go home to their other work.

The collectivities of women clearly have potential strength, although this seems to have declined rather than grown more recently, even as 'empowerment' has became one of the themes of the training sessions they attend. Those cases I have been able to document where women have successfully exercised power relate to very specific contexts or people such as Ana, rather than reflecting the sustained enjoyment of rights and influence.

Individual Empowerment

If collectivities of women have not clearly been empowered by development projects, what about individual women? In addition to the collective empowerment presumed to derive from these projects, individual empowerment was featured through leadership programs which Tomasa and a few other women were invited to join. This would allow them to take charge of local organization of the program during its period of operation. Some of the workshops they attended taught them about human rights, oppression of women, and spousal violence. Some of the messages certainly percolated through, but most women were still motivated by what material resources they could get or useful networks they could build. The leadership role they were being trained in was a managerial one, linking them with wider institutional and political mechanisms. The women's experiential knowledge of these mechanisms leads them to interpret the role in clientelistic ways.[11] Further, the knowledge can be applied only at home and in the community, since they are unlikely to get formal professional jobs with their training.

Many of the women learned the script, but not the practice; Tomasa, however, by her own account, learned leadership – by which I mean she learned how to get things done in the Peruvian bureaucratic structure. For example, it was she who pressured a government sponsored road improvement program (mentioned above) to allow women to participate. She and about ten other women from the community spent a hard month doing manual labour mixing tar and filling in potholes. At the end of this period, it appeared that the necessary paperwork to ensure they would get paid had not been done. Tomasa then undertook to travel to the government offices, pressuring various individuals (some of whom she knew from previous programs) until the money came through. Lorenzo, the male president of the comunidad, was grateful to her for her work and skills, as they compensated for his lack of them.[12]

Tomasa's acquaintance with key figures – her 'social capital'[13] – has been a central part of her strategy. One of her most important contacts was the community nurse, Helena, a young woman from Allpachico. Not all projects are mediated by the nurse, but this position has been a major linchpin for many of the government programs in communities. She[14] determines whether children are malnourished, thus permitting them to receive food from the Vaso de Leche program up to the age of 12, and finds out about other projects through which the state makes food or resources available. This broker role allows her to influence which community woman will be the local organizer of a project and, in some cases, which women can join. Thus, she might select women for further training workshops in regional cities. These workshops often include GAD-type sessions on rights or empowerment.

So far, Tomasa's story seems to indicate that local women can become empowered and gain access to income. However, let us see what became of her in the past few years. Three events served to dislodge Tomasa from her local leadership role and show us how fragile the patronage form of empowerment that pertains in Peru is. First, the nurse with whom she had such a close and productive relationship was tragically killed in a car accident in 1997. Second, Fujimori, through whose party she had negotiated further networks, fled power in 2001. Finally, very messy marital problems in 2002 and 2003 marginalized her from the network being built by another capable community woman, Magloria. As noted above, allegations that her husband was having an affair with another woman in Allpachico made it impossible for both women to participate in the same group.

This last event also demonstrates the depressing outcome of teaching women of the institutional means of support available to them. Tomasa went to the police and to government services with accusations of abuse at the hands of her husband. Legal proceedings began, and Rómulo was ordered to pay support that was clearly beyond his means. He responded by withdrawing completely – he did not attend legal hearings, rarely worked, and did not pay her or the children any support. Although members of the community tried to intercede with both Rómulo and Tomasa, they felt she should not have gone outside the community to deal with the issue. In effect, the use of these outside agencies further undermined both the local women's collectives and the community. She thus lost support from her neighbours that she might otherwise have been able to count on. Meanwhile, the legal proceedings were time-consuming, drawn out, and did not result in any effective settlement, in no way compensating for the decline of community interference. It is not my intention to imply that community solutions are necessarily better than state institutional ones; indeed, I have argued elsewhere that opportunities in the wider economy can relieve women from oppression in the community (Vincent 2000). In this case, however, neither was viable.

Tomasa was able to piece together participation in projects in other communities by mobilizing networks she had built up during her leadership years. This provided her with bits of income and work. Her position here, though, was thoroughly as a client, with no clients of her own under her. She has since moved to Lima, where she lives in the house her father bought there. Not having to pay rent, she is able to make ends meet by selling food in the street. Her time is thoroughly taken up with this, though, and she has no time for joining women's groups there.

For a time Magloria, niece of the mayor of Piedra Blanca in office between 2003 and 2006 and on good terms with the new nurse, took Tomasa's place in Allpachico. Magloria attended the training sessions and was the president of the community chapter of the Vaso de Leche program in 2002. Note that, under the decentralization of the political system over the past ten years, the mayor and council have increasing resources to deliver to constituents.[15] Magloria, as the mayor's niece, was in a good position to argue that projects in which she is interested get funding. When these involve food handouts or temporary work programs to be directed to the people of the community, Magloria could use this to build her own (fragile) system of clients. In fact, in the years since Tomasa's fall from position, Magloria has left Allpachico and the mayor has been replaced.

Conclusion

In this chapter we have seen some evidence that individual women and collectives can exercise power, but in constrained and context-specific ways. Thus, some women develop abilities that allow them to manage others, fitting into hierarchical administrative networks. The models presented to them are connected to domestic femininity, and in realms pertaining to the market or in organizational management.

The position and role of women have clearly changed over time, largely as a result of changes in the economic structure of Allpachiqueños, but also as a result of these gendered interventions which pull them away from subsistence farming towards more capitalist activities. These activities, though, tend to be as consumers, or as workers in the low-paid gender segregated sector.

Still, the collectives embody certain kinds of power. As logistical machines they can efficiently produce feasts, food for sale, or public spectacle in their parades and dances. Further, they can win some battles, although the longer term wars have so far usually been lost. The construction of the new church is a rare exception.

I want to pull out some threads that reveal the implications of these identity-based collectives for the comunidad as a political institution. First, with respect to the comunidad itself, one change over the past twenty years is that women are now regularly elected to various positions on the executive – but usually as members at large (*vocales*) or as secretary. There is still resistance to supporting women for higher positions. When a group of women wished to be presented as a slate of candidates for comunidad elections in 2003, the male head of the electoral committee (ironically, this was Rómulo, who had been the one to remember the language of women's empowerment), refused to sanction them. Given the gradual erosion of the comunidad's power both locally and in the Peruvian political structure (to be discussed further in chapters 7 and 8), it is not clear that the women would have accomplished much even if they had been successful.

The establishment of crosscutting collectives could be seen as part of this attack on the comunidad, but it is worth pointing out that its representatives have not seen the situation this way. Remember that comunidad president Lorenzo was grateful that Tomasa was able to negotiate the road work project, and that Rómulo worked to get some of the projects for women, despite his contempt for women politicians. Lorenzo and Rómulo do not perceive the women's collectives and the projects they participate in as a threat, but rather as ways to bring resources to Allpachico. Their attitudes and the limited benefits the women can access demonstrate that women's power is still thoroughly contained.

7 NGOs, Infrastructure Projects, and Commodification[1]

Chapter 5 examined an NGO-led project, focusing on the Integrated Rural Development/Basic Human Needs approach it represented. Here we reflect in greater depth on the NGO form of delivery itself. In the 1980s around the world, NGOs became the delivery agents of choice in development, alongside the global spread of a neo-liberal economic system (Mitlin, Hickey, and Bebbington 2007). Governments downsized, and work formerly under the purview of the state, as well as development aid in general, was taken up by NGOs, themselves often staffed by out of work civil servants (Gill 1997) or unemployed social scientists (Ávila Molero 2000: 434). As we have just seen in Chapter 6, one aspect of the neo-liberal wave was the introduction of Structural Adjustment Programs, with their attendant hardship for the poor of the Global South, mitigated in Peru by government sponsored workfare projects in the 1990s. Many of these projects aimed to build public infrastructure, in a change of direction from the Integrated Rural Development projects of the 1980s that we examined in Chapter 5. Importantly, these tended to work with local collectives other than the comunidad campesina, such as groups of women as in the last chapter, or groups of service users where the project dealt with a service such as electricity, water, or sewage. This dislocation of local project management reframed the political scene: now people had even less incentive to join the comunidad campesina, because receiving the benefits of the project was not tied to membership as it had been in the project in Chapter 5. Paradoxically, however, the comunidad still had to exist as it provided tools and logistical support for these projects.

The new focus on infrastructure, the increased use of NGOs, and the marginalization of the comunidad are all important trends that will be discussed in this chapter. Ultimately, however, the focus is on one of the effects of all of these: the escalating commodification of labour in community endeavours, which up to that time had been undertaken with comunidad faena obligations. As we will see, this process is confused, and accommodated in contradictory ways by both Allpachiqueños and NGOs.

I begin by reviewing briefly the rise in popularity of NGOs both globally and in Peru, and then turn to a description of a potable water project that took place in Allpachico in the early 2000s. This project, while focused on the same service, water supply, as one in the 1960s that I mentioned in Chapter 4, was quite different in inception and implementation.

NGOs, Governments, and Aid

Edwards and Hulme observe that 'The proportion of total aid from OECD countries channeled through NGOs increased from 0.7 percent in 1975 to 3.6 percent in 1985 to *at least* 5.0 percent in 1993–94' (1996: 3; original emphasis). This rise happened in conjunction with the spread of neo-liberal economics and addresses two aspects of what they call, following Robinson, a 'New Policy Agenda': (1) NGOs rather than states became the preferred option for delivering various services; and (2) civil society groups were seen as important to democratization in order to counter state power (ibid.: 2). This great enthusiasm for NGOs led to a significant amount of discussion about them, both from within the sector and beyond it (e.g., Edwards and Hulme 1996; Fisher 1997; Hillhorst 2003; Lewis 1999; Lewis and Opoku-Mensah 2006).

The term 'non-governmental organization' covers a vast range of institutions in terms of purpose, political ideology, geographical coverage, and so on (Toche 2003). Gill (1997) offers a useful definition for our purpose here, as long as we recognize, with her, that the characteristics of actual NGOs may be more complex than is implied by its distinctions. She indicates that development NGOs are usually assumed to be private agencies mediating between donors and subjects; they are not part of the state nor are they based on membership; they do not operate for profit; and they engage in development activities. As she shows in a case study in Bolivia, however, NGOs may well be complicit with the state agenda (Gill 1997, 2000).

In the mid-1980s the idealistic characterization of NGOs claimed that they delivered aid more cheaply and effectively than states could.

The initial flush of enthusiasm made its way into the policy of institutions such as the World Bank (Siddharth 1995; see also Lewis 2005: 204–5) and the programs of the Canadian International Development Agency (Junta de Gobernadores, Fondo General de Contravalor Perú-Canadá 1997). Tvedt (2006) charges that such claims were not only unsupported by evidence, but were counter to already existing research. Other critics accused NGOs of being coopted by implementing the projects of other organizations rather than developing their own (Zaidi 1999: 266); of permitting foreign agents to meddle in national affairs; of having become too corporate; of being a new form of missionizing (Lewis and Opoko-Mensah 2006); of being led by elites who circulated in and out of government and NGOs (Tvedt 2006); of being inattentive to the politics of their interactions with the people (Fisher 1997); of being unaccountable to the populations they addressed (Edwards and Hulme 1996; Fox and Brown 1998); and of a lack of managerial ability (Tendler cited in Lewis 2005: 216n2).[2] Still, NGOs continued their popularity, being seen by their proponents as the best chance to address flaws in development practice, and by the opponents of development as being the source of possible alternatives (Fisher 1997: 443). Although there was a great variation among NGOs, in general the terrain of development in which they operated shifted to the right, increasingly taking forms that assumed the primacy of capitalist market solutions, as well as a smaller range of responsibility for the state (Cammack 2002; Gill 1997; Zaidi 1999).

This neo-liberal model promoted self-help, and constituted a point of convergence among donors, states, and NGOs. Self-help (as opposed to state support) meshed with the participatory trend in development that we examined in Chapter 4, and NGOs were considered to be peculiarly effective in this regard (Fisher 1997: 443). Thus, a range of strategies was generated to address how to involve populations in their own service provision, especially by governments and donors looking for cost-efficiencies in the provision of rural water and sanitation services (Coirolo et al. 2001: 2; Terry and Calaguas 2003; UNDP n.d.).

The Demand-Responsive Approach (DRA) provides one example. OneWorld (1999) defines DRA in water and sanitation services as 'requir[ing] that consumers be engaged in the process of selecting, financing, implementing and managing water and sanitation services that meet their needs and willingness to pay.' Sara (2003) further explains that 'the ideal demand-responsive model is the market model, in which there exists some level of demand from households in a community for improved water and sanitation services, and services to meet this demand is paid for and contracted out to by community members to providers' [*sic*]. She sees a supportive role for governments as facilitators and rule-makers, rather than as funders. Even then, however, she argues that the inclusion of governments and NGOs distorts the market model. In this view, potable water and sanitation services are goods like any others and consumers must be prepared to pay the costs to enjoy them. If people cannot afford the financial cost, then part of the costs can be defrayed through the contribution of in-kind goods or labour (OneWorld 1999).[3] Thus, participants are expected to calculate the opportunity costs of implementing water and sanitation services and to make economically rational decisions about how to pay for them.

These approaches sometimes acknowledge that there are enormous differences among and within communities, while they still rely on collective mobilization. Coirolo et al. (2001) provide an example in a World Bank document. Their discussion of community-based organizations and the benefits of Community-Based Resource Development (CBRD) refers to the potential to address the needs of marginal and vulnerable groups and notes the corollary advantage that they will build social capital through these processes. The insistence in CBRD philosophy that community responsibility for providing its own services will save money depends on this collective spirit and on the participants not calculating the market value of community contributions. Clearly, however, it is governments and donors, which might otherwise be responsible for the costs of providing basic human needs, that derive the financial benefit, and not necessarily the communities which must shoulder this burden (OneWorld 1999). As we will see below the position of these strategies is contradictory in that community dwellers are conceptualized as consumers who decide to spend their labour and material resources on infrastructure, while this contribution is not acknowledged as a cost.

Despite the growing trend in the 1980s for NGOs to work with governments, the governments themselves often retain a deep suspicion of the sector (Lewis and Opoku-Mensah 2006: 669). As I have already mentioned in Chapter 2, this is certainly the case in Peru, where there is a longstanding tension between governments and NGOs (Alasino 2008; Tanaka 2006; Toche 2003). Both sides have expressed deep suspicions of the other: on various occasions, NGOs have been accused of being involved in narcoterrorism, of being the agents of external forces, or of working for personal gain, while governments are charged with political manipulation of regulations and resources to try to bend the development sector to their political ends.

Peru's history of development NGOs[4] began in the 1960s, amid a ferment of social activism against the traditional Peruvian oligarchy. In the later stages of the military government and in the transition to democracy in 1980, the number of NGOs in Peru started to increase dramatically: in 1977 there were about thirty or forty; in 1984 there were at least 218; in 1990 there were 703; and in 2007 there were over 1,060[5] (Toche 2003: 30; Beaumont and Rossel 1992: 71; Llona 2008). The increase in numbers is continuous, but the reasons for this varied in each era. Toche (2003) recounts that in the 1980s, earlier scepticism by the left towards NGOs diminished, with the result that leftist organizations became involved in local level development and political organization. Up to this point, NGOs had operated largely independently of the state.

These official numbers are not accurate, however, and obscure the strategies of different NGO actors. There is evidence, for example, that some NGOs are registered to be in a position to receive development aid funds, although they may not actually exist. In 2004, three Peruvian students carried out a census for me in the Mantaro Valley, which counted twenty-six working NGOs, while another twenty-six were locally registered but could not be located at the addresses given. Many academics and practitioners I spoke to suggested that this trend to registering NGOs without actually operating them was the result of a regulation that NGOs had to have been in existence for two years before being eligible to receive government assistance. Currently, in order to register with the relevant government agency (APCI), an NGO must indicate that it has some professional experience (APCI 2010). Those I spoke with hinted that politicians and others founded NGOs in order to be prepared if an opportunity arose to get funds.[6]

In contrast to these opportunistic NGOs, others avoid registration in order to elude government interference. The man who mediated the transfer of funds from the foreign country to Agua, the NGO I discuss below which carried out a water project in Allpachico, was carefully strategic about registering only some of the several NGOs under his supervision. He complained that politicians and the state were only interested in the registered NGOs in order to get a share of the wealth. He was concerned to have as little involvement with the state as possible.

In keeping his distance, this foreign NGO director went against the prevailing trend. In the 1990s, the scepticism that had earlier characterized Peruvian NGO attitudes to the state turned to cooptation. Beaumont, Gamero, and Piazza (1996: 35) examine the social politics of NGOs in Peru in the 1990s after the advent of neo-liberalism,[7] noting two important trends: one was the concentration of power in the Ministry of the Presidency, and the other was the use of NGOs to carry out the social welfare functions designed by the Ministry of the Presidency to mitigate the effects of structural adjustment (see also Alasino 2008: 5). Thus, they argue that while NGOs had begun in opposition to the state, after the mid-1980s they began to work in greater cooperation with it (Beaumont et al. 1996: 38).[8] Peru was unusual in increasing the amount of its budget dedicated to social welfare programs after the neo-liberal reforms of the 1990s, due in part to the severe decline in social spending the rough economy of the 1980s had incurred, as well as to Fujimori's interest in making this a keynote of his presidency (18–19). Between 1992 and 1994, NGOs implemented programs that commanded 18 per cent of the state social welfare budget (35).

The shift from independent NGOs to close association with the government is clear in a couple of publications honouring the twenty-fifth and thirtieth anniversaries of DESCO, the oldest development NGO in Peru. The twenty-fifth anniversary fell in 1990, the year of Fujimori's initial election. This publication (Zolezzi 1992) includes twenty-seven chapters, all written by people associated with Peruvian NGOs. The subsequent volume (Sánchez León 1996), commemorating the thirtieth anniversary in 1995, has nineteen contributors: two from a Dutch NGO (which financially supported the publication); six from Latin American think tanks and NGOs; and eleven from Peru. Of the Peruvians, only six represent NGOs, and one of these is a business group. The final two are a representative of the Wiese Bank and, most tellingly of all, a representative of the Peruvian Ministry of the Presidency.

Government attempts to regulate and control the NGO and international cooperation sector continue to the present. Alasino (2008) provides an analysis of the extent to which Peru has been effective in implementing international agreements to improve coordination among different development actors and promote transparency of government and NGO work. His conclusion is that government inter-ference continues, to the point where some international agencies are withdrawing from the country.

Alongside strong government influence in shaping development processes, there has been a neo-liberal impetus towards capitalist mar-ket involvement. In the projects I examine in this chapter, the govern-ment is an evident, if often behind the scenes actor, while the market has a very obvious role. Thus, although some development priorities are repeated from the 1960s in more recent projects, the context differs greatly. For example, Padrón notes that infrastructural works and the local contribution of labour were common in both periods (Toche 2003: 33) with different manifestations deriving from the politicized consci-entization of the 1960s and the capitalist rationality of the 1990s and 2000s. We turn now to examine particular projects, focusing on a water project in the early 2000s, to demonstrate the changing calculations of development actors.

Antecedents

In Chapter 4, I presented a project in the 1960s that built a reservoir and installed public taps in the streets. This allowed comuneros to ac-cess clean water more conveniently than the earlier system of taking water from springs, which were drying up anyway. That project was instigated, designed, and carried out by the comunidad. Although completely autonomous projects still happen, most notably the re-placement of the church over the past ten years, after the 1960s, most have involved significant outside involvement. For example, in the 1970s there was an effort to improve water distribution by laying pipes to take it directly to the houses. Members of the comunidad made a successful request to the government to contribute the pipes to be used, and that seems to have been the extent of the government involvement. The comunidad laid the pipes, but they proved to be too small to carry the water, so the system was never put into opera-tion. Here, in contrast to the earlier project, the technology for what the comunidad aspired to was beyond local engineering expertise, so the mostly autonomous effort was in vain. It did, however, show that the government was a possible source of assistance. As external agents took on greater significance, the precise nature of their involve-ment had an impact on the project. The point at which they became involved (that is, whether they initiated the project or were asked for support at some subsequent stage) and the form of their contribution are particularly important.

As we have seen in Chapter 5, in the 1980s the emphasis in development was on income generation, carried out independently by NGOs. Except for the small workfare projects described in Chapter 6, there has not been a significant project to improve the local economy since the Multi-Need one. Instead, infrastructure has become the focus of the bigger projects.[9] At the end of the Multi-Need project, the comunidad made another autonomous venture into construction of service infrastructure, this time for electricity. The prime movers included influential members of the community, such as a man from the wealthiest family (one with a small mine and some transport trucks), as well as younger people who had lived in places with electricity and yearned to have its benefits. They started by collecting funds from interested residents, and bought a generator with proceeds from the sale of the pickup trucks left to the comunidad by Multi-Need.[10] Thus, the project's resources and organization relied on both the comunidad structure and individual residents. While initially they ran wires from the generator for a few hours of service a day, they also applied to Electro, an NGO which specialized in electrification. Electro was a foreign NGO with financing from its government, a European nation. Eventually Electro carried out a project that connected Allpachico and other neighbouring communities to the regional grid. This stage of the electrification project marks an important shift from the comunidad as local recipient to a committee of future service users, often glossed as the community. It is important to note that only the two main hamlets, Allpachico and Colibrí, got electricity: Electro considered it too expensive to extend the network to residents of the more inaccessible highland part of the comunidad. The NGO did, however, connect less isolated highland hamlets from the neighbouring communities. There was resentment from Allpachiqueños that all of these communities received the same benefits in spite of the fact that only Allpachico had already invested significant resources in electrification from the earlier autonomous phase.

While electricity is sometimes framed as improving quality of life, the project demonstrates the growing involvement in the capitalist economy. With the connection to the grid, Allpachico got access to three-phase electricity, which they hoped would be able to power local small industry, in addition to residential service. With the exception of a short-lived stone cutting business, no small industry has arisen to use the high-powered electricity supply. Apart from its potential to generate income, electricity is a service that must be paid for. Further, electricity only makes sense if one has purchased light fixtures and appliances.

Electro provided materials and technical support, while comuneros provided the unpaid non-technical labour. I noted above that this was a feature of development in the 1960s in Peru. Of course, labour taxes and tribute have been around at least since the Inca Empire. However, the superficial similarity among Inca, Spanish, 1930s Republican, and more recent forms of labour conscription are belied by the very different contexts. As I have argued above, the requirement for unpaid labour in the Demand Responsive Approach in a capitalist system is meant to lower costs. Proponents of this also assume that if people make a valuable contribution to a project they will be more likely to maintain it afterwards, ensuring its sustainability. The labour investment is thus expected to implicate them as owners of the project. This can make them very reluctant to give up ownership to a business to administer the service once the infrastructure is in place. Not only do they see this as the loss of their investment, but now they would have to pay for a service to a business which did not compensate them for their work. The product of their labour would thus be given a market value and alienated: from being an integral part of the community, it would be turned into a commodity and sold.

This is what happened in the electrification project. The initial idea was that the consumers would share the monthly bill equally. However, very soon there arose complaints that some were using far more electricity than others and those who felt taken advantage of refused to pay. When the bill fell into arrears, the regional state-owned utility cut off the electricity. The negotiations with the utility led to the latter taking over the infrastructure, including all of the concrete poles and wire contributed by Electro and put in place with Allpachiqueño labour. Individual metres, paid for by the resident, were installed at each house. People worried that the concrete poles would be replaced by cheaper wooden ones and were resentful and humiliated at the loss of control over the system. Various state attempts to privatize the company through the 1990s and 2000s have made people even more furious. From being collective owners and managers of a project with their own embedded labour and resources, they became individual clients of a business that appropriated their investment without indemnification.

The experience taught Allpachiqueños a bitter lesson in commodi-fication, covering the full range of the dimensions Castree (2003) attri-butes to the process (see Chapter 2). The infrastructure was privatized as an ownable system. It was alienated from the people who produced it. It was individuated in two senses: the people feared that parts of the grid, such as the poles, would be removed from their location, and its incorporation into the regional electrical company technically sepa-rated it from the environment. In being transferred in payment of their debt, it was given a market value and exchanged, in the process attrib-uting to it an abstract comparison with other electrical grids. Finally, in this process its value seemed to be a characteristic of the electrical system itself, rather than linked to the labour that created it.

The electrification project not only began the spate of infrastruc-tural development in Allpachico, but also, importantly, opened the door to service users as the beneficiary group rather than the comu-nidad campesina. Unlike the Integrated Rural Development project of Chapter 5, which was restricted to comuneros, the service user group excluded geographically distant households, who were mem-bers of the comunidad, and included households that were not mem-bers. This history, beginning with local control and ending with a complete loss of ownership of the project, made people very wary of future infrastructure projects. As we will see with the Agua water project, they were suspicious of promises that it belonged to them when their past experience and their shrewd assessment of the real-ity challenged this view.

The Agua Water Project

The water project that took place in the early 2000s exemplifies the growing involvement in the capitalist economy, along with the con-flicts and contradictions accompanying this process. The project shares many features with earlier ones: it was carried out by a foreign-funded NGO; it relied on unpaid contributions of labour; and it involved a collective, in this case a service user group as in the elec-trification project, while also relying on the organizational structure of the comunidad. Its inception is more complex, however, as we will see. While improving the water supply had been a long time concern of the people, as attested by the truncated 1970s project, it was not at the top of their list. Besides, successive mayors of Piedra Blanca had made various (unfulfilled) promises since the 1990s to upgrade the water system, and the earlier electricity project had taught them that it did not pay to show independent initiative.

In 1998 and 1999, I surveyed community residents about their development priorities and how to achieve them.[11] While income generation and community dissension received the most attention, there was some discussion of services. My assistants and I looked around to see if there were any NGOs that could support Allpachico's priorities. We discovered that there were few options. Most were working in areas officially designated as 'in extreme poverty,' which were the higher priority and for which more resources were available. Remember that the average income in the municipality of Piedra Blanca was above this threshold, because of businesses owned by another comunidad.[12] Among the very few possibilities, the most promising was a foreign NGO, which I will call Agua, that sponsored potable water projects, incorporating a conscientization component. The latter conveyed a hope of addressing the widely decried internal conflict.

In 1999, the comunidad of Allpachico[13] held an assembly (poorly attended, as were most general assemblies at this time) to discuss these findings. Although most people still expressed the need for income generation in the discussion, a majority vote established a potable water project as the main priority. It was, after all, the only firm opportunity on the horizon. People agreed that potable water was important in order to address health concerns and the time women and others spent carrying water from the public taps. Farmers were less interested in the residential service, but some hoped there would be enough water for irrigation. They had been disappointed during the Multi-Need project when a pump to draw river water to the fields was sent to another community: Multi-Need felt it had not been sufficiently used in Allpachico. In the discussion, women and returned migrants tended to be most in favour of the water project, but there were few vocal dissenters. The assembly formed a committee to contact the NGO and pursue the matter.

Their background of false promises, failed projects, loss of control of the electricity grid, and the lack of great enthusiasm made Allpachiqueños leery of committing too heavily to the Agua project.[14] By the time of my return to the field in 2000, the committee had missed some important meetings with the NGO and the plans were in disarray. Meetings to address the issue were poorly attended, but a wide range of people did express their continued interest in the project and eventually a new committee was formed and Agua directors agreed to reactivate the project.

Reorganization of the NGO, alongside the difficulty the Allpachico water committee members had in getting to Lima and setting up the project led to several further delays; however, funding was in place and work begun by early 2002. The contract between Agua and the service users group outlined the general responsibilities of each party: Agua was to provide materials for the main infrastructure of the system, as well as technical work and supervision, while the users were to provide unskilled labour, for example, to dig trenches for the pipes. Each registered user would have to purchase household plumbing. A schedule of deadlines for several phases of the project was also part of the contract. Some elements of the project, such as the water capture system, were not included in the contract, and how each party was to fulfil its obligations was not detailed with one exception. Here, the fact that it was not the comunidad, but a list of users that was the recipient of the project became important: Agua required that each individual user had to fulfil all of his or her obligations to receive a connection, rather than the comunidad being able to make decisions about who was to benefit and what participation would be required of each person. The role of the comunidad was reduced to providing support such as lending tools and a place to store project materials – both necessary, but giving little acknowledgement to the comunidad.

The users had decided that each registered user would dig four 10 metre sections of ditch for the pipe to bring the water from the source, which was 1.6 kilometres away, to the reservoir. The distribution system in the settlement would be excavated by faenas. The users also had to repair the existing reservoir, which was cracked and leaking. This work was to have been completed by the end of April 2002. When I arrived in mid-May, it was still not finished. Those who had been allocated sections of trench that were pure rock had no means of digging their sections, and the people were uncertain how to proceed. There was also discussion about the diameter of the pipes to bring the water to the reservoir. Some people thought that larger pipes would be needed, especially those who had some hope of being able to use water for irrigation. There was concern about leaving the trenches open, both in the highlands and in the village, as they posed a danger to unwary livestock and humans. The longer the delay in laying the pipes, the more the earth resettled in the trenches and more work had to be done to re-excavate them. Agua technicians were markedly absent during this time, and many users complained about the lack of technical direction. There was much speculation that the funds had run out and that the project would go no further.

When Agua engineer Milagros finally showed up in July, she explained that she had made it clear that she and the technicians would not return until the users had done their part. This was still not finished, she complained, although the contract outlined a schedule. She also pointed out that those who had not fulfilled their faena obligations would not be connected: her mandate was only to offer materials and assistance to those who complied with the contract. She said she would return in August and, if the users had completed their part, the project would proceed. The users agreed to continue working.

When I returned to Allpachico in 2003, the project was still not finished, although a date for the inauguration of the system had been set. While the pipe from the source to the reservoir had been laid, break-pressure tanks[15] still had to be installed on it. Further, the users had taken the initiative to dig a water capture system at the source, since it was not explicitly mentioned in the contract and they had heard nothing from Agua about it. Engineer Milagros explained that this was something done at the end of the project, and ordered the work redone to meet her technical specifications, thus ensuring that the system would last. This was very hard work, involving climbing one and a half kilometres from the settlement, carrying tools and cement. They had to dig through gravel that became increasingly waterlogged as they excavated. At one point, the trench wall collapsed, causing the workers to complain about safety. In addition to the water capture system, final distribution trenches had to be built in the town across roads, disrupting traffic. The valves for each house connection also had to be installed. Each individual user had to purchase a specific cement case for the valve. Several people had purchased smaller, less expensive cases on the recommendation of one of the villagers who claimed knowledge in the area; Milagros refused to allow these to be installed. Thus, a lot of heavy, hard work and individual monetary investment still had to be carried out so the system could be inaugurated at the end of June, when representatives from the NGO's country would be in Peru to help celebrate. To further complicate matters, all of this took place during the harvest season when people had to get their crops in. A month-long teachers' strike, while rendering some household organization more difficult, did mean that children were available to help out rather than being away at school during the day.

Finally, on 29 June 2003 the inauguration took place. Of 120 original registered houses, seventy-nine had been eligible for connections in May 2003. Only about fifty had connections outside their houses by the end of June, and of these only a handful had any system inside the house to access the water. On this day, the old public taps, connected to a different distribution system, were to be turned off, leaving most households without water. The users had prepared a typical feast and entertainment for the foreign visitors from the funding organization. They arrived, took part in the celebrations, baptized the system, and left for their next engagement.

Diverse Perspectives of the Project

Although the people of Allpachico had supported the idea of the water project, carrying out the negotiations themselves and engaging in the process, most of the period of the project during my visits at least, was marked by complaints and accusations against each other and Agua. The complaints centred on the amount of work involved to get the water. There were differences among the villagers. In this section I point to the views of two major groups in Allpachico: permanent residents with little or no wage or pension income, and current or retired migrants with wage or pension income. Their different points of view revolve around how they calculate the unpaid work necessary to carry out the project.

The Views of Permanent Residents

At the time of the project, Pancho and Mimi (whom we met in Chapter 4), were around 60 years old. They have lived in Allpachico all of their lives, although they have no land or house of their own. Since the mid-1980s they have lived in the house of a migrant to Lima, looking after it in his absence. In addition to sharecropping and working for others, Pancho and Mimi get by through informal exchanges and helping out wealthier villagers and migrants. Mimi's crocheted bedspreads, for example, are gifts to these family and friends from whom they receive various forms of assistance.[16]

The reciprocity between patrons and clients involves a web of mutually beneficial goods and services that are not always monetarily valorized, in contrast to an employer-employee model. Running water would help Mimi, who had to carry water uphill to their house from

the village tap, but the cost of the project was heavy. To them, participating in the faenas meant a loss or potential loss of income. Even when
they did participate, it counted for others; their own access to water in
the future depended on whether the owner of the house they lived in
was willing to install a connection. In addition to their work on behalf
of this house, however, some of the other people with whom they had
arrangements could require them to perform their faenas. Members of
another permanent resident household looked after four houses in addition to their own. If they were required to perform water faenas for
all of these houses it would greatly exceed the household labour supply. Juggling all of these responsibilities meant that some permanent
residents ended up owing days, even if they had worked them. The roll
call taken at faenas was a complicated procedure, because *who* was in
attendance was less important than who they were attending *for*. The
politics of patron-client relations led some clients to support the project,
even while they complained bitterly about its costs. Even for permanent residents who owned their own houses, access to water depended
on having the money to purchase the plumbing supplies for inside the
house.

Pancho and Mimi were not against the idea of having running
water, and indeed it has saved Mimi a fair amount of work. Their
labour contribution was costly, though, and they deeply resented the
fact that it was unpaid. Every day these permanent residents worked
on the project on their own behalf, they were not earning money. This
was in contrast to their experience of the workfare projects organized
in the 1990s and which still take place in neighbouring communities
with the coveted 'in extreme poverty' label. Chevalier (1982) argues
that, in a context in which labour power can be sold for a wage, simple
commodity producers take account of the value of their labour power
in their own production. The potential market value of their labour
power becomes part of their calculations about how to price their
products and spend their time. Similarly, the permanent residents of
Allpachico counted the potential value of their labour. If they had a
real offer of work for a given day, the opportunity cost of contributing to the faena instead was quite high. But even without alternative
paid work, the permanent residents saw their labour contribution as
unrealized income. Even worse, if they carried out a faena as part of
the general services undertaken for a patron, and so still owed on
their own account, they calculated that they had to pay to work. In
Allpachico, poor and rich villagers alike understood the potential

market return on their labour. Indeed, the amount of the fine for non-attendance at faenas was set at the local rate for agricultural workers. This was lower than the mine workers earned in their jobs, but still constituted a financial burden, especially when the number of faenas accumulated. Clearly, both migrant workers and permanent residents counted their labour contribution in commodified ways.

The Views of Wage and Pension Recipients

Jaime and Valerí were in very different economic circumstances from Pancho and Mimi, as they had recently moved back to Allpachico after Jaime's retirement from work in a mining smelter. After years of living in the city, they were accustomed to the comforts of urban life, such as electricity, running water, and sewers. They supported the water project. They had some land, but at that time had not begun to farm all of it, although they had recently grown a few things for their own consumption. They had no children who could either assist with household labour requirements or make demands on household finances. Valerí, through years of city life, had lost the ability to do hard physical work that country dwellers must undertake. Thus, although their household had two adults, only Jaime considered doing jobs demanding strength, as the water faenas did. Jaime had a pension which covered their needs and, although he often participated in the faenas, could afford to pay the fine for those he missed. Still, he complained about the excessive number of work days and the poor technical assistance. Having had a skilled job in the refinery, he found it difficult to be treated as unskilled labour with no input into the technical specifications of the project. He was particularly outraged by the danger he faced when the trench wall for the water capture system collapsed. He also fumed at the cost of fines for too many faenas. He was willing to pay for the service, but saw the costs spiralling beyond his control.

Yolanda and Antonio were a young couple with one child. Antonio worked in a quarry 20 kilometres from Allpachico and only had Sundays off. Yolanda split her time between child care, looking after her mother's store, and helping out her grandmother. In addition, the couple was building their own house in Allpachico, also demanding her time and their income. Yolanda sometimes attended faenas, but the hard work tired her and she resented those who devalued her contribution as a woman. Antonio's income was insufficient, though, to pay the fines for non-attendance. Here, too, the major complaint was about the financial cost of so many work days.

Where the permanent residents complained about the cost of participation in terms of labour and lost wages, the wage and pension recipients focused on the direct expense of fines for not participating. The differences were divisive. G. Smith (1985) discusses how the commodification of labour affects how people calculate the cost of work for the community, as well as considering why people may need to sustain these costs. When rich villagers can replace actual participation in community faenas by a fine, or by a hired replacement for a quantity of money that is less than the well-off peasant could earn elsewhere, then the nature of community ties changes, entering the realm of commodification. As Smith notes, however, commodification is usually only partial – simple commodity producers can rarely afford to give up their access to labour power that is not paid at market values. They are thus forced back into the idiom of community, such as by actually showing up at faenas, in order to be able to draw on community networks and resources in difficult market conditions.

These considerations affected how wage and pension recipients viewed the cost of their participation in the project. This is similar to how CBRD/DRA proponents imagine people will calculate their contribution, by eliding the fine and the work. In effect, the wage and pension recipients saw the two as abstractly comparable as Smith's rich peasants try to do. To a great extent they saw their leisure as something they could purchase by paying a fine, if they could afford to do so.

Another important point of view is that of later returned migrants, not in Allpachico during the project, who balked at the cost of hooking up to the water system, which was calculated as the fines for the total number of days of work multiplied by the rate of inflation. The resulting total was more than hook up costs in urban areas. These villagers tried to argue for lower costs by reverting to the idiom of community, much as G. Smith's (1985) rich peasants were usually forced to do. They claimed that they had been supportive of the comunidad while working away and so should get free access.

The permanent residents had a somewhat different perspective from those with wage or pension income. While various project tasks at the end were undertaken by members of both groups who wished to pay their fines in labour rather than in money, the permanent residents believed that they were contributing far more personal work to the project than richer residents, who, because they could pay the fines and afford the materials for connections inside their houses, might get the water before them. For them the problem was the alienation from the product of their labour, despite their disproportionate share of the cost in labour, fines, and foregone wages.

Given that the number of faenas was a critical factor in the cost for all participants, let us now turn to examine why there were so many.

The Market in the Community

The litany of complaints about the project from villagers and Agua staff alike seemed to indicate that the project was a failure. Certainly resentment and frustration infused the participants throughout the process. Rather than apportioning blame, however, I wish here to draw lessons about the logic of community participation. One of the sources of tension, the contradiction between the expectation of egalitarian community participation and the market calculation of actual contribution of labour power, directly relates to this logic.

This project took place at a time when development practitioners were trying to break the pattern of *asistencialismo* (welfarism), understood as an excessive dependency by the poor on handouts and frequently linked to political manipulation. Requiring community decisions and unpaid labour were considered to counter this. In insisting on equivalent contributions on the part of each beneficiary, Agua tried to ensure that no one was able to take unfair advantage of the project. Indeed, Milagros called attention to how some powerful members of the community were trying to get access to water without having completed any of their required duties. Agua also emphasized the value of the contributions of women and the elderly, again addressing power inequalities in the community, issues that had received critical attention in development circles, as we have seen in chapters 5 and 6 (see also Slocum et al. 1995). Those in charge of organizing the work, on the other hand, were less enthusiastic that so many of the workers were women, and among them, elderly or very young women. They could not work as quickly as the men, the organizers charged, which meant that more faenas were needed. As noted above, Yolanda was sensitive to these complaints. In order to reinforce the notion of equality, Agua refused to allow the donated materials or technical service to be used to connect anyone who had not fulfilled the faena requirements or paid the appropriate fines. Record keeping at faenas was complex but essential, and Milagros closely scrutinized them. Agua's attempts to overcome inequality involved the imposition of rules rather than discussions with the user group, essentially ignoring how local inequalities play out.

These structural requirements of egalitarianism were accompanied by Milagros' insistence in speeches in Allpachico that this was a community project in which the labour component was essential and valuable. Indicating her understanding of the wage and pension recipients' calculations, in 2002, when the project was already behind schedule, she suggested that the fines be raised to four times their current value. She hoped to make the cost of simply paying the fine too great to be borne, because the project depended on having the work done rather than on having the money. While various causes[17] led to delays in the project, the lack of labour to finish the tasks relegated to the users was a major reason.

Agua clearly viewed the users' contribution of unskilled labour as appropriate and expected project beneficiaries to engage in this work with some enthusiasm. As we have seen, much development theory argues that it will ensure that the people truly want the project and are willing to engage in work or financial commitments to achieve it.[18] It did not have the desired effect: the technician overseeing the last stages of the project repeatedly commented on how slowly and half-heartedly the people of Allpachico were working. The slow pace meant that in two weeks in the community he had really only been able to do four days of his own work. In other communities, he said, people would pick up their tools immediately on hearing of their receipt of the project, would work on Sundays and into the night, and get him up early in the morning to do his own part of the job. In Allpachico, he spent much of the time wandering around, despairing whether the project would ever finish.

Looking back at Allpachico's prior experience, we see that Allpachiqueños had already asserted a strong sense of ownership over the electrification project, with humiliating consequences. Indeed, one of the things that delayed the water project was a fear that it, too, would be taken over by a regional water authority. Agua's expectation that the people would enthusiastically embrace their role to work together for a common cause sits awkwardly with the market-informed calculations people actually made about their work, and their understandings of development involving infrastructure. As we saw in Chapter 6, the Fujimori era had taught them that infrastructure projects were supported by government through paying people for their labour. This had ensured that poor people, and especially women, received income for building roads or working on water and sanitation projects. Women embraced this opportunity to earn money and their generally slower pace helped them to earn over more days. In many cases, these projects provided services that the wealthier members of the community wanted – those who had cars or tractors to drive on the roads, or those who had become used to domestic water and sewers from living in cities or work centres. This system, vilified as reflecting asistencialismo, had the advantage of providing something for both rich and poor: services for the former, money for the latter. The reassertion of community in the sense intended by the neo-liberal model imposed in the wake of asistencialismo could not help but grate on the poor who had come to see their community-oriented labour power as having financial value.

A comparative case, involving the government program A Trabajar Urbano, helps to see how the valorization of labour impacts on local perspectives of a water project. Arias and Aramburú (2003) describe participant perspectives on a potable water project in a neighbourhood in the city of Huancayo. Here, the government provided technical supervision and paid eligible poor members of the project for their work in a poverty reduction program, contributing 50 per cent of the cost of the project (Marchesi 2003: 40). The municipality provided 30 per cent of the funding. The people themselves had to contribute financially for the rest of the project (20 percent) as well as participating in weekend faenas. Participants attributed a significant part of the reason for their participation as the need for paid employment. This did not prevent them from complaining about the low wages, but these complaints in themselves indicate that people do calculate the market value of their work. They also connect having physically worked on the project, either through the paid positions or in faenas, with owning the service. Arias and Aramburú (2003: 73) quote their informants as feeling that those who worked owned the project and that others in the neighbourhood who wanted water were viewed as clients. The clients paid more for their water and, in times of scarcity, had less right to it. To the extent that there was a sense of community here, it was limited to the workers who saw themselves as operating a business (ibid.).

This comparative case highlights the ways in which Peruvians have come to understand the commodified value of their labour while not accepting that wages imply that the product of their labour is thereby alienated. Teasing apart the embedded assumptions about market and community, both in project planning and in participant perspectives, is essential to understand the underlying goals of the project from both points of view and the types of tensions that might arise as a result of it.

Conclusion

In subsequent visits to Allpachico I have discovered that the water project is largely viewed as a success by the people. There have been numerous valve failures, requiring digging through the mud to replace them, but those who visit Lima in particular tout the abundant supply of clean water in Allpachico as a great advantage. Thus, their hindsight minimizes the tensions I observed during the implementation. This makes me more hesitant to accept at face value any positive reflections on other projects, though, than to discount the fraught process through which the water system was installed. After all, they always did want the water, which they now have.

The tensions among the different groups over work and fines demonstrate important class-like divisions. The dwindling number of permanent farming households meant there were few able-bodied people to undertake the hard work as a community responsibility. Instead, and in contrast to how Arias and Aramburú described those who had worked on the Huancayo project as owners, those who actually did the work in Allpachico felt that their labour was exploited. In turn, those who hoped to pay the fines or to access the service on return to the community also felt exploited, although for them this was as consumers and in terms of the monetary cost.

The conflicts highlight the contradiction relating to the assumption of market rationality in one aspect, that of cost management through unpaid labour contributions, while simultaneously assuming that this labour will not be evaluated. This was exacerbated by another contradiction presaged in Chapter 4: that of an external agency trying to bring about an ideal community by making requirements about who could work and how users got a right to the water. Agua's very separation from government underscored that the people could not claim the right to affect how the project was organized. This was charity, not a service provided by an elected government. Agua was well-intentioned, but we can see here some of the difficulties inherent in

NGO work with populations who are ultimately seen as recipients of charity and therefore must conform to the NGO's rules.

This project did not cause the infiltration of capitalist rationalization into Allpachico but it was an influential part of the wider process. This experience points to the need to think carefully about market logic and community participation in development projects. We have seen that much of the current turn to community, in this case in the form of service users, is aligned with a neo-liberal interest in extending capitalist market influence. Market rationality reduces costs and is assumed to ensure long-term commitment. However, this strategy also depends on a sense of community that implies a non-market calculation of mutual responsibility. In contrast, poor participants in the Allpachico water project persisted in calculating their contribution in terms of market rationality. Appeals to community conflicted with their understanding of the value of their labour power. We continue the discussion of the different evaluations of labour power and projects in Chapter 8.

8 Participatory Budgeting: Accounting, Accountability, and Politics[1]

In this chapter, I return to the state as actor in development. In a radical shift from the big projects described in chapters 5 and 7 that were run by NGOs, the state has become the major source of development funds through municipal participatory budgeting. Gradually, beginning in the late 1990s Allpachico started to get more resources from the municipal district to which it belonged, Piedra Blanca. Don Jorge, serving a term as president of the comunidad campesina in 2004, was enthusiastic. 'We used to just get what we called a subsidy,' he said, '400 or 500 soles that didn't begin to cover what we needed to do for our people.'[2] Then things began to change. First, the mayor gave funds to fix up the plaza, and then he donated a satellite dish so they could get access to television.

Finally the government seemed to be taking responsibility for rural development, after largely empty promises going all the way back to independence from Spain in 1824, and even giving people a say in how the resources would be spent, as well as implementing procedures to ensure transparency. Representatives of civil society groups attended workshops where they proposed projects, which were then approved or rejected after a technical appraisal. The size of the projects increased. Never before could Allpachico have hoped to get municipal support for a sewage system, (completed over 2006 and 2007 with a budget of about 100,000 soles), to replace the aging school building (started in 2008 with a budget of over 80,000 soles), or provide the medical post with its own up-to-date facility (planned, with a budget of 60,000 soles).

But there is something curious about those big-budget projects: although the community asked for them, none of them seem to be in particularly high demand. About half of the people who live in All-pachico, including many who worked on the project, have not connected to the sewage system. Enrolment in the school has plummeted from 103 students in 1987 to about fifteen in 2008 and the number of teachers declined from four to two. And few people say they like the nurse who has worked at the medical post for years; several simply go elsewhere for their health needs.

How could participatory budgeting be so ineffective? Why was there so little interest in accepting the numerous and clear invitations to participate in decision-making over these resources? And why did complaints of fiscal mismanagement and corruption continue despite the disclosure of municipal accounts?

The law proclaimed goals of eliciting citizen engagement, alleviating political corruption, and ensuring the allocation of public resources to the most acute problems.[3] Far from deepening democracy, the actual process reflects a significant level of state control; it also shows, however, how the community resists state attempts to reformulate the 'local.' Further, close attention to the accounting methods used by the various participants uncovers some interesting differences. On the surface, participatory budgeting applies a capitalist rationality similar to the cost-saving principles around unpaid labour and community investment in the project discussed in Chapter 7. In participatory budgeting, citizens must allot scarce resources to carefully considered priorities. The situation is not straightforward, however. Certain funds accessed in the system permit municipal officials considerable flexibility, while others are extremely restrictive. This dilutes and sometimes overcomes the community's freedom to choose its own projects and potentially allows politicians to continue to manipulate funds for their own ends. The accounting logic applied by members of the community to the fiscal information made available through transparency measures critiques the hierarchical assumptions of value embedded in technical evaluations, leading to more scepticism than acceptance.

The choices made through the process are not simply the product of state and local level political interference, though. The social norms that bind a community's collective existence drive them to choose certain kinds of projects that may not appear to be at all useful. There is a strong ethic to apply resources directed to the community to generally beneficial projects, rather than ones that might provide only a few with a significant personal advantage.

This chapter begins by reviewing the rise in popularity of participatory budgeting globally, placing the Peruvian system in this context. Then I outline the Peruvian participatory budgeting process. The chapter ends with an extended analysis of what has happened in Allpachico.

State Reform and Participatory Budgeting

In earlier chapters we have seen how the Peruvian government's adaptation of neo-liberalism led to political clientelism, the rise of NGOs, and the growing infiltration of capitalist rationality among the population. At the end of the 1990s, after a sustained period during which the state receded in favour of the private sector,[4] it returned in a discourse of democratization and governance. Hewitt de Alcántara (1998) notes the infusion of neo-liberalism into state practice as she comments on the elastic ways in which governance has been conceptualized by various government, civil society, and free market actors in the last two decades. In an echo of the sentiments behind the Basic Human Needs approach, she argues for a change in the overall economic regime to address poverty as the most effective way to achieve democratization, against the trend for technical or institutional restructuring.[5] This is not a call for local autonomy, but an argument for closer interrelations between citizens and government (Hewitt de Alcántara 1998: 112–13; see also Gaventa 2004; Grompone 2005).

This link between governance and participatory strains of development manifested itself in the growing popularity of municipal participatory budgeting (Goldfrank 2007). Participatory budgeting involves the distribution of state, locally generated, and other resources to public fora which decide municipal spending priorities. The mechanism simultaneously proclaims the contribution of the state and devolves responsibility (and potential blame) for decision-making to the people. It is a hybrid that might variously be seen as aligned with the neo-liberal interest in downsizing government and intensifying capitalism, or, alternatively, as according power to the people to establish their own autonomous direction. Reflecting this range of possibilities, the precise structure and experience of participatory budgeting varies widely, affecting the outcomes (see, e.g., Baiocchi 2003; Cabannes 2004; Dickovick 2006; Goldfrank 2006, 2007).

In Peru, as we have seen in Chapter 6, the state did not retreat from local service provision as much as in other countries. Instead, President Alberto Fujimori took a prominent role in directing state social funds to his followers during Peru's structural adjustment in the 1990s. This meant that addressing political corruption, the widely touted neo-liberal justification for structural adjustment programs, had to be revisited when he left office. One element of this was to replace the hypercentralism of his regime by decentralized political structures. Various projects to decentralize Peruvian government and build local government have taken place over the years even before this period. Remy's (2005b) history of local government indicates that the 1984 municipal law already referred to community participation. With some notable exceptions, those early moves were ineffective, and all were truncated by the violence of the late 1980s and 1990s and lack of interest on the part of central governments in inducing real change. I focus here on the resurgent interest in devolving power and resources to local governments since 2003, when the new laws on municipal government and participatory budgeting were passed.

The history of political decentralization in Peru demonstrates how important it is to recognize the particularities of different governments, rather than reifying the state. According to Dickovick (2006), decentralization was deployed by strong central governments who restructured power to regions or to municipalities in attempts to limit opposition power. For example, the APRA government of Alan García created regional governments in the late 1980s as a way of shoring up power in the face of probable national electoral defeat in 1990. In turn, Fujimori disbanded the regions and made a tentative attempt at creating municipal governments in the early 1990s. This was short-lived, and the Fujimori regime returned to a strong highly centralized structure. As the country adapted to the post-Fujimori era, Alejandro Toledo, elected president in 2001, reinstated regions in an initial decentralization move. Then, when his party lost the elections to fill the regional governments, he starved them of resources, bypassing them in favour of supporting municipalities. Thus, Dickovick (2006) concludes, the municipal and participatory budget laws of 2003 were the product of a powerful unitary state government forced into decentralization while trying to undermine the influence of opposition parties. Ironically, therefore, decentralization in Peru has been a centralized government strategy.

This context is important as the evidence suggests that top-down decentralization is not as effective as bottom-up (Eaton 2004 cited in Dickovick 2006: 3; Heller 2001).[6] Cabannes' (2004) largely positive view of participatory budgeting includes two Peruvian cases in which the policy was implemented autonomously in advance of legislation.

When participatory budgeting is entrenched into law, the possibility of achieving broad participation and responsible local governments becomes less certain (Cabannes 2004: 40). Remy (2005a, 2005b), an important analyst of Peruvian participatory budgeting, agrees, pointing to the technocratic nature of the legislated process.[7]

Meléndez (2005) adds a depressing analysis of Peruvian politics to this mixture. Party politics, with their established ideological platforms, have given way to a personalistic style of leadership. This has resulted in a web of cronyism[8] around a person. He notes the high number of amateur 'electoral entrepreneurs' entering politics (Degregori and Meléndez 2007; Meléndez 2005) for personal benefit, undermining the probity of government at all levels.

These analyses of the political obstacles to effective participatory budgeting are supplemented by a few others which document the problems and successes of specific cases. In Peru, the case of Villa El Salvador[9] is the best known. A pioneer in participatory budgeting having incorporated participatory governance laws since its inception in the 1970s (Chambi Echegaray 2001), Villa El Salvador's experience informed the design of the national law requiring municipalities to institute the process (Hordijk 2005: 233). Among the problems encountered, Hordijk lists obstruction by actors opposed to the processes or to specific projects, a lack of technical capacity to manage the projects, limited funds, and a fragmentation of projects dealing with local practical concerns rather than with broader strategic needs.[10] This last has been partly addressed by a requirement to develop a long-term plan with which specific projects must comply. The tendency in the majority of the corrective measures, however, has been to focus on the local and the technical. Thus, the annual guidelines distributed by the Ministry of the Economy and Finance (MEF) have become more detailed and restrictive, leading to top-down control that undermines the effectiveness of participatory budgeting, as we have just noted. These guidelines show that, ironically, if budgetary decentralization was supposed to address citizens' distrust of the government, the degree of government regulation reflects the government's deep suspicion of the people. Let us now turn to the guidelines for a brief overview of how participatory budgeting happens.

Participatory Budgeting in Peru

The participatory budgeting guidelines published for the 2008 process for the 2009 fiscal year are much more detailed than those for 2003.[11]

I will outline these most recent steps here in general terms to give an idea of what the process has been working towards, focusing on the municipal level (the process is also carried out at the regional level).

The process involves eight steps. 'Preparation,' the first step, requires the local government to have an integrated development plan (*plan de desarrollo concertado*), a list of problems in the district that require attention, details of proposals from the previous year, a report of past projects undertaken through participatory budgeting or other mechanisms, and to have set the amount to be spent.

Second, they must announce that the process will take place and invite participants. Third, the participatory agents are to be identified and registered. These agents include the mayor, councillors and representatives of a wide range of civil society groups. The 2008 instructions mention universities, public development agencies, youth groups, business groups, professional colleges, socially based organizations, communities, associations of people with disabilities, and other associations of groups at risk because of poverty, ethnicity, violence, or gender (Chapter 2 of R.D. No. 021-2008-EF/76,01). The organizations represented by the agents must have been in existence for three years and be legally registered. This requirement involves a degree of bureaucratic formalization at odds with the apparent wish for a broadly representative group including the more vulnerable sectors of society. The long list of groups implies a greater interest in involvement than is the case, at least in Allpachico, as we will see.

Once the agents have been identified and registered, the fourth phase, training, takes place.

The fifth phase, the workshops, constitutes the centrepiece of this democratic decentralization experiment. Here the participants review the integrated development plan and the diagnosis of the district. They establish priorities in social, economic, environmental, and institutional areas and audit the accounts of the previous year. They are informed of the amount of money in the participatory budget for the current year. I will explore the different ways in which the accounts are understood in some detail below. In this phase the participants also establish criteria by which to prioritize the problems to be addressed. A suggested point allocation system for different characteristics is included in the instructions for each year, and has become more complex as the years pass. As we will see, the 'suggested' character of the table is overlooked in practice. Proposed projects are prioritized through this point system. Because I refer to this in some detail below,

I quote the guidelines for the 2004 process at some length here. The guidelines for the 2008 process are a more complicated version of the same general principles, including:

> 2. The criteria for prioritization should, in general, bring together the principal goals of the society for development. In Annex 4 there is a *suggested* [emphasis added] matrix of prioritization criteria. These criteria include levels of poverty by income and by Unsatisfied Basic Needs of the beneficiary population; the effect on local employment; vulnerable groups such as children, gestating and lactating mothers, the elderly and people with disabilities, among other groups.
> 3. The workshop establishes points according to the criteria mentioned above, and applies these to establish a priority of action. *Both the criteria and the point system should be validated and reconsidered in this Workshop.* [emphasis added].[12] (re Talleres de trabajo de definición de criterios de priorización in R.D. No. 010-2004-EF/76.01; my translation)

The prioritized projects then undergo a technical evaluation in the sixth phase. Here each project is accorded a profile with its costs, technical feasibility, a description of the problem it is addressing, and a justification of this solution. The preparation and cost of these profiles was a significant problem for small rural districts.[13]

In the seventh phase the participatory agents approve the integrated development plan and the list of prioritized projects. The eighth phase, the submission of accounts that is embedded in the workshops the following year, finishes the cycle.

In Allpachico this system is dramatically different in two fundamental ways from what happened earlier: it is more open and participatory, and it assigns significant resources to public projects. Don Jorge's enthusiasm is easily understood – now the community can get more than a park bench, a few bags of cement, or water pipes that lead nowhere.

Democratization, State Control, or Citizen Empowerment? The Case of Allpachico

Democratization implies a situation in which a responsible government interacts with an engaged and interested citizenry. The objectives of the Peruvian participatory budgeting law, however, outline the responsibilities of citizens and dictate the limits of their role. We have seen above how analyses of participatory budgeting report success when it is not formalized and citizens retain an informal but determined role in decision-making. In contrast, the Peruvian process arose out of the interests of state-level political actors. Can democratization in the form of citizen empowerment be legislated? The case of Allpachico shows a very unequal balance between the role of political leaders and law, on one hand, and of citizens' ability to make decisions about how best their needs might be addressed, on the other. Participants in the process have to work through a confused mixture involving the rigidities of formal dictates and the promise of flexibility through their input. By wading through the rules and what are perceived as rules, along with local understandings of the process, we can see how public input into resource spending gets subverted by actual or apparent top-down regulation.

We have become acquainted with Allpachico over the earlier chapters: its status as a comunidad, coexisting with a broader community of people who identify with the place; its limited resources, reliance on labour migration and the diversified economy of the residents; and the declining population over time. We have not so far paid much attention to the municipality of Piedra Blanca, to which Allpachico has belonged since the late nineteenth century. The district is small with a population of about 1,500. The political centre is in the town of Piedra Blanca. In addition to Allpachico there are two other comunidades campesinas in the municipality. One is small and poor like Allpachico, but the other has significant communal enterprises including a dairy farm, a soft drink factory, and a mine. This comunidad is also located in the town of Piedra Blanca, and I will refer to it as Piedra Blanca CC. It is Piedra Blanca CC's businesses that raise the municipal average income to above the threshold of 'extreme poverty' that would have made the people eligible for various programs for the poor. Thus, as I have mentioned earlier, because of Piedra Blanca CC's resources – to which only its members have access – the other two poorer communities are excluded from these programs. Piedra Blanca CC has a further advantage in its location which, along with its resources, gives it increased exposure in the municipality.

Each community, however, does have a right to a share of the municipal funds and input into how these were spent. I was quite interested in finding out how the community had chosen the projects it did. All were infrastructural – a sewage system, a school – rather than productive projects, such as investment in farming or other collective endeavours which could provide steady income to Allpachiqueños for the long term.[14] These projects were at odds with earlier priorities of Allpachiqueños. As I mentioned in Chapter 7, I had asked community members in 1998 and 1999 what they thought were the most important issues that might be addressed through a development project. Income production was the clear preference: 70 per cent said work and income were the greatest problems in 1998. Younger men and women wanted non-agricultural employment in small local production, and older farmers wanted improvements to agriculture. In addition to these, there was a significant contingent, led by retired workers who had returned from work centres to live in Allpachico, who expressed a wish for infrastructural services such as potable water and a sewer system.

When I asked why people had chosen infrastructure over production in the participatory budgeting consultations, I got two kinds of answers. First, there was a common response that government regulations directed how funds were spent by allocating fewer points in the participatory budgeting evaluation process for productive projects. This response relates to some of the rigidities of fund allocation that I will address here as 'accounting.' I address the impacts of these on the community under 'politics.' Also under 'politics' I discuss the second response: that choosing a project such as a carpentry workshop to make furniture for local sale would create conflict.

We now turn to a discussion of the financial dimension of participatory budgeting.

Accountability and Accounting

An ethnography of the different structures, practices, and understandings of accounting goes a long way to unravelling the hesitations about the process which accompany the enthusiasm for the resources. For years I have heard various complaints about accounts in Allpachico. Suspicions (there is rarely proof) about the disappearance of public funds inform how people approach the participatory budgeting system. For example, Allpachiqueños have been very aware of being at the mercy of the rules and practices of outside organizations concerning finances. Thus, throughout the 1990s, Allpachico was not eligible for various state programs because it had not complied with public reporting and registration requirements. In addition, the unwillingness of NGOs to open their books to beneficiary communities has been sharply resented.[15]

Suspicion is directed not only at politicians, bureaucrats, and NGO workers, but also internally. Concern about the proceeds from the sale of the Multi-Need trucks provides one example, but there is also a litany of treasurers of committees who vanished with the funds or turned over little or no money to their successors. This is a widespread complaint in Peru and explains the heavy emphasis on accountability in government procedures. Accounting itself, who gets to decide what information is counted and divulged, how resources are valued and attributed, has long been a terrain of contestation. We begin with a look at some of the structures of access to money, and then turn to examine how people understood the costs and transfers of money in participatory budgeting.

State Control: Structural Accounting

How much money is in the participatory budgeting purse, what other funds might be accessed, and what money is available for projects apart from the participatory budgeting fund are part of the structure of accounting that can undermine public confidence in the system. In addition, the municipal council has a great deal of discretion over some of these funds, while others are strictly tied to specific ends, both of which extremes are at cross-purposes with the promise of public decision-making that is implied in participatory budgeting. Much of what goes on here reflects state domination of the participatory budgeting system, although other actors such as the international donor community and the local government also exercise some control.

Municipalities get core resources from a state fund called Foncomun. The amount is based on the number of voters but has a minimum of eight basic tax units (UITs) per month[16] – 28,000 soles in 2008. Municipalities also get revenue from taxes on primary resource exploration in the region, if such exists, as well as from service fees and local taxes. These resources must also cover basic administrative costs, building expenses, salaries, and so on. How much goes to these administrative expenses and how much goes into the participatory budgeting purse is left to the mayor and councillors. This is one feature of the system that demonstrates the control retained by elected officials that prevents them from merely carrying out public spending instructions year by year. It also leaves a degree of uncertainty about where the money kept out of participatory budgeting is actually going.

The Foncomun and municipal revenue funds are those over which the participants in the budgeting process have the most control. Nevertheless, it was surprising that NGO workers, municipal officials, and participatory agents frequently referred to how the criteria given by the government dictated what they could do.[17] I have indicated above that the guidelines clearly state that the criteria are suggested and that they should be validated and reconsidered by the workshops. Why was there this contradiction?

Some of the answer seems to lie in the need to supplement Foncomun funds – after administrative expenses, there may be little left of the monthly disbursement. Thus, the mayor and councillors also seek funds from other state, NGO, or international help for projects. A glance at the list of projects to be undertaken in 2007 in Piedra Blanca, as listed in the integrated development plan for 2007–15, shows partnerships with other state programs: Foncodes (support from Foncodes became a part of regular disbursements to districts in 2008; it is for social and productive infrastructure), the Ministry of Women and Development (MIMDES), the Ministry of Housing Construction and Sanitation, A Trabajar (a state-run workfare program that pays unskilled workers), and the Council of Ministers. In addition to state sources, Caritas (an international NGO), the Italian bilateral fund (Fondo Italo-Peruano), and other agencies are mentioned. The problem with this, as Osvaldo, one of the councillors, pointed out, is that these organizations provide funding for specific things. In 2008 environment and health were high on the agenda of the international donors, so Osvaldo said they would ask for projects in these areas – before the participatory budgeting process meant to elicit local ideas even began. The councillor representing Allpachico, Yolanda, spent much of her time tracking downs hints of things that might be available from different sources – wheelchairs (in a region with few paved streets or sidewalks), tree seedlings, or medical supplies. She gets frustrated that people do not take advantage of the things she comes up with. Certainly some of the projects and items that arise address needs and desires of the populace. However, the tail of funding too often wags the participatory budgeting dog, making the promise of public input that much more illusory.

Other sources of funds add to the confusion. The municipality might get one-time payments from ceding rights or selling something. For example, a telephone company made a payment to the municipality for the right to lay cable through the district to connect the Mantaro Valley to Lima. The cable went through Allpachico, and a certain amount of money was paid to the municipality of Piedra Blanca to compensate. No one seemed to know what it was spent on. Alfonso, a former president of Allpachico, thought 86,000 soles had gone to rebuild a reservoir in Piedra Blanca and said that the mayor of the time had explained this. The mayor elected in 2007 said it was not clear what his predecessor had spent it all on: some 44,000 soles was spent on improving the gravel road between Piedra Blanca and Allpachico and the rest of an original 80,000 soles went somewhere else, although he could not remember. A second disbursement of 47,000 soles, he said, disappeared during the election campaign.

Access to these other funds allows the mayor and councillors to accede to some of the numerous requests they get for school supplies, materials to construct a kindergarten toilet, a prize for a soccer tournament, and so on. Yolanda says she used to wonder what the district council did with its budget but now she says she see there is never enough and even uses her monthly salary to pay for small items.

These constant requests allow elected officials to demonstrate responsiveness to the electorate, but they also detract from the message of participatory budgeting. They can appear to be a return to the days when projects were seen as gifts of the mayor. This is the case of Trebol's water tanks.

Trebol is a hamlet in decline: once seven homes, now there are only three families living there, half an hour's walk uphill from Allpachico village. The electricity, water, and sewage projects that Allpachico village has enjoyed over the past two decades did not reach Trebol, although these households were still obligated to contribute their labour to these projects. When I talked to people of Trebol or Kutru, a further hour's walk away, they usually found it hard to come up with suggestions for what they needed.[18] How was it that they got the water tanks, then? The answer I got was that, during the electoral campaign in 2006, the soon-to-be-mayor offered the people of Trebol tanks near their homes to capture water so they would not have to carry it from a spring from which livestock also drank.

I walked up to Trebol in 2008 to see the tanks, put in since my visit the year before. A short distance from two of the occupied houses is a cement tank with a pump and a drain. Fabiola was washing her laundry there, evidently enjoying the relative ease of the task. She did not know how it came about, she said, but it was great to have.[19] She proudly told me her son had worked as a mason on the project. Felicidad, a young woman from the third home, which had its own tank, was also pleased and looked forward to more things from this mayor. He clearly made good on his promises. She did not see the point of participating as a representative in the participatory budgeting process, though, since there were so few people in Trebol that their projects would be drowned out by the majority – 'somos tres gatitos, no más' – we're only three little kittens up here. For these residents, the old fashioned system of asking authority figures for help seemed to work better than collective prioritizing. The possibility of getting funds and materials other than through the participatory budgeting kept the practice of requesting gifts alive, and as a consequence, an air of clientelism lingers.

This situation arises, in part, because of the lack of alternative sources of funding. The municipality has come to be the major provider of resources for Allpachico, displacing the NGOs that filled this role in an earlier era. This is not the case for all communities. Comparative work on four other communities, undertaken by four Peruvian students for me, included one case in which the comunidad managed more money than the municipality, because of collective farming.[20] In these cases, the comunidad is better able to control the process to support its own goals, as we will see below.

Cultural Accounting

Apart from these structural features of the budget, relating to sources and uses of specific moneys, people also discussed the values attributed to different items. Transparency requirements meant that people saw some of the details of project expenses. Through their reactions, we can see how poorly the budgeting relates to local realities.

Many people were frankly horrified by the high cost, especially of technical labour. While some men in Allpachico have had what passes for high-waged work in the mining sector,[21] in general incomes are extremely low. The most common stable waged work comes from young men employed to quarry rock at various mines in the region; they get between 800 and 1,500 soles a month. Don Luciano said the average pensioner gets 350 to 400 soles a month. The wage for agricultural workers ranges between 10 and 12 soles a day; domestic servants might get 300 soles a month; and when Judith got 17 soles a day on a municipal work project, she counted that generous.

People are also precisely aware of prices for materials such as cement. They often have home repairs to do, or are asked to 'collaborate' in materials for community projects, and keep a close eye on price fluctuations for cement, lumber, wire, and so on.

This awareness of their own earning power and of prices makes them very suspicious of budget items and amounts made public in the participatory budgeting process. Why did the project to build a new school run out of money before it was finished? Could it be because of the high cost of the feasibility study (*estudio de efectividad*) – 20,000 soles of the total budget of 80,000? Or because three different technicians were involved? How could the small water tanks in Trebol have cost as much as 3,000 soles? Someone must be profiting. Thus, despite the measures in support of accountability, people still complain of a lack of transparency.

The 'someone' is taken to be politicians and contractors, combining to fleece public coffers. Unsubstantiated rumours circulated about irregularities in the 2007 municipal election – lights going out at a crucial point in counting the ballots and when they came back on, the tally was in favour of a different candidate, or charges that candidates were paying for votes. Pascal, who might occasionally earn 10 or 15 soles a day as an agricultural worker, was outraged at the 3,000 soles a month earned by the mayor[22] and 800 soles by the councillors. This in itself was taken as proof of corruption.

The amount of money being injected into the community was believed to make people opportunistically greedy, leading to inflation in land prices. As he reviewed the possible locations for a new medical post in 2008, Ricardo noted that some owners were offering abandoned buildings for as much as 24,000 soles. To put this in context, in 2004 Carolina found the asking price of 4,000 soles to buy the house she was renting to be too much.

Another part of the accounting practice concerns the value of contributed labour, an issue discussed in Chapter 7. Several people noted that projects in Allpachico, unlike other communities in the district, were less expensive because the people contributed the unskilled labour. This was felt to lead to a greater likelihood that their project would be selected in the process because it could fit in the budget and showed community support, but there were two areas of tension. First, there was resentment that people get paid for their unskilled work elsewhere. Projects since the Fujimori era in the 1990s have been welcomed for the income or handouts they offered rather than for what they embodied. As we will see below, many understand 'productive' projects to be those which give them a wage, however temporary.

The second point of tension was that the value of this unskilled labour was included as part of the value of the project. In one project valued at 80,000 soles, 17,000 was attributed to unpaid labour. As Ricardo asked, where did this amount go? How can it be given a monetary value if it was never materialized as money? Again, someone, or some other community, must be benefitting. In Chapter 7 we saw that people do calculate the value of their unpaid labour contributions and trace it as a loss, a subsidy, or a transfer of value to someone else. Although the intention may have been to acknowledge the community contribution, its appearance in accounting tables makes the people suspect that the value was more than symbolic and that someone had pocketed their wages.

A similar confusion crops up over ownership of the public buildings and infrastructure that have been paid so much attention in development recently. We saw in Chapter 7 that Allpachiqueños were outraged when the local electrical grid they had worked so hard for was transferred to the regional state-run company, signifying to them that their resources were given for free to a business that now charged them for using what they themselves had constructed. Similar concerns over the alienation of the product of their labour came to the fore with the school project, as rights of ownership over materials were debated when they tore down the old school and built a new one. The old school was close to eighty years old, and had been built and maintained with comunidad labour and resources. As part of the political establishment of the comunidad campesina, and to get state supported education, it was transferred to the state in the 1930s, although in practical terms responsibility for its upkeep was taken by the comunidad. The materials left over after demolition, such as beams, or windows, became involved in a tug-of-war between the school director and the comunidad. The director insisted they were state-owned and that she would be denounced if they went missing. She wanted to sell them to have money for APAFA, the school parents' association.

The comunidad's position was that while the school might legally belong to the state, the people had built the school. Furthermore, they were investing resources in the use of the tractor, purchases of gas and oil and payments for customary coca, cigarettes, and drinks along with their donated labour during the faenas to clean up the mess. Their contribution was thus being appropriated by the state, leaving them with no claim to the building and materials. They even found it difficult to arrange to buy the materials.

The accounting procedures described here were confusing and contradictory in the eyes of Allpachiqueños. How could their labour be acknowledged as valuable – almost a quarter of the entire value of the project – at one time, and at another give them no rights to used materials they themselves had contributed in the first place? How could skilled labour and materials cost so much more than their own experience informed them was reasonable? Far from reassuring citizens about government accountability to them, accounting transparency fed suspicions about costs and values, further entrenching distrust of politicians and state processes.

Politics: Why Bother Participating?

So far we have examined how confusion and suspicion are raised by the rules surrounding different sources of funding, and by different calculations of value. Now we turn our attention from the economic considerations to the political ones. As I have discussed above, participants in the process believe that government regulations direct what the funds can be used for. Here we examine the impact of this in the community, manifested primarily in a widespread lack of interest. While the regulations were imposed by state-level political actors pursuing their own goals, local political objectives also affect the process. Local politicians and community members alike try to avoid conflict by choosing the most unobjectionable projects, rather than risky ones with more potential to address local poverty if they are successful, but that accomplish nothing if they are not.

The lack of enthusiasm presents a conundrum, given that participatory budgeting offers much more funding for Allpachico than the community has ever had. Why was there so little interest in naming representatives from the comunidad or other community groups? It was striking in 2008 that the people were far more engaged in a crisis over the satellite dish (a gift from an earlier mayor) that provided one channel at a time to villagers with televisions than with the participatory budgeting process. The operator had resigned because of difficulties collecting the 2 soles (about 67 cents) a month fee and complaints about the channels selected. If no one would turn on the system, change the channels, and collect fees, the company would cut them off and they would lose television access. This issue raised hackles, got people to meetings, and was bitterly disputed.

In contrast, the participatory budgeting process was treated with apathy. No community organization other than the comunidad campesina planned to send a representative. When the comunidad campesina's former representative, Don Gustavo, refused to serve another term, no one wished to take his place. Finally, Don Jorge agreed.

Allpachico was not the only constituency in district to exhibit low interest. Two meetings to train the participating agents at the municipal office were cancelled for lack of attendance.

The community did not ignore the process altogether: there was informal discussion about various projects. This discussion demonstrates how external control of decision-making led to a lack of community interest. A couple of people had proposed a project to make small plazas in front of their houses, but it had been turned down. Pancho, then president of the comunidad, told me that even his proposal to fix up the main plaza had been rejected as not fitting current government priorities. The legal assessor for Piedra Blanca confirmed that they were discouraging building communal centres and sports fields. These were not felt to make optimum use of funds.

Others were concerned about the proposal to build a new medical post. The current post is lodged in the community centre. It is too small, and dust from the meeting room upstairs falls on things. Although a new post had been approved for 2008, construction could not go ahead because a location had not been set aside. This project had been on the minds of Allpachiqueños for years, and they had usually agreed that it should be on a property outside the village. Villagers told me, though, that this location could not get official approval as security would be impossible to organize. The new post would have drugs and equipment that could get stolen.[23] Other locations in town were bandied about but the choice was stalled over the inflated prices demanded by some landowners, as mentioned above, and the difficulty of choosing from whom to purchase.

These two cases show how the imposition from above over which choices were allowable and which were not dampens people's enthusiasm for participating in the process. Further, projects are supposed to fit into the district plan, which covers the period 2007–15. There had been some consultation over this plan (although there seems to have been more extensive consultation over the earlier 2003–6 plan). If the projects and goals were already listed there, what was the point in further participation, especially since there seemed to be so many restrictions on proposals?

The sense that the decisions are preordained limits not only enthusiasm but also conflict over different possibilities. Thus, it may be not only the power of government suggestion, but also local political processes which lead to a preference for infrastructural projects.[24] In 1998–99, most people suggested income-earning as a major need; four years later, in 2003, the first municipal-sponsored workshop to elicit local needs turned this on its head, putting infrastructural items as top priorities.[25] A sewage system, reconstruction of the suspension bridge, and a multi-use sports field were placed above above the number four spot called 'productivity,' specified as reforestation and nutrition. The only other item that addressed the local economy involved workshops to produce goods for a local market, listed in eighth place (Municipalidad Distrital de Piedra Blanca 2003: n.p.). The difference was not because of who was asked; there was a significant overlap in those who attended this session and those who had given me a different list a few years earlier.

One reason for choosing infrastructure over production may have to do with selecting common rather than acute needs. Where there is a great diversity in sources of income, infrastructural services may be the only overlapping concern. In Allpachico, as we have seen in Chapter 4, there is a shrinking number of aging villagers who farm or have livestock; a significant group, partly overlapping this, who have pensions; and a third category of younger households in which the man has a volatile wage from work in rock quarries in the area. The common denominator where everyone's interests overlap, even though it may be a low priority for those who may be thinking of leaving Allpachico, ends up being buildings and service grids.

In contrast, in communities where there is a longstanding and widespread dedication to a collective endeavour, there are different outcomes. For example, Piedra Blanca CC's communal enterprises provide employment for some comuneros as well as giving some economic stability to the comunidad (although all of these businesses have suffered ups and downs). In 2008, Piedra Blanca CC intended to ask for electricity to be extended to the dairy farm so they could make a greater range of products to sell. The integrated development plan for the whole municipality of Piedra Blanca for 2007–15 (Municipalidad Distrital de Piedra Blanca 2007: 139–150) lists various projected goals over the short, medium, and long terms to address land based infrastructure (*acondicionamiento territorial*), social development, productive economic development, and local development, management, and administration. Under productive development, the majority of the items are for Piedra Blanca town or the annexes of Piedra Blanca CC: seven of seventeen are for Piedra Blanca town alone, while a further three are for the town's annexes. Six items deal with promotion of activities at a district-wide level: artisanal and small industry, small animal husbandry, dairy husbandry (only relevant now to Piedra Blanca CC), agriculture, farming committees, and grain mills.

Two of these, the artisanal or small industry workshops and the grain mill, are specific ways in which the people of Allpachico might earn an income. Neither of these is explicitly on the list of 2007 and 2008 projects included in the plan, although close to 58,000 soles of a list of priority projects for 180,000 soles of Foncodes money is for 'Productive projects in the district and annexes' (Municipalidad Distrital de Piedra Blanca 2007: 135–6, my translation). This is the top priority, but is not broken down into specific projects. No projects of this sort were planned for 2008 for Allpachico, although there are two obvious small industries that could have been started: the woodworking and clothing workshops originally planned in the Multi-Need project (described in Chapter 5) could have been reactivated with relatively little cost. In both cases, however, there would be difficult decisions about who would be invited to participate. These would be selective projects that would use communal resources to help a few, offering nothing to the rest.

My survey of four other peasant communities provides further support for the notion that where there is a collective enterprise or a common economic activity, people prioritize productive projects in support of this in the participatory budgeting process. Alternatively, where there is greater diversity of sources of income, there is a concomitant greater investment in roads, buildings, and so on. These latter communities do not seem to initiate productive enterprises with participatory budgeting funds.

I have suggested that infrastructure is a *common* denominator: the choices made reflect an interest in finding projects that address the whole population as opposed to serving the needs of only a few. The issue of envy – who would get to benefit from the project – was a constant theme in Allpachico projects. Complaints about favouritism in the selection process have been rampant since the projects of the 1990s, when project participants would get food handouts. Whenever projects have privileged various needy groups as beneficiaries, such as parents of young children, or single mothers, or households without wage income, those who have been left out have responded with the lament that 'we are all poor, we are all in need.'[26] The question of who would be able to work in a productive enterprise seems to be far too divisive to get started. Villagers who have requested to rent productive equipment belonging to the comunidad, such as a welding machine or sewing machines, have been turned down, because authorities have preferred to let the machinery decay rather than facing charges of favouritism.[27]

Requests by individuals to rent community equipment reflect a growing reluctance to engage in collective production. Although there is little creative enthusiasm to initiate a comunidad enterprise, a great deal of energy and creativity has gone into personal initiatives – stone-cutting, bread making, guinea-pig raising, tailoring, trout farming, and so on. A lack of capital prevents most of these from getting started, while an inability to generate sufficient profit has sunk others. Despite these failures, people clearly prefer investing in their own businesses to depending on the comunidad to generate jobs.

Whether collective or individual, production projects face a real danger of failure. Among the threats listed in the SWOT (i.e., strengths, weaknesses, opportunities, and threats) analysis carried out for the district development plan for 2007–15 were: a great degree of competition in agricultural product markets; instability of prices of agricultural goods; low prices for non-metallic minerals (Piedra Blanca CC has a non-metallic mineral mine); and uncontrollable diseases (presumably in crops and livestock) (Municipalidad Distrital de Piedra Blanca 2007: 126). The broader survey of four communities indicated that low prices for agricultural products were a common complaint in two of them. The huge scale of these problems puts success in doubt, making productive projects less attractive to politicians.

They are also less attractive to people. When I asked about productive projects that would provide people with an income, the most common assumption among the people was that I was referring to workfare. That is, they hoped for components that would pay participants for unskilled labour, rather than a collective enterprise that would generate income. Infrastructure projects that required people to dig holes, carry materials, or clean areas were highly attractive to them when part of the budget could be used to pay them. What the project built was a minor concern. As discussed above in the section on accounting, Allpachiqueños contributed free unskilled labour to their participatory budgeting projects. While this may have helped guarantee they got the project, it also rubbed against one of the goals many had for participatory budgeting.

Projects producing physical results are politically safe (but maybe not actually safe, given the number of schools built by Fujimori which have fallen down because of poor construction). Other kinds of initiatives, such as training, can backfire. Few women were interested in attending a workshop for making a sweet pastry (*churros*) held by the municipality in 2008. It would have meant giving up a Friday afternoon to go all the way to the town of Piedra Blanca to learn to make something of little use.

Infrastructural projects that provide a service that all could potentially enjoy avoid these problems. They have an additional attraction in being the kinds of things comunidad leaders have long tried to provide to mark their period of office. When talking to any of the men who have served on the comunidad executive, I would hear of which communal building or service was due to them. Don Máximo claimed credit for the current community meeting hall (built with the Multi-Need project); Don Leonardo took credit for the truncated water project in the 1970s; both Máximo and Federico claim the foreign Multi-Need project discussed in Chapter 5; and old Don Adán said that when he was on the executive in 1935, they brought the bell for the church from Oroya. The list could go on, and several people claim credit for each large project.

Local politicians, and those with larger constituencies alike, benefit from having a concrete marker of their contribution. Plaques, or writing in the cement, frequently indicate the mayor (or more recently the governing period to draw attention away from the mayor alone and to the council in general) who presided over its inauguration. The project can be completed – or at least started – before the end of one's term of office.

Conclusion

Participatory budgeting seems to offer the perfect compromise between a responsible state and an engaged citizenry, but Allpachico's experience demonstrates how the complex of political strategies, culturally based perceptions, and structural factors limit its potential. Transparency has fuelled suspicion, the requirements imposed by diverse funding sources subvert public decision-making, and the choices may be of minimal value.

Participatory budgeting promotes integration into capitalism, but in extremely uneven and contradictory ways. As with the water project, participatory budgeting assumes capitalist rationalization to make scarce resources meet priorities. The accounting system privileged technical over vernacular skills, and tried to calculate all inputs, including unpaid labour, in monetary terms. These elements carried their own contradictions, which were exacerbated by the politicians who pursued their own personal and political strategies that were often at odds with the goals of the policy.

Allpachiqueños in turn had their own perspectives and objectives. These demonstrate that there is a sense of community, one that pressures them to favour projects that are widely beneficial rather than supporting a favoured few. This sense of community, though, is not the warmly cooperative image held by development planners. Rather, like Gavin Smith's (1989) analysis of Huasicancha, community is a habit of interaction, integrally mixed with the uses the members make of it. Thus, the practice of community in Allpachico arises from the diverse economic positions of the members and tends towards goals that are common to all. The uses made of the community are not necessarily opposed to capitalism in general. People have accepted the commodification of their labour – as long as it is compensated – along with the purchase and sale of market commodities. What they balk at in participatory budgeting is the privatization to only a few members of the government of resources they see as a public good.

9 Conclusion: Immanent Development in Capitalism

This examination of development projects in Allpachico has demonstrated mixed results. On the positive side of the ledger, Allpachico now has residential running water, a sewer system, electricity, and a new school, and some people have used participation in projects to get food or income to help them survive economic crisis or general poverty. But there have also been failures, unintended consequences and accompanying effects. In the introduction I sketched the theoretical architecture for this book, delineating an historically informed political economy analysis of development, involving actors who strategize with the tools and barriers offered by the immediate and larger structures. Some of the chapters have made little reference to this theoretical literature as they grappled with more specific debates about development trends. I now want to take up again the bigger issues to tie together the major themes of this book and to think about the effects of the projects.

History

There has been an obvious focus on history through the book, both through the long trajectory described in chapters 3 and 4, and in the recognition that people's experience of past projects informs their reactions to subsequent ones. This deference to historical formation follows the work of Gavin Smith (1989; Narotzky and Smith 2006), as well as of Nash (2001), Sider (1988), and Wolf (1982). These writers demonstrate the importance of analysing how people use their accumulated knowledge to negotiate changing circumstances as well as how these circumstances themselves are the product of historical struggle. Thus, both local experience and wider contexts are important to chart. In the case of the Andes, we can see this through a quick glance at the constitution and use of collective social forms. Starn (1994) charges that the focus of foreign researchers on communities is a sign of their 'andeanism,' which he sees as an imposed orientalist construction. In contrast, here I have insisted on the historically and contextually contingent character of community, comunidad, and other collective forms. Prehistorically, groups joined to share or exchange produce, especially across ecological zones, as we saw in Chapter 3. Gradually, those who planned production and redistribution eased their way out of manual labour. The Inca Empire both drew on and scaled up the effective organization of labour, to the point where the demands of accumulation for hierarchical reciprocity were probably not sustainable. Inca collective patterns and reciprocal rights changed under the Spanish: while indigenous leaders who retained control were still held to account by their followers, both leaders and commoners also looked for new opportunities offered by the new regime, whether for freedom, position, or wealth. Thus, collective rights and forms were transformed as they were avoided or exploited in the new regime at different moments and by different people. When Huanca curaca Felipe Guacrapáucar asked for more rights over his followers from the Spanish Crown in the late sixteenth century as redress for Huanca sacrifices in the fight against the Inca, he was using the argument of tradition to place himself to take advantage of the new possibilities. His followers, in turn, busily escaped from traditional obligations to avoid excessive tribute payments in wealth and labour.

Collective forms have continued to have purchase over the centuries, constantly changing along the way. As I have discussed in Chapter 4, when the comunidad campesina was established in the 1920 Constitution, President Leguía claimed to be acknowledging traditional forms. With its promise of state support and legal rights, the comunidad actually positioned peasants to participate more fully in the modern political economy. Different yet again were the collectivities of the women's groups described in Chapter 6, of the service users' groups in Chapter 7, and the local citizens' groups of Chapter 8. All of these forms imply a connection to traditional Andean social patterns, although I have endeavoured to show that each is quite distinct, both in the intended use and in the ways people actually put them into practice.

This critical analysis of long history helps to avoid Starn's (1994) criticism of essentialist andeanism. It is also important to acknowledge the shorter and more localized history of recipients of development projects rather than approaching them as if they were a blank slate. Prior experience inevitably affects how people view their future opportunities. Thus, each iteration of collective forms draws on its predecessors. It also provides a resource both for Allpachiqueños, and, as we have seen, for external agencies who wish to avoid market costs for labour power. Allpachiqueños have experienced a range of labour practices, including communal faenas, inter-household reciprocal exchanges, permanent and short-term waged work, and welfare type work for food or money. Each carries its own significance, costs, and benefits. Over time Allpachiqueños have come to perceive their labour power in ever more commodified ways. In chapters 6, 7, and 8 we have seen that as more elements of development projects were designed outside of the community, the rewards of participation came to be the fringe benefits such as food or money, rather than the product of the project itself. Thus, after the Fujimori era, when women were enticed to join projects (and, often, political parties) through handouts, the unpaid labour contributions required in the water project described in Chapter 7 and the various participatory budgeting projects in Chapter 8 came as a disappointment. This is in stark contrast to earlier periods when decision-making, planning, implementation, and fund raising were all in the hands of the comunidad. The result is that communal labour comes to be seen as something owed external agencies in return for immediate or future considerations for the participants, rather than an obligation to the local polity.

At the same time that they seek possible income wherever it may come from, Allpachiqueños are deeply concerned about depending on external agents and markets. The ambitious Multi-Need project described in Chapter 5 continues to play a big role in their perspectives on this. It is seen by many as an opportunity missed becaue of the national political and economic turmoil, or to the cupidity of grasping individuals. They hope for another project of the same size, and for the workshops originally set up twenty years ago to be finally put in place. Still, the failures of that project make people very hesitant to depend on collective commercial production. The pitfalls of potential theft and mechanical problems along with unstable and highly competitive markets are all too visible to them.

Political Economy of Development

The history I have presented has focused on political and economic arrangements, both those that contextualize development and those that
inform development practice. In the introduction, I pointed to Eric
Wolf's idea of 'structural power': 'Structural power shapes the social
field of action so as to render some kinds of behavior possible, while
making others less possible or impossible' (1990: 587). Thus, he goes
on to explain, 'what capitalist relations of production accomplish . . .
is to make possible the accumulation of capital based on the sale of
marketable labor power in a large number of settings around the
world.' This accumulation is central to capitalist structural power, although the settings can vary widely. Distinct social settings are transformed over time as they are gradually reoriented to capitalistm. As I
observed in Chapter 3, although there were many similarities in manifestation and methods of solution between the political and economic
crises of the late sixteenth and late twentieth centuries, there was a critical difference arising from the former's context of feudal conquest and
the latter's capitalist system. The sixteenth-century version of governance brought indigenous peoples into towns so they could be better
monitored and guided by Spanish authorities. In contrast, that of the
late twentieth century involved the decentralization of administration
of power to the people themselves, inviting them into the world of capitalist rationalization. Where the former required force, the latter sought
to reduce the cost of governing by giving the incentive of funds to encourage acquiescence to both the government political and the capitalist hegemonic projects.

That the overall structure in which the development projects described here took place is capitalist, I take as a given. Žižek comments
that capitalism is taken as an unquestionable fact in the world today
(cited in Smith 2006: 623). Further, capitalism is continually deepening
and spreading as new types of products (water, body parts, genetic
material) and the workers to produce them are accessed.[1] Allpachico
is integrated into this wider process as the people engage in livelihood
activities in the region and beyond. The projects that have taken place
in the community show a further way in which capitalism spreads.
These projects not only reflect various trends in development practice,
they also exhibit uneven and contradictory commodification. On one
hand, Allpachiqueños have been encouraged to produce goods for

sale on capitalist markets, to purchase commodities, to sell their labour power, and to learn the peculiar mindset of capitalist rationality. On the other, they have been encouraged *not* to value their labour in communal projects, and to engage in non-capitalist collectives. They have also been forced to undertake subsistence production or petty commodity production to deal with economic crisis in the capitalist sector.

As a result, in rural peasant communities in the Andes, learning the assumptions of capitalist processes takes place against the continued importance of subsistence agriculture and a variety of social relations related to this. The process of absorption into capitalism situates these people as marginal actors, often operating through informal exchanges. As Narotzky and Smith (2006; see also Smith 2006) argue, informal economies are not parallel to or outside of formal ones; rather, in their Spanish example, they may be deliberately invoked by governments to produce conditions attractive to political domination or capitalist investors.

Similarly, in Allpachico, processes of commodification have been accompanied by pressures that work both with and against a purely capitalist system. Let us review four areas that reflect these contradictory processes: the production and sale of commodities, the purchase of commodities, the sale of labour power itself as a commodity, and the promotion of capitalist accounting systems.

The Production and Sale of Commodities

I have commented that Allpachico is poor in resources, with little arable land, poor pasture, and little else that could be exploited. This has meant that there has been quite limited commodity production in the community. By the time of the Multi-Need project, Allpachiqueños had long been involved in labour and product markets. People had long sold goods they produced, such as food during fiestas, and the 1935 census lists a few weavers, shoe makers, and a bread maker. These would have been very occasional businesses, complementing other activities. In contrast, the never fully functioning Multi-Need workshops presented the possibility that Allpachiqueños could stay in the village and work steadily at a job there. This was innovative in its proposed scale and dedication to market production. Importantly, the project took place when Peru's economy was particularly unstable and during a period of political violence. The capitalist economy and state direction of it were in crisis. As formal employment declined and hyperinflation discouraged the use of money, Allpachiqueños stayed in or returned to the community where they could at least survive. Agriculture's role in the Peruvian economy had long been in decline as the result of government policy to import cheap food in support of industry (Hopkins 1998: 89). Given the poor prospects for market agriculture in these environmental and economic circumstances, the agricultural technicians focused on subsistence production that would allow people to eat. The subsistence agriculture the agronomists had in mind during the first phase was their view of traditional Andean techniques. However, both land-rich Allpachiqueños, who pressed successfully for a tractor and other mechanical aids, and the Peruvian NGO staff who took over in the second phase (which took root after President Fujimori's neo-liberal reforms stabilized the economy), had other ideas. In the second phase, industrial inputs firmly replaced the labour-intensive terracing and composting promoted by the foreigners. Both of these tendencies, the 'indigenous' and the technical inputs, reflect the complex infiltration of capitalism. In the first phase, avoiding industrial inputs to agriculture made sense to the NGO staff, given their cost and the low returns on agricultural produce, especially in a period of economic crisis. This retrenchment because of market conditions did not entail complete avoidance of markets, though, as the associated small industries show.

These small industries were short lived, if they got started at all. Similarly, inclusion of industrial agricultural inputs of the second phase did not imply production for markets. Mayer and Glave (1999) provide a detailed analysis of peasant accounting practices for potato production in two regions of Peru during the economic crisis of the mid-1980s. They show how peasants refer to costs, market conditions, and so on as they make their decisions about production and sales, but argue that the actual accounting is a hybrid that sidesteps the valorization of all inputs the way an economist would. Similarly, in Allpachico, subsistence production typically uses a combination of commercial inputs to increase yield and other methods to meet taste preferences.

The various gendered projects aimed at women from the 1960s on have also promoted commercial production on a smaller scale than Multi-Need's workshops, but were no more successful. As we have seen, in many cases the things the women were taught to produce, such as pasta-covered containers, were probably unsalable. Informal sector selling, especially by women and children, continues in Allpachico, in the region, and in Lima. This income can be essential to household survival. Informal sector work is not fully capitalist, however, depending on undervaluing labour and other non-monetized inputs in order to make a profit on the monetized ones.

The Purchase and Consumption of Commodities

Clearly, Allpachiqueños have not become capitalist producers and sellers of commodities. Capitalist patterns have advanced more in teaching women to be consumers of commodities, although, again this is not without conflicts. Remember Jacinta's fury, described in Chapter 6, when she and other women in the Vaso de Leche program were told to replace their home-grown potatoes and cheap oil and sugar with more expensive foods. The nutritionist who proposed this new diet was clearly working from the assumption that a whole variety of foods were available and accessible to consumers, and that health was simply a matter of consumer choice.[2] While not all development workers are so insensitive to the culture and resources of the people with whom they work, for at least the past twenty-five years that I have visited Allpachico, it is both normal and expected that projects dealing with nutrition will provide industrial goods available in capitalist markets. This introduces the people to commodified foods and presents them as desirable. At the same time, many development practitioners, such as Milagros, the Agua engineer, loudly proclaim the merits of traditional Andean crops such as potatoes and quinoa. These two trends are not in opposition to each other. Rather, the aestheticized valorization of the traditional is largely the urban middle class counterpart to the rural peasant regard for the industrial. Consumer choice makes both possible in a capitalist economic structure.[3]

Many of the infrastructure projects, too, require or promote capitalist consumption. Electricity serves no purpose without light fixtures and appliances, and the bill itself must be paid. Although there were no monthly bills for use, the water and sewage projects required plumbing fixtures inside houses. These are not insignificant costs for those at the lower end of the economic scale and require either the generation of money to pay for them or the willingness to do without their convenience. Both tendencies are evident in Allpachico. While those with pensions and high enough wages are pleased with their urban style comforts, others continue to go to bed when it gets dark instead of turning on a light, or refuse to pay their electricity or television bill. Still, the younger generations at least aspire to have the services and all they imply, so capitalist consumerism has a very firm toe hold.

Capitalist Rationality

The infrastructure projects of chapters 7 and 8 applied capitalist accounting procedures even while they relied on free inputs, such as labour. They assumed that people would make their decisions based on prioritizing their needs in order to allocate scarce resources. The Demand Responsive Approach described in Chapter 7 is an extreme version of the promotion of capitalist prioritizing in development projects, which is very much in contradiction with its expectation of the contribution of free labour. The water project carried out in Allpachico shared some of this contradiction: on one hand the engineer emphasized that the community owned the project, while on the other she retained the right to decide on the materials used, the technical specifications, and even the organization of labour. Both this and the participatory budgeting project privilege formal technical qualifications, valuing them significantly more than the experiential knowledge the Allpachiqueños had. In addition to these mixed messages, the conflicts over the evaluation of items in the accounts demonstrate the uneven ways capitalism has infiltrated here. While Allpachiqueños resist many of the assumptions of capitalist accounting, they have come to calculate their labour power in commodified ways. This is the element of capitalism that has been most completely adopted.

The Commodification of Labour Power

Allpachiqueños have sold their labour power for a wage for decades. In 1929 they purchased land from Huaripampa with their earnings. Through the mid-twentieth century, most men had at least short periods of work in the regional mining and transport industries, many of them staying for their full working careers. Those jobs vanished as a result of changes in the sector and to economic crisis in the 1980s. As the Peruvian economy stabilized after 1990, both men and women looked for jobs, reflecting the entrenchment of proletarianization. Gradually, too, the previously non-monetized work and services that had been carried out in Allpachico started to be valorized. We saw this infiltration of commodification in the calculations of participants in the water project in Chapter 7. Further, the gendered projects of chapters

5 and 6 show how women have been given sewing and managerial skills and work experience in the workfare projects. These initiatives correlate with the trend for women to choose employment rather than informal sector selling that had been their primary money-earning activity.

Proletarianization is linked to the poor prospects for market oriented agriculture and small industry in Allpachico. By default, it is the major conduit for the integration of Allpachiqueños into capitalism. But while they have come to depend on their wages, community development practices demand that they donate their labour to community projects for free. We have seen the contradictions and frustrations involved in this in chapters 7 and 8.

Class

The peculiar characteristics of Allpachico, poor in resources and rich in labour power, have thus tended to position its people as proletarians in the wider economy, rather than dividing them into internal class fractions. The majority of younger Allpachiqueños hope for jobs rather than to work in their fields. I have, however, observed throughout this book how differences among people, based on economic activity, gender, and life cycle[4] led to distinct perspectives on the projects. In the economic crisis of the 1980s, people were led to engage in increasing numbers of exchanges with ever more partners, both within and outside of Allpachico. Many of the exchange relationships were fragile, quickly broken when they became costly. As the economy has stabilized, there has been a downward trend in the number of relationships. With fewer households carrying out agriculture, there is less need to share labour or tools with others. The economic activities now providing income are varied, with the younger generations seeking jobs. The result is that there is less need for Allpachiqueños to depend on each other for survival. Thus, the conflicts that arise are less likely to concern one person taking advantage of another in production, and are more often about differential access to the external resources offered in development projects: *envidia* (envy) rather than exploitation.

I do not wish to minimize the conflicts within Allpachico, nor the role of economic differences in fostering them. The major class formation that is taking place, however, is not within the community, but between Allpachiqueños as workers and their employers.

Community, Comunidad, Collective

Links to the wider political economy are clear in the many current for-mulations of the local. Most of these collectivities are often called into being by external agents, such as the state or an NGO, but some of them are also heavily used by their members. The comunidad is clearly weakening in Allpachico with frequent internal conflicts and a lack of interest among comuneros. It is, however, surviving in the face of some significant challenges presented not only by government policy, which now allows for the privatization of land and disintegration of the co-munidad, but also in the tendency for external development agents to reorganize the local. We have seen this through the women's groups discussed in Chapter 6, the service users' group created by the Agua water project in Chapter 7, and the government participatory budget-ing provisions encouraging other civil society groups apart from the comunidad to participate in planning.

These collectivities are conduits as much as or more than they are ways of organizing locally: they are constituted to manage the institu-tional relationship between development subjects and external agents. As conduits to the larger structure, they are formed in conjunction with how their architects and the people in them see that structure as operating. Thus, the comunidad indígena was established in part to organize indigenous men as labour for state projects and thus facilitate their incorporation in the capitalist work force. At the same time, com-munities requested comunidad status as a way of accessing state and other resources to support their members' participation in capitalist markets.

The challenges to the comunidad, in the form of competing groups formed on the basis of gender or of service use, imply new forms of mediation with wider processes. The service users' groups in particu-lar promote a relationship unidimensionally linked to the consumption and organization of a specific service, very different from the multi-dimensional comunidad with its economic centre in agriculture, and more like a city neighbourhood with residents who go off to their dif-ferent jobs. Similarly, the government policy that regulates participa-tory budgeting encourages a wide range of civil society groups, many organized around single goals like the Vaso de Leche committee.

The fragmentation of identity and associations has made sense in the world of niche marketing, but as we have seen, so far it has been resisted in Allpachico. This resistance is a testament to the strength of the comunidad as a collective polity. However, it is also evidence that local economic conditions are not conducive to further fragmentation. If Allpachiqueños have demonstrated that they are very willing to participate in capitalist product and labour markets when these offer opportunities, they have also experienced hardship from inadequate wages, low prices for their products, and national economic crisis. Institutions such as the comunidad can be reinvigorated in new ways in time of need and the people are not prepared to lose this safety net.[5]

The Inevitability of Capitalist Development

The projects described here exude the assumptions and rationalizations of capitalism. This has long been a criticism of development, leading some, such as Escobar (1995) to seek alternatives to development. Cowen and Shenton (1996) argue that alternative development is simply another trustee-led capitalist project. As I outlined in the introduction, Cowen and Shenton draw a distinction between the pre-modern understanding of development as an automatic internally generated sequence and the modern usage of the term as something that can be deliberately put into action. They further argue that intentional development is the attempt by trustees (a term they take from Auguste Comte) in charge of the society and the economy to fix the problems engendered by capitalist processes. Unemployment, caused by overproduction or technical innovation, for example, might be dealt with through workfare, paying unemployed workers to construct public infrastructure. In this way, labour power is kept available for when it is needed again. Thus, in colonial Africa, Cowen and Shenton see a link between agrarian policy and the mitigation of capitalist crisis: 'Development doctrine for British Africa was a part of the 1945–51 Labour government's response to the 1947 sterling crisis and the final withdrawal from India. It was a late-imperial doctrine to maximise production in African colonies to meet British needs' (1998: 32). A few years later, circumstances having changed, the policy also changed: from production to serve the needs of British workers, the goal now was to expand agriculture in Africa to address unemployment there (Cowen and Shenton 1998: 33).

Similarly, many of the projects described in this book were intended to deal with problems in the capitalist economy. This is most obviously the case with the workfare type projects that Fujimori made so much use of in the 1990s. The current participatory budgeting projects can be seen to absorb excess labour, slowing migration to overpopulated Lima by improving conditions in rural areas, improving access through road construction to isolated areas, and improving the health and education of potential workers.

In their effects, development projects and policies also go beyond mitigation of crisis in the capitalist state through the role they play in spreading worker skills and capitalist rationality. These were not necessarily the explicit intentions of the project designers. Nevertheless, these designers were technically trained people who were products of the dominant ideas of the era, that is, capitalist ideologies. What they saw as possible, therefore, tended to assume participation in capitalist markets. In this way, intentional development *is* the immanent development of capitalism.

Not only are development practitioners and the projects they design the product of capitalism, but intentional development is immanent to capitalism in another way. Capitalism is essentially expansionist, as Sweezy (1997) reminds us, in search of markets for goods, cheap labour, raw materials, investment opportunities, and so on. As we have seen, the projects that have taken place in Allpachico have supported these goals in encouraging consumerism, framing the people as workers, orienting them to consider how resources in the community could be sold, and teaching them the rationality of capitalist business. Internationally, development is invoked as not only a moral imperative, but as necessary to support the capitalist economy. Thus, former Canadian Prime Minister Jean Chretien elided development and global business in a speech to the United Nations in support of the New Partnership for Economic Development in Africa: 'For the developed world as a whole, implementing NEPAD means making development assistance more effective and doing more to ensure that we are open to business with Africa. For business worldwide, this means re-evaluating commercial opportunities in Africa as the new economic conditions take hold that NEPAD seeks to create, to revisit the stereotype, all too deeply rooted, that investing money in Africa doesn't pay' (Chretien 2002).

States offer development assistance to other states in support of their own interests. When they provide support for development NGOs, such as by matching donations, states in effect encourage citizen donors and NGOs to subsidize state priorities. Žižek (2009) argues that well-intentioned development and other current trends towards social responsibility are markers of an emerging hegemonic form of capitalism that uses this as ideological window dressing to obscure ongoing exploitation.

But if intentional development is inevitable and part of immanent capitalist development that continually intensifies and expands, it is implemented by people with their own goals in a world in which there are other possibilities. Alongside the incentives and benefits, the people of Allpachico experience the contradictions and frustrations that arise from their experiences with development; therein lies the basis for the future.

Glossary

Asistencialismo: 'welfarism'; used to denigrate people's expectation of handouts from the state.

Ayllu: a group linked by kinship or the idiom of kinship.

Barrio: a neighbourhood or residential cluster.

Bosta: dried animal dung, used as stove fuel.

Cabildo: a community council.

Comedor popular: a 'soup kitchen' that offers low cost meals to people; the women who run it receive free meals and sometimes food supplements. They usually receive donations from NGOs or the state.

Comunera/comunero: a registered female/male member of a *comunidad indígena* or *comunidad campesina*.

Comunidad campesina: the designation given to the *comunidad indígena* after the 1969 Agrarian Reform.

Comunidad indígena: a legal territorially based political institution, requiring proof of existence 'since time immemorial' and communal work and property; established in the 1920 Constitution.

Criollo: referring to people of Spanish descent born in a Spanish colony.

Curaca: indigenous leader.

Encomienda/encomendero: the *encomienda* involved rights given to Spaniards after the Conquest to the labour of indigenous people; the holder of the *encomienda* was the *encomendero*. In principle, the *encomendero* was a trustee with the obligation to care for the indigenous people, in particular by providing religious instruction to them.

Faena: community work bees; *comuneros* who do not attend *faenas* are fined.

Forastero: outsiders who live in an area outside of their place of origin; in the colonial period they had fewer rights to land but also fewer obligations to pay tribute.

Hacienda: a large landholding.

Indigenismo/indigenista: *indigenismo* was a Peruvian political and cultural movement beginning in the late nineteenth century and extending to the mid-twentieth century; it involved the promotion of indigenous rights and culture, often in romantic ways; *indigenista* is the adjective.

Peón: an agricultural labourer.

Reducción: indigenous settlements established by the Spanish to facilitate Spanish control over the people; many were set up after Viceroy Toledo's reform of 1570.

Vaso de Leche: a program initiated by Lima mayor Alfonso Barrantes in 1984 and subsequently established throughout Peruvian municipalities to give food supplements to children under the age of seven.

Notes

1 Introduction: Development in History in Peru

1 All names of people and most of the places in and around Allpachico are pseudonyms.

2 I am alert to the sharp critiques of anthropological (mis)representations (e.g., see Starn 1994 with respect to debates about 'andeanism'). The claims I make about Allpachico's experiences are my interpretation of its unique character and history, some features of which it may share with other Andean communities. I am writing from the position of a Euro-Canadian woman, trained in Canada as an anthropologist, who has been acquainted with Allpachico since 1984.

3 Antonio Raimondi, a nineteenth-century Italian explorer and scientist is cited as reporting: 'El Perú es un mendigo sentado en un banco de oro' (R.L.S. Antonio Raimondi – no. 132 n.d.).

4 See Li (2007) for an excellent ethnography of development in one region over time.

2 Anthropology, Development, and Capitalism

1 See, e.g., Harvey (1989) on the coalescence of flexible accumulation in global capitalism over the past 30 years.

2 Narotzky and Smith (2006) present a particularly rich descriptive analysis of the historical development of a Spanish regional economy, noting both the role of policy and global capitalist expansion from outside the region, as well as the particular patterns of life that arose within it.

3 Wolf (1982: 158–94), e.g., documents how furs became a commodity, with tragic consequences, among North American indigenous peoples – perhaps

simultaneously providing a spur for the development of capitalist production relations in England as factories developed to provide cloth to trade to the Iroquois (1982: 4). In another example, water is currently in the process of being commodified throughout the world.

4 Services that can be purchased extend now even to human body parts (Scheper-Hughes 2000).

5 Some discussions of 'social capital' tend to objectify social relations (e.g., Woolcock and Narayan 2000; see discussion in Long 2001: 132–55). Also, women might use their degree of intimacy with a friend to determine how much they need to spend at her Tupperware party (Vincent 2003).

6 De Soto's (1987) paean to informal sector entrepreneurialism in Peru has been popular among proponents of neo-liberalism.

7 For comprehensive reviews of development theory and practice, see, e.g., Kitching (1982); Kothari (2005); Leys (1996); Long (1977); Nederveen Pieterse (1998).

8 Sachs implicitly acknowledges Rostow in a subsection titled 'On the Eve of Takeoff' (2005: 31), although it should be noted that he also invokes Polanyi in 'The Great Transformation' (2005: 35).

9 One of the most renowned authors of this type of approach is Robert Chambers (1983, 1992, 1994a, 1994b, 1994c, 1997, 2008), whose work since the 1980s has tried to 'put people first.' He has sparked an enormous interest in participatory practices – ways to involve the subjects of development in gathering information, developing solutions, contributing to or acknowledging projects, and so on. Olivier de Sardan (2005: 8–9) criticizes this as 'ideological populism.'

10 I am grateful to Susanne Matheson for her assistance in this task.

11 Among the *indígenistas* were major cultural, political, and intellectual figures such as Clorinda Matto de Turner, Dora Mayer, José Carlos Mariátegui, Victor Raúl Haya de la Torre, and José María Arguedas. The ideology spanned a period from the late nineteenth to the mid-twentieth century.

12 I was ably assisted in this by Manuel Gilvonio at the Universidad Nacional del Centro (UNCP) in Huancayo, and his students Patricia Tumialán Núñez, Rosa Flores Javier, and Janeth Castañeda Calderón, and I gratefully acknowledge their contribution.

13 Some people charged that elected officials were among those who founded NGOs in order to be able to take advantage of their knowledge of where money was available. A debate in the Peruvian Congress on a bill to improve the auditing and supervision of NGOs is fascinating for the perspectives and allegations aired (Congress of Peru 2003).

14 Hackenberg and Hackenberg (2004: 394) say, 'NGO is the least specific and most inclusive of the terms in the postmodern vocabulary with which we must work in the future.' Their illuminating summary highlights NGOs with multimillion dollar budgets from USAID among other funders, which, although they employ anthropologists in high-level positions, were unknown to the American Society for Applied Anthropology.

15 Bolton, Greaves, and Zapata (2010) for a recent collection with appraisals of the project. Babb (1985) and Stein (2003) have produced earlier informed analyses.

16 That is, of the English language debate. Vicos has also been discussed in Peru (Ávila Molero 2000; Degregori 2000).

17 The project is still used in introductory anthropology texts as an example of successful anthropological development practice (e.g., Harris 1995: 261, 263; Scupin 2006: 478).

18 More recent accounts continue to make this complaint (Phillips and Edwards 2000; Stirrat 2000).

19 It is interesting that Holmberg's initial publication of 'participant intervention' took place in the fledgling journal of the Society for Applied Anthropology, *Human Organization*, in 1955, and that Doughty's acceptance lecture of the Malinowski award was published in that journal 50 years later.

20 Doughty (2005) complained that it was unfair to use contemporary standards to judge a project from 50 years ago. Mitchell (2010) also notes the modernist outlook of the Vicos era and explains how his own ideas have changed since then.

21 Pribilsky (2010: 184) is more cautious, noting the dismay felt by Holmberg and Mangin at public discussions of Vicos as an emblem of U.S. capitalist expansion.

22 I discuss this movement further in Chapter 4.

23 While the earlier works defending the project emphasized its pioneering nature as an integrated rural development project, by the 1980s Doughty acknowledged counterparts in Mexico and India and placed the project as part of the contemporary 'broad attempt to improve the status of disadvantaged people' (1987b: 438), using methods also typical of the period. Nevertheless, he still presented the project as novel.

24 Mangin (1979: 75) says there had already been considerable criticism by 1961.

25 See also Köhler (1981), who comments on the difficulty of getting the peasants to agree to have their houses sprayed with DDT!

26 The book is actually more wide-ranging, as it builds on Stein's earlier work in the 1980s.

3 Somos libres? Political Structures of Development in History in the Peruvian Central Highlands

1 I take *hegemony* to be a process in which groups try to achieve or maintain political domination (Kurtz 1996). At certain historical moments, there may be a dominant group with little opposition, but this does not imply that all members of the society support this group. Rather, many may acquiesce, either through fear of reprisal or through lack of any viable alternative. When historical conditions change, these groups may coalesce around symbols and actors who seem to offer a more acceptable vision. Thus, both dominant factions and those hoping to displace them or to achieve autonomy from them, are constantly fashioning and refashioning messages and mechanisms of power. This implies that the messages and symbols themselves must transform to accommodate new realities and perceptions of possibilities. This understanding of hegemonic process acknowledges that social actors may respond to powerful incentives or messages of dominant groups, thus changing the political architecture. The more successful a dominant group's hegemonic process, the more other groups must build their own strategies on the dominant terms, including political structures, economic forms, language, religion, symbolism, etc. As an example, conquered indigenous leaders may be co-opted by colonial powers through a combination of force and incentive, although they may also represent themselves to their followers as upholding indigenous claims (see, e.g., Carstens 1991).
2 See Ekholm Friedman and Friedman (2008) for enlightening reexaminations of history.
3 Huayna Capac was the father of Huascar and Atahualpa, who were engaged in a civil war over the empire when the Spaniards arrived in 1532. He died around 1527 (Espinoza Soriano 1990: 98).
4 European colonizers around the world followed two distinct strategies: in one they left a semblance of the indigenous political structure, and in the other they replaced it with a European-style one. See, e.g., Mamdani (1996) for a discussion of direct and indirect rule in Africa.
5 Spalding (1974) provides a thoughtful analysis of how the role of the curaca changed through the colonial period, showing how they gradually turned to European methods to extract personal benefit to themselves, turning away from traditional methods which had been oriented to

collective management. See also Silverblatt (1995), who traces the discursive shift in the seventeenth century through which the Andean people came to use the Spanish identification of them as 'Indians' as their struggle for political place went from resistance to Spanish power to rights within the colony. Just as, under the Incas, the Huancas had become united as an ethnic group, so under the Spanish, the Andean people became united as 'Indians.'

6 That is, a *'nation'* in the imagined community sense of Benedict Anderson (1991).

7 Millennarian movements are a type of revitalization movement. They call for the intervention of supernatural forces to bring about the end of the world as it is, and the renewal of a proper traditional order. They are often related to situations in which a group of people has experienced a sudden decline in fortunes as a result of foreign conquest, as happened in the Ghost Dances in the American West in the late nineteenth century (Wallace 1956).

8 See Gonzales de Olarte (1995) and Alvarez Rodrich (1995) for discussions of ineffective economic policies between 1964 and 1994. The global economic situation and the way in which Peru related to it differed greatly, of course, between the 1560s and the 1980s and 1990s.

9 Not all priests were favourably disposed to the indigenous people. Rowe (1957: 183–90), e.g., discusses a range of ways in which the Catholic Church dealt with indigenous people from priests who kept concubines and exploited indigenous people, to an inquisition in the eighteenth century, along with more benevolent actions.

10 Sempat Assadourian (1994: 154) disagrees with Espinoza Soriano, arguing that only a few ethnic groups supported the Spanish and that the resistance was much greater.

11 Sendero Luminoso was ideologically Maoist, but some interpreters claimed that it incorporated pre-Hispanic indigenous revivalist ideas through a secondary emphasis on the work of José Carlos Mariátegui (Comisión de la Verdad y Reconciliación, Perú 2004: 98–100). For critical discussions of the extent to which Sendero Luminoso was actually indigenist, or was merely interpreted by analysts as being so as they emphasized the group's exotic 'otherness,' see Mayer (1991), Starn (1995), and Starn, Degregori, and Kirk (1995: 305–7).

12 The period of violence in Peru in the 1980s and 1990s can also be seen to have fed into the ambitions of President Fujimori and his assistant Vladimiro Montesinos, who were able to parlay their heavy-handed methods of dealing with presumed terrorists into political success. Even before

Fujimori came to power in 1990, the military had been sent into areas of
the country that had been relatively free from the daily presence of the
state. That is, the indigenous people of Ayacucho neither had much access
to national resources and influence, nor were they subject to much state
supervision. Of course, during the colonial era, this was less true, given the
importance of mining in Ayacucho.

13 He also meddles with morality and household architecture, mandating
that houses have a separate sleeping apartment for daughters so that they
are not exposed to their parents' sexual relations (Matienzo 1967: 53).

14 In a pat coincidence, Fujimori's capture of Abimael Guzmán in 1992 was
the beginning of the decline of Sendero Luminoso and of the consolidation
of the neo-liberal era in Peru.

15 Hemming (1983: 410) calls him a 'conscientious servant of the Crown and
a man who wished to protect the Indians' and 'honest and honourable but
cold and unfeeling' (392).

16 From the Conquest on in Peruvian history, technological innovations have
been described as deriving from the Spanish, or other nonindigenous
sources (e.g., Lohmann Villena 1970), or in the current trend of sustainable development, from the pre-Conquest past (e.g., Straughan 2003). Few
sources mention how indigenous knowledge or practices affected the development of technology in the past. One exception is Miller (1986), who
has reflected on how Peruvians (but perhaps not Peruvian indigenous
people) contributed to railway construction in the nineteenth century.

17 This is located just below the ruins of Huajlas, several hundred metres
above the river and long abandoned by this time.

18 The official designation was delayed until 1896 (Adams 1959: 31).

4 Community Development: Definition, Context, and History in Allpachico

1 Khan's work in Comilla and Orangi constitute convincing cases of community empowerment.

2 See Peters (1996), Harrison (2002), and Mohan and Stokke (2000), who see
continued problems in the conceptualization of the local in participatory
approaches.

3 Chambers (2008: 91) responds to criticism of PRA, singling out the Cooke
and Kothari (2001) collection, by charging that the concerns were often
outdated, focusing on early problems that had since been addressed, ill
informed, or based on the critics' own poor practice. For other critiques
of participatory practice, concerning political relations and context of

development, see Gill (2000), Long (2001), Pottier (1997), Vincent (2005a), and Webster and Engberg-Pedersen (2002).

4 The two sides were not always opposed. Many indigenistas promoted the incorporation of the indigenous people through education as the best way to ensure their own future (Davies 1974: 37).

5 The early part of the twentieth century saw the florescence of pro-indigenist sentiments, involving José Carlos Mariátegui, Dora Mayer, and Victor Raúl Haya de la Torre, among others. Mariátegui was an influential socialist writer who promoted the indigenous communities as a foundation for the development of a Peruvian socialist state. Mayer was an activist who commented on the treatment of the peasantry. Haya de la Torre was the founder of the APRA (American Popular Revolutionary Alliance) party in 1924 and its leader until his death in 1979.

6 Piel (1967: 381, my translation) summarizes the indigenista writers' attitude to Indians as a monolithic eternity: 'If we follow our writers from Ancash in 1885 to Huancane in 1923, it would be "eternally" the same scenario which would be reproduced. Even an observer as discerning and sympathetic as Luis E. Valcárcel tells us: "They were an unformed, ahistoric mass. They didn't live, they seemed eternal as the mountains, as the sky."' The indigenista novelists (e.g., Clorinda Matto de Turner, Ciro Alegría, and even much of anthropologist José María Arguedas's fiction) certainly seem to favour this romantic vision of the indigenous people, portraying them as the eternal dupes of wily landlords or corporations, dupes because of their allegiance to a higher ideal. Pribilsky (2010) observes that there were two strains of indigenismo: one more cultural, such as the above, and the other more socialist, following José Carlos Mariátegui.

7 Mossbrucker (1990: 96–7) is one of the few others who distinguishes between the people and the comunidad in Peru (see also Grondín 1978). See Halperin (1998) for a discussion of the concept of 'practicing communities,' based on her work in the United States.

8 Velasco was, in turn, removed from power by the more conservative General Morales Bermúdez in 1975. Democracy was restored in 1980 when Belaúnde returned to power in the elections that also marked the public beginning of the Maoist guerrilla organization, Sendero Luminoso (Shining Path).

9 As I noted in Chapter 2, Enrique Mayer (2010) argued that the Vicos project provided the template for the agrarian reform with its emphasis on collective production.

10 The number of comunidades recognized did not pick up until the late 1980s in the crisis-ridden regime of Alan García. Half of these, though,

were from Puno which had not seen many communities seek recognition until that time for historical reasons (Trivelli 1992: 27–30).

11 García headed the American Popular Revolutionary Alliance Party (APRA), founded in the 1920s by Victor Raúl Haya de la Torre as part of the socialist side of the indigenista movement. The party has, however, strayed from its socialist roots, having allied with the oligarchy in the 1950s, moved to populism in the 1980s and becoming firmly bourgeois in the 2000s (Manrique 2009).

12 Although Robles Mendoza sees García's funding of comunidad projects as unprecedented, Belaúnde had set up a fund called Cooperación Popular in the 1960s, offering support to poor communities to undertake their own projects (Parodi Trece 2000: 367).

13 Revisiting debates of the 1950s and 1960s, Urrutia (1992, 2001), Mayer (1996), and Golte (1992), among others, reject the notion that the peasant community is a relic of a pre-hispanic past, with its homogeneous and egalitarian communitarian structure surviving into the present. Rather, they argue that there are many types of communities, products of historical experience and of particular responses to state legislation (see also Mossbrucker 1990; Pajuelo 2000; Starn 1992). Among these, Mayer stands out as an emphatic defender of the ongoing viability of the comunidad.

14 *Hiladora* does not have the dual meaning in Spanish that it has in English, as both spinner and spinster/single woman: these women's marital status is separately listed.

15 We will return to the school in Chapter 8.

16 Similarly, Mallon (1983: 263–5) discusses the Yanamarca Valley, noting that while income from migrant labour supported infrastructural projects in their home villages, there were also tensions as the migrants then believed that this contribution exempted them from the need to donate their labour to community projects.

17 The 1987 data are based on interviews with representatives of 64 of the 89 households then resident in Allpachico. Most of these were from the hamlet of Allpachico proper, where 47 of 52 households were included. Four of those not included consisted of elderly single adults, so this age and economic activity category is underrepresented. From the highland hamlet of Trebol, I interviewed representatives of all three households, but did not do any interviews with people from the farthest hamlet, Kutru, where there were nine households at the time. In Colibrí, the other hamlet by the river, I interviewed 10 of 25 households. For the 2007 data, I was assisted in doing a census by someone who lives in Allpachico; she listed those living in Allpachico, Trebol, and Kutru. The 2007 data are thus more inclusive

than the 1987 data with respect to three of the four hamlets, but have no information about Colibrí. The long-standing tensions between the hamlets of Allpachico and Colibrí mean that there is less interaction between residents of those two hamlets.

18 Another major demographic change has been the reduction in family size. Where Tina had seven children, now women tend to have only one or two.

19 One man said that they had received pipes from the government, but this probably refers to a 1970s project which was never completed.

20 This is in contrast to the community of Cajas, within 30 km in the Mantaro Valley. Alberti and Sanchez (1974: 103–6) recount that Cajas received both government support for some of the materials and for technical supervision.

21 This predates the Multi-Need project to be discussed in Chapter 5.

22 Referring to legal battles over land in Mexico, Nuijten (2004) describes the constant promise of state intervention as a 'hope-generating machine,' luring peasants to continue to participate in a formal process that has continually failed them.

5 Teach a Man to Fish (and a Woman to Sew) . . . Integrated Rural Development and Basic Human Needs

1 The Comilla project in Bangladesh and the Puebla project in Mexico are other common models for Integrated Rural Development (Ruttan 1984).

2 Rondinelli (1979) lays the blame on the contradiction generated when governments tried to maintain a firm grasp on the content and form of development, in the face of a strategy that could only work if the people were accorded decision-making ability. As we will see in Chapter 8, this criticism is more recently relevant to the Peruvian participatory budgeting policy.

3 The *State of the Microcredit Summit Campaign Report 2009* begins with the announcement: 'In 2007, more than 100 million of the world's poorest families received a microloan' (Daley-Harris 2009: 1). For descriptions of microcredit programs see, e.g., Bernasek and Stanfield (1997) and Bornstein (1996). For critical analyses of microcredit, see, e.g., Brett (2006), Ehlers and Main (1998), Goetz and Gupta (1996), Hulme and Moore (2006), Kabeer (2005), and Sick (1997).

4 See also Gardner (1997) and Mosse (2005) on projects with changing goals over time.

5 For more detailed discussions of the political violence in Peru, see, e.g., Degregori (1990), Degregori and Rivera Paz (1993), Poole and Rénique (1992), Starn (1995), and Stern (1998).

6 See M. Smith (1991) on the vulnerability of development workers.

7 Cajamarca is a department in northern Peru.

8 Purchased firewood became quite common in the 1990s.

9 See Chapter 6 for further discussion of WID, GAD, etc. The incorporation of sewing and knitting machines in Peruvian development projects was widespread: during a 1997 educational seminar trip to Peru, in which I participated as a supervisor, I was struck by the number of different projects in Lima and in southern Peru that had this as a component aimed at women.

10 See, e.g., Bennholdt-Thomsen (1984), Rogers (1980), and Labrecque (1988). These writers complain that women in Third World countries are being turned into housewives or otherwise taught activities that correspond to the subordinated women's gender roles in the countries that fund the development projects. This is also discussed in Chapter 6.

6 Developing People: Gender and the Turn to Individuals as Foci of Development

1 While women were the most high profile target of individualized development, children and youth also received attention. Children had already been recipients of aid, especially through such NGOs as Save the Children (founded in 1919) and World Vision (founded in 1947). See http://www. savethechildren.net/alliance/about_us/index_byyears.html 1920s and http://www.wvi.org/wvi/wviweb.nsf/maindocs/E7809E562722923A8825 7375007659B0?opendocument.

2 See Rathgeber (1990) for a good overview of WID, WAD and GAD.

3 See also the four elements examined by Stromquist (2002).

4 It is worth mentioning here an earlier form of organization among Allpachiqueños sharing a common characteristic: migrants. Since perhaps the 1920s migrants' associations were common ways for men from a community who worked elsewhere to create a social network in work places away from home. They also served to generate resources for projects in their community of origin (e.g., Laite 1981; Mallon 1983; Paerregaard 1997; G. Smith 1989). In Allpachico, migrants helped with the purchase and transport of the church bell and built the first suspension bridge across the river around 1950. Through these contributions they could maintain their rights as members of the community, and also assert themselves as patrons. With the economic crisis and the disappearance of jobs in the regional mining towns, the Allpachico migrant associations disappeared during the 1980s. I am told there are groups of Allpachiqueños in Lima,

who meet to play soccer but do no other organizing. Thus, while the migrant men have contributed in the past, there is little evidence today of this collective spirit. Individual men remember the experience, and also make claims to their part in it. Further, these men, working during the heyday of Allpachiqueño migration, were able to invest some of their earnings either in productive resources in the community or elsewhere. Those who returned to Allpachico have pensions and can enjoy a somewhat better quality of life than their neighbours, depending on how long they worked, when they retired, and so on. There is occasional resentment expressed towards either particular migrants or migrants in general by other Allpachiqueños, over their wealth or their lack of willingness to contribute their labour to comunidad projects. In contrast to the organizations discussed in the rest of this chapter, then, the migrants were self-organized and shared a position of power relative to other Allpachiqueños. However, as we will see, there is a common tendency to individualization, and none of the groups have proved to be particularly sustainable over time.

5 Stromquist (2002: 30) charges that such education is reformist, not transformative, and does little to empower women.

6 Some do, however, make savoury food, such as tamales or hoof jelly, for sale. These can be made with a stove, and are time-consuming special foods.

7 Young women are less likely to be heavily engaged in these agricultural tasks now, partly as a result of the messages projects sent about women's proper role.

8 I consider the distinct implications of NGO- and government-sponsored projects in chapters 7 and 8.

9 They must also participate in parades when the mayor demands it.

10 This committee is connected to the comunidad, but would not exist were it not for the initiative of the women involved. Thus, it is really self-created.

11 In a similar case, a Peruvian researcher and community worker said he was disconcerted when women participants in a community leadership workshop all said they wanted to become heads of NGOs, a position they saw as having lucrative access to resources (Javier Ávila Molero, personal communication). See also A. Moser (2004).

12 See Vincent (1999) for a discussion of the continuities and changes in local gender roles.

13 The notion of social capital has become another development trend (e.g., Bebbington 2004; Fox and Gershman 2000; Mosse 2006; Woolcock and Narayan 2000), but not one that has so far made an explicit appearance in Allpachico.

14 All of the nurses in Allpachico and neighbouring communities have been women.

15 I return to this in Chapter 8.

7 NGOs, Infrastructure Projects, and Commodification

1 Part of this chapter is based on Vincent (2005b).

2 I should point out that there has continued to be widespread confidence in NGOs specializing in the area of human rights (Nash 2001; Youngers 2003). In Peru, the human rights sector has been much more independent of government since it was concern over the Fujimori government's human rights abuses that led to a growth in this area (Youngers 2003).

3 IRC (2003) recognizes that not all communities can afford the cost and suggests that very poor communities may need funding assistance. This would lead to some communities receiving more subsidies than others. This would not go unnoticed in Peru, where there is a high degree of sensitivity about who or which regions get support, as we see in various complaints by Allpachiqueños throughout this book.

4 For a more detailed history of NGOs in Peru, see Alasino (2008); Beaumont, Gamero, and Piazza (1996); Beaumont and Rossel (1992); Llona (2008); Sánchez León (1996); Toche (2003); and Zolezzi (1992).

5 Ávila Molero (2000: 429) cites figures of 218 for 1988 and 900 for 1996. If all sets of figures are accurate, then there was an increase of almost 500 in the two years between 1988 and 1990. In addition to the 1,060 officially registered NGOs in 2007, there were 142 ENIEX (foreign organizations involved in international technical cooperation) and 406 IPREDAs (private non-profit institutions receiving donations for assistance or educational purposes) (Llona 2008).

6 I am grateful to Patricia Tumialán Núñez, Rosa Flores Javier, and Janeth Castañeda Calderón, all then students in the Department of Anthropology at the Universidad Nacional del Centro in Huancayo, for undertaking the census. Manuel Gilvonio Perez assisted me in supervising them.

7 Beginning in August 1990, Alberto Fujimori undertook a Structural Adjustment Program to reorganize Peru's economy and government structure in order to be able to regain the support of the International Monetary Fund, the World Bank, and the International Development Bank. This support had been lost under the previous presidency of Alan García when he announced linking payments on Peru's foreign debt to export earnings. The World Bank accorded a loan of $300 million in 1992 in recognition of Fujimori's efforts (Gonzales de Olarte 1998: 18, 22, 41).

8 Congressman Luis Guerrero, e.g., a political chameleon who has represented five political parties of different leanings in his career as mayor of Cajamarca, member of Congress, and vice-presidential candidate, started his career in a development NGO and has continued his interest in and links to them (Anonymous 1996; Joseph 1997; Somos Perú 2000).

9 The change of focus from productivity to infrastructure parallels increased interest in the latter at the global level. Among the U.N. Millennium Development Goals (MDGs) proclaimed in 2000 is a target to halve the proportion of those without access to potable water. Support for water provision globally increased slowly between 1990 and 2004 (Clermont 2006). This tendency has been evident in Peru where the state has taken a central role, spending nearly $400 million on rural water projects in the 1990s, and establishing a dedicated state office on water, PRONASAR, in 2002 (PRONASAR 2006: 7). Thus, to some extent, Allpachico's opportunity to pursue a potable water project is a result of these national and international goals.

10 As mentioned in Chapter 5, the sale of the trucks raised concerns about where the proceeds went.

11 Susanne Matheson (in 1998) and Fabiana Li (in 1999) were most able assistants in this work. The surveys were random and informal but with consistent questions. We reached about half of the households throughout the comunidad with 43 respondents in 1998, supplemented by focus groups in 1999.

12 I return to this in Chapter 8.

13 That is, there was an elision between the hopes and expectations of some community members with the organizational apparatus of the comunidad.

14 Elsewhere (Vincent 2005a) I have elaborated on Allpachico's unhappy history of failed development projects, beyond those involving water distribution.

15 Break pressure tanks prevent the water from building up too much pressure as it runs downhill.

16 Note that she does not sell them – Mimi sees more potential in ties of reciprocity than in market exchange.

17 Over the life of the project, other reasons for delays included illness on the part of key Agua personnel, reorganization of the NGO, shortage of materials, and problems with the transport of materials.

18 Arguably, sustainability is more likely to be achieved through training to be able to maintain the technology, something Agua worked to ensure, and through an organizational structure that will be effective in enforcing rules, exacting penalties for misuse, repairing the system, and so on.

8 Participatory Budgeting: Accounting, Accountability, and Politics

1 An earlier version of this chapter was originally published as Vincent (2010).
2 The Peruvian currency has had a volatile exchange rate history with the U.S. dollar and has been converted twice over the time I have done field-work there: in 1985 the inti replaced the sol at a rate of 1,000 soles to one inti; and in 1990 the nuevo sol replaced the inti at a rate of 1,000,000 intis for one nuevo sol. The rate has stabilized over recent years. Here are some rough average exchange rates for the following periods: May 2000 – U.S. $1 = 3.47 soles; June 2006 – U.S. $1 = 3.37 soles; June 2007 – U.S. $1 = 3.21 soles; June 2008 – U.S. $1 = 2.92 soles.
3 See Article 3 'Objetivos' of the Ley No. 28056 Ley Marco del Presupuesto Participativo.
4 Of course, the state never really disappeared, as Kingfisher and Maskovsky observe (2008: 117). Rather, while the numbers of government employees and services for citizens declined, the role of facilitating trade and invest-ment, especially across borders, accelerated in support of global capitalist expansion.
5 It has been shown that restructuring in the form of political decentraliza-tion, a central element in the governance discussion and closely associated with participatory budgeting, does not necessarily lead to deeper democra-tization (Faletti 2005; Heller 2001).
6 Goldfrank (2006), in a broad comparison of Latin American cases, points to the failure of participatory budgeting to lead to more accountability and participation and better municipal government, partly because of how the laws were designed by actors with other objectives in mind. Further reasons had to do with local political resistance and conflictive society.
7 She criticizes the evaluation of the participants' 'dream list' of projects which she describes as a 'black box,' the internal workings of which are a mystery (2005a: 140). Further, she charges that the there is no guarantee that the participants in the workshops are representative of the population.
8 This has been encapsulated in Peruvian political analysis as *otoronguismo*, literally 'jaguarism,' deriving from the quip 'jaguars don't eat jaguars.' De-gregori and Meléndez explore this in the Fujimori era, focusing on elements of cynicism, pragmatic individualism, and venality (2007: 16) that they argue characterize the politics of the time. Recent discussions in the major national newspaper, *El Comercio,* demonstrate the ongoing relevance of oto-ronguismo (see, e.g., the editorial '¡Hasta dónde puede llegar el otorongu-ismo!' 27 Sept. 2008).

9 Note that Villa El Salvador is seen as the Peruvian success story to compare with the famous Brazilian Porto Alegre case (Hordijk 2005; Chambi Echegaray 2001; for Porto Alegre see, e.g., Abers 1998; Baiocchi 2001).

10 Benefits have also been noted, from the provision of services which did not exist before, and an increase in public participation in the local governance (Hordijk 2005). It is possibly linked to an increase in local tax revenues as people become aware that their taxes go to local projects (Cabannes 2004: 36).

11 The formatting is different between the two years, but the presentation appears much denser in 2008, as well as covering 28 pages (R.D. No. 012–2008-EF/76.01), compared with 16 for the instructions published in 2004 (R.D.No. 10–2004-EF/76.01).

12 '2. Los criterios para la priorización deben, en general, recoger las principales aspiraciones de la sociedad en términos del desarrollo. En el numeral 4 del Anexo se señala una matriz sugerida de criterios de priorización. Estos criterios incluyen niveles de pobreza por ingresos y por Necesidades Básicas Insatisfechas de población beneficiaria de las acciones: efecto en el empleo local; grupos vulnerables tales como niños, madres gestantes y lactantes, ancianos y personas con discapacidad; entre otros.

3. En función a los criterios antes mencionados se establecen puntajes que ayudarán a establecer una prioridad de las acciones. Tanto los criterios como los puntajes señalados en este Instructivo deben ser validados o reconsiderados en este Taller.'

13 This point was originally suggested to me by Manuel Gilvonio. I subsequently heard complaints from people in Piedra Blanca and Allpachico about this.

14 A Peruvian government presentation indicates that a heavy proportion of the spending is on infrastructure (Salhuana Cavides 2008). The same tendency has been noted in participatory budgeting outside Peru (Goldfrank 2007; Jeppesen 2002).

15 As we will see below, opening the books does not necessarily alleviate suspicion.

16 The *unidad impositiva tributaria* (UIT) is an amount used in various government calculations. It has risen steadily by about 100 nuevos soles per year from 2,900 soles in 2000 to 3,500 in 2008.

17 In all my interviews and conversations, only one person, someone who works for a multilateral agency, indicated that the people could choose what they wished.

18 Fabiola did tell me that improving the track so crops and lumber could be moved to market and getting the track lit so they could walk safely

at night would be good, but I have heard few other concrete suggestions from hamlet residents.

19 The lack of awareness of sources of funding and origins of projects was widespread among many women in the community. On the other hand, other women had detailed knowledge of programs and had been central to attracting them to Allpachico in the past.

20 The four anthropology students from the Universidad Nacional del Centro del Perú (UNCP) were: Tatiana Salas Bilbao, Andrea Ccahuana Belito, Gabriel Gilvonio Condeza, and Francis Obispo Romero in 2008. Professor Manuel Gilvonio assisted me in supervising their work.

21 The regional gold standard in terms of pay in 2006 was for permanent blue-collar workers at the American-owned Doe Run mining operation in La Oroya, who earned between 1,500 and 5,000 soles a month (CEPEMA 2007). By this time no one from Allpachico worked there, although the facility under other ownership had been a major employer in the past.

22 Data from the Ministerio de Economía y Finanzas indicates a maximum of 1,820 soles a month for the mayor of this district (MEF n.d.), so Pascal's charge may not be accurate

23 Being in town did not prevent sewing machines and motors for carpentry tools from being stolen in the early 1990s. See Chapter 5.

24 It is worth pointing out, however, that there is cross-fertilization between all arenas. Some people commented during the water project discussed in Chapter 7 that the mayor had become more visible in local support to avoid being upstaged.

25 Jeppesen (2002) notes the same tendency in Bolivia. Similarly, Medeiros (2001) observes the translation into technical concrete projects of people's needs, again for Bolivia.

26 See also Chapter 6.

27 A. Moser (2004: 222) cites Maruja Barrig as making the same point with respect to why Peruvian grassroots women's organizations do not choose productive projects.

9 Conclusion: Immanent Development in Capitalism

1 In the United States, e.g., surrogate mothers are learning to see their bodies as sites of production when they gestate babies for others, even while they may conceptualize their actions in the idiom of generosity (Ragoné 1996). Note that Ragoné does not argue that surrogacy is a capitalist relation.

2 In 2010, I was told by an intern about to go to the Mantaro Valley in Peru that the organization she was to work for was suggesting people in a

highland village purchase sweet potatoes for their vitamin C content. Sweet potatoes are grown in coastal Peru and tend to be used as a luxury food for special meals. Carrots, which are grown in the valley, would be a better choice, although again, they would have to be purchased by those living at higher altitudes.

3 See also Pratt (2007) with respect to commodification and local, authentic, and organic foods.

4 Life cycle here is meant to link an individual's life stage to wider historical patterns, especially as these relate to economic opportunities. See Vincent (2000).

5 This is not only a feature of the Global South. In Spain, e.g., the effect of unemployment is cushioned by reliance on family (Anonymous 2010). Family also continues to be enormously important in Allpachico.

References

Abers, Rebecca. (1998). From Clientelism to Cooperation: Local Government, Participatory Policy and Civic Organization in Porto Alegre, Brazil. *Politics and Society* 26/4: 511–37.

Adams, Bill. (1993). Sustainable Development and the Greening of Development Theory. In F.J. Schuurman, ed., *Beyond the Impasse: New Directions in Development Theory*, 207–22. London: Zed.

Adams, Richard. (1959). *A Community in the Andes: Problems and Progress in Muquiyauyo*. Seattle, WA: University of Washington Press.

– (1964). Politics and Social Anthropology in Spanish America. *Human Organization* 23/1: 1–4.

Alasino, Enrique. (2008). *Peru: Kingdom of the NGO? Donor Harmonisation: Between Effectiveness and Democratisation: Case Study III*. Madrid: FRIDE.

Alberti, Giorgio, and Rodrigo Sanchez. (1974). *Poder y Conflicto en el Valle del Mantaro, 1900–1974*. Lima: Instituto de Estudios Peruanos (hereafter IEP).

Almy, Susan. (1977). Anthropologists and Development Agencies. *American Anthropologist* 79/2: 280–92.

Alvarez, Rodrich A. (1995). Del Estado Empresario al Estado Regulador. In J. Cotler, ed., *Peru 1964–1994: Economía, Sociedad y Política*, 69–91 Lima: IEP.

Anderson, Benedict. (1991). *Imagined Communities: Reflections on the Origin and Spread of Nationalism*. London: Verso.

Andreas, Carol. (1989). People's Kitchens and Radical Organizing in Lima, Peru. *Monthly Review* 41/6: 12–21.

Anonymous. (1996). El Autobombo: El Ampe y el Gobierno. *Caretas* 1412. http://www.caretas.com.pe/1412/ampe/ampe.htm, accessed 18 April 2002.

Anonymous. (2010). Europe in Search of a Job: Spanish Unemployment. *Economist* 395/8677: 55.

APCI (Agencia Peruana de Cooperación Internacional). (2010). Website re 'Preguntas Frecuentes: Preguntas Acerca Inscripción de ONGD.' http://www.apci.gob.pe/pregunta_frecuente.php?TIPO=ONGD, accessed 12 June 2010.

Apthorpe, Raymond. (1972). The New Generalism: Four Phases in Development Studies in the First U.N. Development Decade. *Development and Change* 3/1: 62–73.

Arce, Alberto, and Norman Long, eds. (2000). *Anthropology, Development and Modernities: Exploring Discourses, Counter-Tendencies and Violence*. London: Routledge.

Arguedas, José María. (n.d.). Evolución de las Comunidades Indígenas. In *Dos Estudios sobre Huancayo*, 1–87. Huancayo: Universidad Nacional del Centro del Perú.

– (1968). *Las comunidades de España y del Perú*. Lima: Fondo Editorial Universidad Nacional Mayor de San Marcos.

Arias, Rosario, and Carlos Aramburú. (2003). Documento de Análisis del Discurso de las y los Beneficiarios de los Programas Estatales (ATU y CP). In Carlos Aramburú, ed., *Proyecto de Desarrollo Comunitario Auto-Sostenible en Perspectiva Comparada, Informe Final de Investigación –1era Etapa*, 64–122. Lima: CIES.

Ávila Molero, Javier. (2000). Los Dilemas del Desarrollo: Antropología y Promoción en el Perú. In Carlos Iván Degregori, ed., *No Hay País Más Diverso: Compendio de Antropología Peruana*, 413–42. Lima: Red para el Desarrollo de las Ciencias Sociales en el Perú.

Babb, Florence. (1985). Women and Men in Vicos: A Peruvian Case of Unequal Development. In William Stein, ed., *Peruvian Contexts of Change*, 163–210. New Brunswick, NJ: Transaction Books.

Baiocchi, Gianpaolo. (2001). Participation, Activism, and Politics: The Porto Alegre Experiment and Deliberative Democratic Theory. *Politics and Society* 29/1: 43–72.

– (2003). Emergent Public Spheres: Talking Politics in Participatory Governance. *American Sociological Review* 68/1: 52–74.

Basadre, Jorge. (1970). *Historia de la República del Perú, 1822–1933*. Lima: Editorial Universitaria.

Bauer, Ralph. (2001). Encountering Colonial Latin American Indian Chronicles. *American Indian Quarterly* 25/2: 274–311.

Bauman, Zygmunt. (1996). On Communitarians and Human Freedom: Or, How to Square the Circle. *Theory, Culture and Society* 13/2: 79–90.

Beaumont, Martín, Julio Gamero, and M. del Carmen Piazza. (1996). *Política Social y ONGs*. Lima: DESCO.

Beaumont, Martín, and María Alejandra Rossel. (1992). Las ONGDs en el Perú: Elementos Para un Balance Crítico. In Mario Zolezzi, ed., *La Promoción al Desarrollo en el Perú: Balance y Perspectivas*, 63–80. Lima: DESCO.

Bebbington, Anthony. (2004). Social Capital and Development Studies 1: Critique, Debate, Progress? *Progress in Development Studies* 4/4: 343–49.

Blondet, Cecilia. (2002). *El Encanto del Dictador: Mujeres y Política en la Década de Fujimori*. Lima: IEP.

Bondet, Cecilia, and Carmen Montero. (1995). *Hoy: Menú Popular, Comedores en Lima*. Lima: IEP.

Bennholdt-Thomsen, Veronika. (1984). Subsistence Production and Extended Reproduction. In Kate Young, Carol Wolkowitz, and Roslyn McCullagh, eds., *Of Marriage and the Market: Women's Subordination Internationally and Its Lessons*, 41–54. London: Routledge and Kegan Paul.

Bernasek, Alexandra, and James Ronald Stanfield. (1997). The Grameen Bank as Progressive Institutional Adjustment. *Journal of Economic Issues* 31/2: 359–66.

Boesten, Jelke. (2003). Poor Women in Peru: Reproducers of Poverty and Poverty Relievers. *Women's Studies Quarterly* 31/3–4: 113–28.

Bolton, Ralph, Tom Greaves, and Florencia Zapata, eds. (2010). *50 Años de Antropología Aplicada en el Perú: Vicos y Otras Experiencias*. Lima: IEP.

Bonilla, Heraclio. (1978). The War of the Pacific and the National and Colonial Problem in Peru. *Past and Present* 81: 92–118.

Bornstein, David. (1996). *The Price of a Dream: The Story of the Grameen Bank and the Idea that Is Helping the Poor to Change Their Lives*. New York: Simon and Schuster.

Boserup, Ester. (1970). *Women's Role in Economic Development*. New York: St Martin's Press.

Brett, John. (2006). 'We Sacrifice and Eat Less': The Structural Complexities of Microfinance Participation. *Human Organization* 65/1: 8–19.

Brohman, John. (1996). *Popular Development: Rethinking the Theory and Practice of Development*. Oxford: Blackwell.

Browman, David. (1974). Pastoral Nomadism in the Andes. *Current Anthropology* 15/2: 188–96.

– (1976). Demographic Correlations of the Wari Conquest of Junin. *American Antiquity* 41/4: 465–77.

Cabannes, Yves. (2004). Participatory Budgeting: A Significant Contribution to Participatory Democracy. *Environment and Urbanization* 16/1: 27–46.

Cameron, Maxwell. (1997). Political and Economic Origins of Regime Change in Peru: The Eighteenth Brumaire of Alberto Fujimori. In Maxwell Cameron and Philip Mauceri, eds., *The Peruvian Labyrinth: Polity, Society, Economy*, 37–69. University Park, PA: Pennsylvania State University Press.

Cammack, Paul. (2002). Neoliberalism, the World Bank and the New Politics of Development. In Uma Kothari and Martin Minogue, eds., *Development Theory and Practice*, 157–78. London: Palgrave.

Carstens, Peter. (1991). *The Queen's People: A Study of Hegemony, Coercion, and Accommodation among the Okanagan of Canada*. Toronto: University of Toronto Press.

Castree, Noel. (2003). Commodifying What Nature? *Progress in Human Geography* 27/3: 273–97.

CEPEMA. (2007). Perú – Doe Run en La Oroya: Impacto en los Derechos de las Mujeres. In *Estudios de los Impactos de los Proyectos de Inversión Extranjera en los Derechos Humanos: Aprender de las Experiencias de Comunidades en las Filipinas, Tibet, la República Democrática del Congo, Argentina y Perú*. n.p.: International Centre for Human Rights and Democratic Development. Http://www.dd–rd.ca/site/publications/index.php?lang=es.

Cernea, Michael. (1996). *Social Organization and Development Anthropology*. Washington, DC: World Bank.

Chambers, Robert. (1983). *Rural Development: Putting the Last First*. London: Longman.

– (1994a). The Origins and Practice of Participatory Rural Appraisal. *World Development* 22/7: 953–69.

– (1994b). Participatory Rural Appraisal (PRA): Analysis of Experience. *World Development* 22/9: 1253–68.

– (1994c). Participatory Rural Appraisal (PRA): Challenges, Potential and Paradigm. *World Development* 22/10: 1437–54.

– (1997). *Whose Reality Counts? Putting the First Last*. London: Intermediate Technology.

– (2008). *Revolutions in Development Inquiry*. London: Earthscan.

Chambi Echegaray, Gina. (2001). Desarrollo Local con Gestión Participativa – Villa El Salvador, Peru. Lima: Amigos de villa. http://www.amigosdevilla.it/Documentos/Presupuesto_partecipativo.pdf, accessed 28 Aug. 2008.

Chevalier, Jacques (1982). There Is Nothing Simple about Simple Commodity Production. *Studies in Political Economy* 7: 89–124.

Chretien, Jean. (2002). Text of Jean Chretien's Sept. 16 speech to the UN. *CP24 Toronto's Breaking News*. http://www.cp24.com/servlet/an/local/CTVNews/20020916/chretien_un_text_020916?hub=CP24Sports.

Cleaver, Frances. (1999). Paradoxes of Participation: Questioning Participatory Approaches to development. *Journal of International Development* 11: 597–612.

Clermont, Florence (2006) *Official Development Assistance for Water from 1990 to 2004*. Paris: World Council & World Water Forum. http:// www.

worldwatercouncil.org/fileadmin/wwc/Library/Publications_and_
reports/FullText_Cover_ODA.pdf

Cochrane, Glynn. (1971). *Development Anthropology*. Oxford: Oxford University Press.

Cohen, Jon. (1987). *Integrated Rural Development: The Ethiopian Experience and the Debate*. Uppsala: Scandinavian Institute of African Studies.

Coirolo, Luis, Keith McLean, Mondonga Mokoli, Andrea Ryan, Parmesh Shah, and Melissa Williams. (2001). *Community-Based Rural Development: Reducing Poverty from the Ground Up*. http:wbln0018.worldbank.org/ESSD/ardext. nsf/11ByDocName/CommunityBasedRuralDevelopment, accessed 16 April 2004.

Collins, Jane. (1984). The Maintenance of Peasant Coffee Production in a Peruvian Valley. *American Ethnologist* 11/3: 413–38.

Comisión de la Verdad y Reconciliación, Perú. (2004). *Hatun Willakuy: Versión Abreviada del Informe Final de la Comisión de la Verdad y Reconciliación*. Lima: Comisión de Entrega de la Comisión de la Verdad y Reconciliación.

Concha Posadas, Rafael Ruben. (1971). No Title. *El Correo*, 23 Oct.

Congress of Peru. (2003). *Diario de los Debates: Segunda Legislatura Ordinaria de 200228ᵃ J Sesión Jueves 22 de mayo*. http://www2.congreso.gob.pe/Sicr/DiarioDebates/Publicad.nsf/SesionesPleno/05256D6E0073DFE905256D870068 17BA, accessed 5 July 2006.

Contreras, Carlos. (1988). *Mineros y Campesinos en los Andes*. Lima: IEP.

Cooke, Bill, and Uma Kothari. (2001). The Case for Participation as Tyranny. In Bill Cooke and Uma Kothari, eds., *Participation: The New Tyranny?* 1–15. London: Zed.

Cotler, Julio. (1983). Democracy and National Integration in Peru. In Cynthia McClintock and Abraham Lowenthal, eds., *The Peruvian Experiment Reconsidered*, 3–38. Princeton, NJ: Princeton University Press.

Cowen, M.P., and R.W. Shenton. (1995). The Invention of Development. In Jonathan Crush, ed., *Power of Development*, 27–43. London: Routledge.

– (1996). *Doctrines of Development*. London: Routledge.

– (1998). Agrarian Doctrines of Development: Part II. *Journal of Peasant Studies* 25/3: 31–62.

Crabtree, John. (1998). Neopopulism and the Fujimori Phenomenon. In John Crabtree and Jim Thomas, eds., *Fujimori's Peru: The Political Economy*, 7–23. London: Institute of Latin American Studies, University of London.

Crewe, Emma, and Elizabeth Harrison. (1998). *Whose Development? An Ethnography of Aid*. London: Zed.

D'Altroy, Terence. (1987). Transitions in Power: Centralization of Wanka Political Organization under Inka Rule. *Ethnohistory* 34/1: 78–102.

D'Altroy, Terence, and Christine Hastorf. (1984). The Distribution and Contents of Inca State Storehouses in the Xauxa Region of Peru. *American Antiquity* 49/2: 334–49.

Daley-Harris, Sam. (2009). *State of the Microcredit Summit Campaign Report 2009*. Washington, DC: Microcredit Summit Campaign.

Davies, Thomas M. (1974). *Indian Integration in Peru: A Half-Century of Experience, 1900–1948*. Lincoln, NE: University of Nebraska Press.

De Soto, Hernando. (1987). *El Otro Sendero*. Bogota: Instituto Libertad y Democracia.

Degregori, Carlos Iván. (1990). *El Surgimiento de Sendero Luminoso: Ayacucho 1969–1979*. Lima: IEP.

– (2000). Panorama de la Antropología en el Perú: Del Estudio del Otro a la Construcción de un Nosotros Diverso. In Carlos Iván Degregori, ed., *No Hay País Más Diverso: Compendio de Antropología Peruana*, 20–73. Lima: Red para el Desarrollo de las Ciencias Sociales en el Perú.

Degregori, Carlos Iván, and Carlos Meléndez. (2007). *El Nacimiento de los Otorongos: El Congreso Durante los Gobiernos de Alberto Fujimori (1990–2000)*. Lima: IEP.

Degregori, Carlos Iván, and Carlos Rivera Paz. (1993). *Perú 1980–1993: Fuerzas Armadas, Subversión y Democracia: Redefinición del Papel Militar en un Contexto de Violencia Subversiva y Colapso del Régimen Democrático*. Lima: IEP.

del Castillo, Laureano. (1992). ¿Tienen Futuro las Comunidades Campesinas? *Debate Agrario* 14: 39–53.

Deustua, José. (1994). Mining, Markets, Peasants and Power in Nineteenth-Century Peru. *Latin American Research Review* 29/1: 29–54.

Dewind, Adrian. (1975). The Miners of Peru. *Science and Society* 39: 44–72.

Di Domizio, Anna, Stefano Marani, and Ricardo M. Salazar Mucha. (1987). *Diagnóstico de los Recursos Naturales y Propuestas para la Reestructuración del Territorio de una Comunidad Campesina, Junín, Perú*. unpublished report, in the author's possession.

Dickovick, J. Tyler. (2006). Municipalization as Central Government Strategy: Central-Regional-Local Politics in Peru, Brazil, and South Africa. *Publius: The Journal of Federalism* 37/1: 1–25.

Diez, Alejandro. (1999). Diversidades, Alternativas y Ambigüedades: Instituciones, Comportamientos y Mentalidades en la Sociedad Rural. In Víctor Ágreda, Alejandro Diez, and Manuel Glave, eds., *SEPIA VII: Perú: El problema agrario en debate*, 247–326. Lima: SEPIA.

Dobyns, Henry F., and Paul L. Doughty. (1971). A Note to Anthropologists. In Dobyns et al., eds., *Peasants, Power and Applied Social Change*, 18–20. Beverly Hills, CA: Sage.

Dobyns, Henry F., Paul L. Doughty, and Harold Lasswell. (1971a). Introduction. In Dobyns et al., eds., *Peasants, Power and Applied Social Change*, 9–17. Beverly Hills, CA: Sage.

–, eds. (1971b). *Peasants, Power and Applied Social Change: Vicos as a Model*. Beverly Hills, CA: Sage.

Doughty, Paul. (1987a). Against the Odds: Collaboration and Development at Vicos. In Donald D. Stall and Jean J. Schensul, eds., *Collaborative Research and Social Change: Applied Anthropology in Action*, 129–57. Boulder, CO: Westview.

– (1987b). Vicos: Success, Rejection and Rediscovery of a Classic Program. In Elizabeth M. Eddy and William L. Partridge, eds., *Applied Anthropology in America*, 2nd ed., 433–59. New York: Columbia University Press.

– (2005). Malinowski Award Lecture, 2005: Learn from the Past, Be Involved in the Future. *Human Organization* 64/4: 303–16.

– (2010). Trayectorias Antropológicas: Vicos y el Callejón de Huaylas, 1948 a 2006. In Bolton et al., eds., *50 Años de Antropología Aplicada en el Perú*, 83–122. Lima: IEP.

Earle, T., T. D'Altroy, C. Hastorf, C. Scott, C. Costin, G. Russell, and E. Sandefur. (1987). *Archaeological Field Research in the Upper Mantaro, Peru, 1982–83: Investigations of Inka Expansion and Exchange*. Los Angeles, CA: Institute of Archaeology, University of California.

Edelman, Marc, and Angelique Haugerud, eds. (2005). *The Anthropology of Development and Globalization,*. Malden, MA: Blackwell.

Edwards, Michael, and David Hulme. (1996). Introduction: NGO Performance and Accountability. In Michael Edwards and David Hulme, eds., *Beyond the Magic Bullet: NGO Performance and Accountability in the Post–Cold War World*, 1–20. West Hartford, CT: Kumarian.

Eguren, Fernando, Laureano del Castillo, and Zulema Burneo. (2009). Los Derechos de Propiedad Sobre la Tierra en las Comunidades Campesinas. *Economía y Sociedad* 71: 29–38.

Eguren, Fernando, Pedro Castillo, and Laureano del Castillo. (2008). *El Agro Peruano y Los Decretos Legislativos de 2008*. Lima: CEPES.

Ehlers, Tracy Bachrach, and Karen Main. (1998). Women and the False Promise of Microenterprise. *Gender and Society* 12/4: 424–40.

Ekholm Friedman, Kajsa, and Jonathan Friedman. (2008). *Historical Transformations: The Anthropology of Global Systems*. Lanham, MD: AltaMira Press.

El Comercio. (2004). Integrantes de ONG Aprodebi Entran en Claras Contra-
dicciones. *El Comercio*, a6, 3 July.

– (2008). ¡Hasta dónde Puede Llegar el Otoronguismo! *El Comercio*, 27 Sept.
2008. http://www.elcomercio.com.pe/edicionimpresa/Html/2008–09–27/
hasta-donde-puede-llegar-otoronguismo.html, accessed 27 Oct.
2008.

Equipo Peru-Need, Programa Sierra. (1996). *Informe Evaluativo y Balance de Trabajo con la Comunidad Campesina de 'Allpachico.'* Unpublished report, in the
author's possession.

Escobar, Arturo. (1995). *Encountering Development: The Making and Unmaking of
the Third World*. Princeton, NJ: Princeton University Press.

Espinoza Soriano, Waldemar. (1969). *Lurinhuaila de Huacjra: Un Ayllu y un Cu-
racazgo Huanca*. Huancayo: Casa de la Cultura.

– (1973). *Historia del Departamento de Junín*. Huancayo: Enrique Chipoco Tovar.

– (1986). *La Destrucción del Imperio de los Incas*. Lima: Amaru Editores.

– (1990). *Los Incas: Economía, Sociedad y Estado en la Era del Tahuantinsuyo*. Lima:
Amaru Editores.

Faletti, Tulia (2005) A Sequential Theory of Decentralization: Latin American
Cases in Comparative Perspective. *American Political Science Review* 99/3:
327–46.

Fairhead, James. (1993). Representing Knowledge: The 'New Farmer' in Research Fashions. In Johan Pottier, ed., *Practicing Development: Social Science
Perspectives*, 187–204. London: Routledge.

Favre, Henri. (1973). Remarques sur la Lutte des classes au Pérou pendant
la Guerre du Pacifique. In Centre d'Études et de Recherches sur le Pérou
et les Pays Andins. First Colloquium. *Littérature et Société au Pérou du XIX-
ième Siècle à Nos Jours*, 55–81. Grenoble: Université des langues et lettres de
Grenoble.

Ferguson, James. (1994). *The Anti-Politics Machine: 'Development,' Depoliticiza-
tion, and Bureaucratic Power in Lesotho*. Minneapolis: University of Minnesota
Press.

Fisher, William. (1997). Doing Good? The Politics and Anti-politics of NGO
Practices. *Annual Review of Anthropology* 26: 439–64.

Flores Galindo, Alberto. (1983). *Los Mineros de la Cerro de Pasco, 1900–1930*.
Lima: Pontificía Universidad Católica del Perú.

– (1987). La Crisis de la Independencia: El Perú y Latinoamérica. In Alberto
Flores Galindo, ed., *Independencia y Revolución 1780–1840*, 7–16. Lima: Instituto Nacional de la Cultura.

– (2010). *In Search of an Inca: Identity and Utopia in the Andes*. New York: Cambridge University Press.

Foucault, Michel. (1973). *The Order of Things: An Archaeology of the Human Sciences*. New York: Vintage.

Fox, Jonathan, and L. Dave Brown, eds. (1998). *The Struggle for Accountability: The World Bank, NGOs and Grassroots Movements*. Cambridge, MA: MIT Press.

Fox, Jonathan, and John Gershman. (2000). The World Bank and Social Capital: Lessons from Ten Rural Development Projects in the Philippines and Mexico. *Policy Sciences* 33/3–4: 399–419.

Frank, Andre Gunder. (1967). *Capitalism and Underdevelopment in Latin America: Historical Studies of Chile and Brazil*. New York: Monthly Review Press.

Fraser, Nancy. (2005). Reframing Justice in a Globalizing World. *New Left Review* 36: 69–88.

García de Castro, Lope. (1921). Letter from Acting Viceroy Lic. García de Castro to His Majesty, 6 May 1565. In R. Levillier, ed., *Gobernantes del Perú: Cartas y Papeles*, vol. 3, *Siglo XVI*, 59–60. Madrid: Sucesores de Rivadeneyra.

Gardner, Katy. (1997). Mixed Messages: Contested 'Development' and the 'Plantation Rehabilitation Project.' In Grillo and Stirrat, eds., *Discourses of Development*, 133–56.

Gardner, Katy, and David Lewis. (1996). *Anthropology, Development and the Post-modern Challenge*. London: Pluto.

Gaventa, John. (2004). Towards Participatory Governance: Assessing the Transformative Possibilities. In Hickey and Mohan, eds., *Participation*, 25–41.

Gill, Lesley. (1997). Power Lines: The Political Context of Nongovernmental Activity in El Alto, Bolivia. *Journal of Latin American Anthropology* 2/2: 144–69.

– (2000). *Teetering on the Rim: Global Restructuring, Daily Life, and the Armed Retreat of the Bolivian State*. New York: Columbia University Press.

Goetz, Anne Marie, and Rina Sen Gupta. (1996). Who Takes the Credit? Gender, Power and Control over Loan Use in Rural Credit Programs in Bangladesh. *World Development* 24/1: 45–63.

Goldfrank, Benjamin. (2006). Los Procesos de 'Presupuesto Participativo' en América Latina: Exito, Fracaso y Cambio. *Revista de Ciencia Política* 26/2: 3–28.

– (2007). Lessons from Latin America's Experience with Participatory Budgeting. In Anwar Shah, ed., *Participatory Budgeting*, 91–126. Washington, DC: IBRD/World Bank.

Golte, Jürgen. (1992). Los Problemas con las 'Comunidades.' *Debate Agrario* 14: 17–22.

Gonzales de Olarte, Efraín. (1998). *El Neoliberalismo a la Peruana: Economía Política del Ajuste Estructural, 1990–1997*. Lima: IEP.

– (1995). Transformaciones sin Desarrollo: Peru 1964–1994. In Julio Cotler, ed., *Perú 1964–1994: Economía, Sociedad y Política*, 41–68. Lima: IEP.

Goodsell, Charles. (1974). *American Corporations in Peruvian Politics*. Cambridge, MA: Harvard University Press.

Grillo, Ralph. (1985). Applied Anthropology in the 1980s: Retrospect and Prospect. In Grillo and Rew, eds., *Social Anthropology and Development Policy*, 1–36.

Grillo, Ralph, and Alan Rew, eds. (1985). *Social Anthropology and Development Policy*. London: Tavistock.

Grillo, R.D., and R.L Stirrat, eds. (1997). *Discourses of Development: Anthropological Perspectives*. Oxford: Berg.

Grompone, Romeo. (2005). Argumentos a Favor de la Participación en Contra de sus Defensores. In Patricia Zárate Ardela, ed., *Participación Ciudadana y Democracia: Perspectivas Críticas y Análisis de Experiencias Locales*, 13–86. Lima: IEP.

Grondín, Marcelo. (1978a). *Comunidad Andina: Explotación Calculada*. Santo Domingo: Secretaría de Estado de Agricultura de la República Dominicana.

– (1978b). Peasant Cooperation and Dependency: The Case of the Electricity Enterprises of Muquiyauyo. In Long and Roberts, eds., *Peasant Cooperation and Capitalist Expansion in Central Peru*, 99–128. Austin, TX: University of Texas Press.

Guijt, Irene, and Meera Kaul Shah, eds. (1998). *The Myth of Community: Gender Issues in Participatory Development*. London: Intermediate Technology.

Hackenberg, Robert A., and Beverly H. Hackenberg. (2004). Notes toward a New Future: Applied Anthropology in Century XXI. *Human Organization* 63/4: 385–99.

Halperin, Rhoda. (1998). *Practicing Community: Class, Culture and Power in an Urban Neighbourhood*. Austin, TX: University of Texas Press.

Hardt, Michael. (1995). The Withering of Civil Society. *Social Text* 14/4: 27–44.

Harris, Marvin (1995). *Cultural Anthropology*, 4th ed. New York: Harper Collins.

Harrison, Elizabeth. (2002). 'The Problem with the Locals': Partnership and Participation in Ethiopia. *Development and Change* 33/4: 587–610.

Hart, Keith. (1973). Informal Income Opportunities and Urban Employment in Ghana. *Journal of Modern African Studies* 2/1: 61–89.

Harvey, David. (1989). *The Condition of Postmodernity*. Oxford: Blackwell.

Hastorf, Christine. (1990). The Effect of the Inka State on Sausa Agricultural Production and Crop Consumption. *American Antiquity* 55/2: 262–90.

Hays-Mitchell, Maureen. (2002). Resisting Austerity: A Gendered Perspective on Neo-liberal Restructuring in Peru. *Gender and Development* 10/3: 71–81.

Heller, Patrick. (2001). Moving the State: The Politics of Democratic Decentralization in Kerala, South Africa and Porto Alegre. *Politics and Society* 29/1: 131–63.

Hemming, John. (1983). *The Conquest of the Incas*. London: Penguin.

Hewitt de Alcántara, Cynthia. (1998). Uses and Abuses of the Concept of Governance. *International Social Science Journal* 50/1: 105–13.

Hickey, Sam, and Giles Mohan. (2004a). Towards Participation as Transformation: Critical Themes and Challenges. In Hickey and Mohan, eds., *Participation*, 3–24.

–, eds. (2004b). *Participation: From Tyranny to Transformation? Exploring New Approaches to Participation in Development*. London: Zed.

Hillhorst, Dorothea. (2003). *The Real World of NGOs: Discourses, Diversity and Development*. London: Zed.

Himes, James R. (1981). The Impact in Peru of the Vicos Project. In George Dalton, ed., *Research in Economic Anthropology*, 141–213. London: IAI.

Holmberg, Allan. (1955). Participant Intervention in the Field. *Human Organization* 14/1: 23–6.

– (1971a). Experimental Intervention in the Field. In Dobyns et al., eds., *Peasants, Power and Applied Social Change*, 21–32. Beverly Hills, CA: Sage.

– (1971b). The Role of Power in Changing Values and Institutions of Vicos. In Dobyns et al., eds., *Peasants, Power and Applied Social Change*, 33–64.

Hopkins, Raúl. (1989). The Impact of Structural Adjustment on Agricultural Performance. In John Crabtree and Jim Thomas, eds., *Fujimori's Peru: The Political Economy*. London: Institute of Latin American Studies, University of London, 88–105.

Hordijk, Michaela (2005). Participatory Governance in Peru: Exercising Citizenship. *Environment and Urbanization* 17/1: 219–36.

Hulme, David, and Karen Moore. (2006). Why Has Microfinance Been a Policy Success in Bangladesh (and beyond)? Paper presented at the Seminar on Policy Success in Developing Countries, Manchester, UK, 20 May 2005. http://www.sed.man.ac.uk/idpm/staff/documents/DH_KM_130306_Microfinance_Bangladesh_Policy_000.pdf.

Hunefeldt, Christine. (1997). The Rural Landscape and Changing Political Awareness: Enterprises, Agrarian Producers, and Peasant Communities, 1969–1994. In Maxwell Cameron and Philip Mauceri, eds., *The Peruvian Labyrinth: Polity, Society, Economy*, 107–33. University Park, PA: Pennsylvania State University Press.

IRC (International Red Cross). (2003). *Thematic Overview Paper: Financing and Cost Recovery.* http://www.irc.nl/content/view/full/7583, accessed 28 April 2004.

Isbell, William. (1972a). Las Culturas Intermedias: 220 aC–600dC. In D. Bonavia et al., *Pueblos y Culturas de la Sierra Central del Perú,* 44–51. Lima: Cerro de Pasco.

– (1972b). Huari y los Orígenes del Primer Imperio Andino. In D. Bonavía et al., *Pueblos y Culturas de la Sierra Central del Perú,* 52–65. Lima: Cerro de Pasco.

Jelin, Elizabeth, and Brenda Pereyra. (1990). *Caring and Coping: Households, Communities and Public Services in the Making of Women's Daily Lives.* Buenos Aires: CEDES. http://www.cedes.org.ar/Publicaciones/Doc_c/Doc_c35.pdf, accessed 14 Jan. 2010.

Jennings, Justin. (2006). Core, Peripheries, and Regional Realities in Middle Horizon Peru. *Journal of Anthropological Archaeology* 25/3: 346–70.

Jeppesen, Anne Marie Ejdesgaard. (2002). Reading the Bolivian Landscape of Exclusion and Inclusion: The Law of Popular Participation. In Neil Webster and Lars Engberg-Pedersen, eds., *In the Name of the Poor: Contesting Political Space for Poverty Reduction,* 30–51. London: Zed.

Joseph, Jaime. (1997). The Round Table for Consensus Building in Cajamarca, Peru. *Grassroots Development* 21/1: 40–5.

Junta de Gobernadores, Fondo General de Contravalor Perú–Canadá. (1997). *Visión y Estrategia del Fondo General Contravalor Perú–Canadá, 1996–2000.* Lima: Fondo General de Contravalor Perú–Canadá. In the author's possession.

Kabeer, Naila. (1994). *Reversed Realities: Gender Hierarchies in Development Thought.* London: Verso.

– (2005). Is Microfinance a 'Magic Bullet' for Women's Empowerment? *Economic and Political Weekly,* 29 Oct., 4709–18.

Kamat, Sangeeta. (2002). *Development Hegemony: NGOs and the State in India.* New Delhi: Oxford University Press.

Khan, Akhter Hameed. (1997). The Orangi Pilot Project: Uplifting a Periurban Settlement near Karachi, Pakistan. In Anirudh Krishna, Norman Uphoff, and Milton Esman, eds., *Reasons for Hope: Instructive Experiences in Rural Development,* 25–40. West Hartford, CT: Kumarian.

Kingfisher, Catherine, and Jeff Maskovsky. (2008). Introduction: The Limits of Neoliberalism. *Critique of Anthropology* 28/2: 115–26.

Kitching, Gavin. (1982). *Development and Underdevelopment in Historical Perspective: Populism, Nationalism and Industrialisation.* London: Methuen.

Köhler, Ulrich. (1981). Integrated Community Development: Vicos in Peru. *Research in Economic Anthropology* 4: 111–40.

Kothari, Uma, ed. (2005). *A Radical History of Development Studies*. London: Zed.

Kurtz, Donald V. (1996) Hegemony and Anthropology: Gramsci, Exegetes, Reinterpretations. *Critique of Anthropology* 16/2: 103–35.

Kymlicka, Will. (2007). Multicultural Odysseys. *Ethnopolitics* 6/4: 585–97.

Labrecque, Marie France. (1988) Développement: La Question des Femmes. Le Cas de la Création des Unités Agricoles et Industrielles pour les Femmes, État du Yucatán, Méxique. *Documents de l'ICREF*, no. 18.

Laite, Julian. (1978). Processes of Industrial and Social Change in Highland Peru. In Norman Long and Bryan Roberts, eds., *Peasant Cooperation and Capitalist Expansion in Central Peru*, 72–97. Austin, TX: University of Texas Press.

– (1981). *Industrial Development and Migrant Labour in Latin America*. Austin, TX: University of Texas Press.

Laos, Alejandro, ed. (2004). *Comunidades Campesinas En El Siglo XXI: Situación Actual y Cambios Normativos*. Lima: Grupo ALLPA. http://www.landcoalition.org/pdf/05_ALLPA_Comunidades_Campesinas_en_siglo_XXI.pdf, accessed 4 June 2010.

Lash, Scott. (1996). Postmodern Ethics: The Missing Ground. *Theory, Culture and Society* 13/2: 91–104.

Laurie, Nina. (1997). Negotiating Femininity: Women and Representation in Emergency Employment in Peru. *Gender, Place and Culture* 4/2: 235–51.

Lewis, David. (1999). Revealing, Widening, Deepening? A Review of the Existing and Potential Contribution of Anthropological Approaches to 'Third Sector' Research. *Human Organization* 58/1: 73–81.

– (2005). Individuals, Organizations and Public Action: Trajectories of the 'Non–Governmental' in Development Studies. In Uma Kothari, ed., *A Radical History of Development Studies*, 200–21. London: Zed.

Lewis, David, and David Mosse, eds. (2006). *Development Brokers and Translators: The Ethnography of Aid and Agencies*. Bloomfield, CT: Kumarian.

Lewis, David, and Paul Opoku-Mensah. (2006). Moving Forward Research Agendas on International NGOs: Theory, Agency and Context. *Journal of International Development* 18/5: 665–75.

Leys, Colin. (1996). *The Rise and Fall of Development Theory*. London: EAEP, Indiana University Press and James Currey.

Li, Tania Murray. (2007). *The Will to Improve: Governmentality, Development and the Practice of Politics*. Durham, NC: Duke University Press.

Llona, Mariana. (2008). El Gobierno Aprista y las ONG: Un Nuevo Ciclo de Disputa por los Derechos. *Perú Hoy*, no. 13. http://www.desco.org.pe/apc–aa–files/d38fb34df77ec8a36839f7aad10def69/completo_PH_jul08.zip.

Lohmann Villena, Guillermo. (1967). Étude Préliminaire. In Guillermo Lohmann Villena, ed., *Juan de Matienzo Gobierno del Perú*, i–lxix. Paris: Institut
Français d'Études Andines.
– (1970). La Minería en el Marco del Virreinato Peruano. In *La Minería Hispana
e Iberoamericana: Contribución a Su Investigación Histórica, Estudios*, vol. 1,
639–55. León: Cátedra de San Isidoro.
Long, Norman. (1977). *An Introduction to the Sociology of Rural Development.*
London: Tavistock.
– (2001). *Development Sociology: Actor Perspectives.* London: Routledge.
Long, Norman, and Bryan Roberts, eds. (1978). *Peasant Cooperation and Capital-
ist Expansion in Central Peru.* Austin, TX: University of Texas Press.
Lowenthal, Abraham, (1983). The Peruvian Experiment Reconsidered. In
Cynthia McClintock and Abraham Lowenthal, eds., *The Peruvian Experiment
Reconsidered*, 415–30. Princeton, NJ: Princeton University Press.
MacEwan Scott, Alison. (1979). Who Are the Self-Employed? In Ray Bromley
and Chris Gerry, eds., *Casual Work and Poverty in Third World Cities*, 105–29.
New York: Wiley.
Mallon, Florencia E. (1983). *The Defense of Community in Peru's Central High-
lands: Peasant Struggle and Capitalist Transition, 1860–1940.* Princeton, NJ:
Princeton University Press.
– (1995). *Peasant and Nation: The Making of Postcolonial Mexico and Peru.* Berke-
ley, CA: University of California Press.
Mamdani, Mahmood. (1996). Indirect Rule, Civil Society, and Ethnicity: The
African Dilemma. *Social Justice* 23/1–2: 145–6.
Mangin, William (1979). Thoughts on Twenty-Four Years of Work in Peru: The
Vicos Project and Me. In George Foster et al., eds., *Long-Term Field Research
in Social Anthropology*, 64–84. New York: Academic.
Manrique, Nelson. (1981). *Las Guerrillas Indígenas en la Guerra con Chile.* Lima:
Centro de Investigación y Capacitación.
– (1987). *Mercado Interno y Región: La Sierra Central 1820–1930.* Lima: DESCO.
– (1988). *Yawar Mayu: Sociedades Terratenientes Serranas, 1879–1910.* Lima:
DESCO.
– (2009). *'¡Usted Fue Aprista!' Bases Para una Historia Crítica del APRA.* Lima:
Fondo Editorial de la Pontificia Universidad Católica del Perú and
CLACSO.
Marchand, Marianne. (2009). The Future of Gender and Development after
9/11: Insights from Postcolonial Feminism and Transnationalism. *Third
World Quarterly* 30/5: 921–35.
Marchesi, Giancarlo. (2003). Estudio de Caso I: El Programa a Trabajar Urbano
– Obra de Agua Potable del Barrio Las Lomas. In Carlos Aramburú, ed.,

Proyecto de Desarrollo Comunitario Auto-Sostenible en Perspectiva Comparada, Informe Final de Investigación – 1era Etapa, 33–46. Lima: CIES.

Matienzo, Juan de. (1967). Gobierno del Perú. In Guillermo Lohmann Villena, ed., *Juan de Matienzo Gobierno del Perú,* 1–366. Paris: Institut Français d'Études Andines.

Matos M.R. (1972). Alfareros y Agricultores. In D. Bonavia et al., *Pueblos y Culturas de la Sierra Central del Perú,* 34–43. Lima: Cerro de Pasco.

Mayer, Enrique (1972). Censos Insensatos: Evaluación de los Censos Campesinos en la Historia de Tangor. In John Murra, ed., *Iñigo Ortiz de Zúñiga's Visita de la Provincia de León de Huánuco en 1562,* vol. 2, 339–65. Huánuco, Peru: Universidad Nacional Hermilio Valdizán.

– (1991). Peru in Deep Trouble: Mario Vargas Llosa's 'Inquest in the Andes' Reexamined. *Current Anthropology* 6/4: 466–504.

– (1996). *Propiedad Comunal y Desarrollo.* http://www.andes.missouri.edu/andes/especiales/em_congreso.html, accessed 22 July 1999.

– (2010). Vicos como Modelo: Una Retrospectiva. In Bolton et al., eds., *50 Años de Antropología Aplicada en el Perú,* 237–76.

Mayer, Enrique, and Manuel Glave. (1999). 'Alguito para Ganar' (A Little Something to Earn): Profits and Losses in Peasant Economies. *American Ethnologist* 26/2: 344–69.

McNamara, Robert S. (1973). *Address to the Board of Governors, Nairobi.* http://siteresources.worldbank.org/EXTARCHIVES/Resources/Robert_McNamara_Address_Nairobi_1973.pdf, accessed 19 May 2006.

Medeiros, Carmen. (2001). Civilizing the Popular? The Law of Popular Participation and the Design of a New Civil Society in 1990s Bolivia. *Critique of Anthropology* 21/4: 401–25.

MEF (Ministerio de Economía y Finanzas). (n.d.). *Medidas Sobre los Ingresos de los Alcaldes.* http://www.mef.gob.pe/GOB_LOCAL/goblocal.php.

Meléndez, Carlos. (2005). Mediaciones y Conflictos: Las Transformaciones de la Intermediación Política y los Estallidos de Violencia en el Perú Actual. In Victor Vich, ed., *El Estado Está de Vuelta: Desigualidad, Diversidad y Democracia,* 159–83. Lima: IEP.

Mendoza Melendez, Eduardo. (n.d.). *Historia de la Campaña de la Breña.* Lima: Archivo del Centro de Estudios Históricos Militares del Perú.

Miller, Rory. (1986). Transferring Techniques: Railway Building and Management on the West Coast of South America. In R. Miller and H. Finch, *Technology Transfer and Economic Development in Latin America, 1850–1930,* 1–35. Liverpool: University of Liverpool, Institute of Latin American Studies.

Millones, Luis. (1973a). Un Movimiento Nativista del Siglo XVI: El Taki Onqoy. In Juan Ossio, ed., *Ideología Mesiánica del Mundo Andino*, 85–94. Lima: Prado Pastor.

– (1973b). Nuevos Aspectos del Taki Onqoy. In Juan Ossio, ed., *Ideología Mesiánica del Mundo Andino*, 97–101. Lima: Prado Pastor.

Mitchell, William. (2010). Esperanza Antropológica y Realidad Social: El Proyecto Vicos de Cornell Vuelto a Examinar. In Bolton et al., eds., *50 Años de Antropología Aplicada en el Perú*, 123–52. Lima: IEP.

Mitlin, Diana, Sam Hickey, and Anthony Bebbington. (2007). Reclaiming Development? NGOs and the Challenge of Alternatives. *World Development* 35/10: 1699–720.

Mohan, Giles. (1997). Developing Differences: Post-structuralism and Political Economy in Contemporary Development Studies. *Review of African Political Economy* 24/73: 311–28.

Mohan, G., and K. Stokke. (2000). Participatory Development and Empowerment: The Dangers of Localism. *Third World Quarterly* 21/2: 247–68.

Moser, A. (2004). Happy Heterogeneity? Feminism, Development, and the Grassroots Women's Movement in Peru. *Feminist Studies* 30/1: 211–37.

Moser, C. (1993). *Gender Planning and Development: Theory, Practice and Training*. London: Routledge.

Mossbrucker, Harald (1990). *La Economía Campesina y el Concepto 'Comunidad': Un Enfoque Crítico*. Lima: IEP.

Mosse, David. (2005). *Cultivating Development: An Ethnography of Aid, Policy and Practice*. London: Pluto.

– (2006). Collective Action, Common Property, and Social Capital in South India: An Anthropological Commentary. *Economic Development and Cultural Change* 54/3: 695–724.

Mumford, J. (1998). The Taki Onqoy and the Andean Nation: Sources and Interpretations. *Latin American Research Review* 33/1: 150–65.

Municipalidad Distrital de 'Piedra Blanca'. (2003) *Plan de Desarrollo Distrital 2003–2006*. Unpublished document, in the author's possession.

– (2007) *Plan de Desarrollo Distrital 2007–2015*. Unpublished document, in the author's possession.

Murra, John. (1978). Los Límites y las Limitaciones del 'Archipiélago Vertical' en los Andes. *AVANCES: Revista Boliviana de Estudios Históricos y Sociales*, no. 1: 75–80.

Narotzky, Susana, and Gavin Smith. (2006). *Immediate Struggles: People, Power and Place in Rural Spain*. Berkeley, CA: University of California Press.

Nash, June. (2001). *Mayan Visions: The Quest for Autonomy in an Age of Globalization*. London: Routledge.

Nolan, Riall. (2002). *Development Anthropology: Encounters in the Real World.* Cambridge, MA: Westview.

Nugent, David. (1994). Building the State, Making the Nation. *American Anthropologist* 96/2: 333–69.

Nuijten, Monique. (2004). Between Fear and Fantasy: Governmentality and the Working of Power in Mexico. *Critique of Anthropology* 24/2: 209–30.

Olivier de Sardan, Jean-Pierre. (2005). *Anthropology and Development: Understanding Contemporary Social Change.* London: Zed.

OneWorld. (1999). *Water and Sanitation: The Demand Responsive Approach in Rural Water and Sanitation. Report of an Electronic Discussion.* http://oneworld.org/thinktank/water/, accessed 18 Sept. 2003.

Orellana Valeriano, Simeon. (1973). Huacjlasmarca, un Pequeño Poblado Huanca. *Anales Científicos de la Universidad Nacional del Centro del Perú*, no. 2: 75–132.

Paerregaard, Karsten. (1997). *Linking Separate Worlds: Urban Migrants and Rural Lives in Peru.* Oxford: Berg.

Pajuelo, Ramón. (2000). Imágenes de la Comunidad: Indígenas, Campesinos, y Antropólogos en el Perú. In Carlos Iván Degregori, ed., *No Hay País Más Diverso: Compendio de antropología peruana*, 123–79. Lima: Red para el Desarrollo de las Ciencias Sociales en el Perú.

Parodi Trece, Carlos. (2000). *Perú: 1960–2000, Políticas Económicas y Sociales en Entornos Cambiantes.* Lima: Universidad del Pacífico.

Parpart, Jane, Shirin Rai, and Kathleen Staudt. (2002). Rethinking Em(power)ment, Gender and Development: An Introduction. In Jane Parpart, Shirin Rao, and Kathleen Staudt, eds., *Rethinking Empowerment: Gender and Development in a Global/Local World*, 3–21. London: Routledge.

Parsons, Jeffrey, and Ramiro Matos Mendieta (1978). Asentamientos Prehispánicos en el Mantaro, Perú – Informe Preliminar. In R. Matos M., ed., *El Hombre y la Cultura Andina, III Congreso Peruano*, vol. 2, 540–55. Lima: III Congreso del Hombre y la Cultura Andina.

Pastor, Manuel. (1992). *Inflation, Stabilization, and Debt: Macroeconomic Experiments in Peru and Bolivia.* Boulder, CO: Westview.

Peters, Pauline. (1996). 'Who's Local Here?' The Politics of Participation in Development. *Cultural Survival Quarterly* 20/3: 22–5.

Phillips, Sue and Richard Edwards. (2000). Development, Impact Assessment and the Praise Culture. *Critique of Anthropology* 20/1: 47–66.

Piel, Jean. (1967). À Propos d'un Soulèvement Rural Péruvien au Début du Vingtième Siècle: Tocroyoc (1921). *Revue d'Histoire Moderne et Contemporaine* 14: 375–405.

– (1970). The Place of the Peasantry in the National Life of Peru in the Nineteenth Century. *Past and Present*, no. 46: 108–33.

Pieterse, Jan Nederveen. (1998). 'My Paradigm or Yours? Alternative Development, Post-Development, Reflexive Development.' *Development and Change* 29: 343–73.

Pigg, Stacy Leigh. (1992). Inventing Social Categories through Place: Social Representations and Development in Nepal. *Comparative Studies in Society and History* 34/3: 491–513.

Pike, Frederick. (1967). *The Modern History of Peru*. New York: Praeger.

Pitt, David. (1976a). Development from Below. In Pitt, ed., *Development from Below*, 7–19.

–, ed. (1976b). *Development from Below: Anthropologists and Development Situations*. The Hague: Mouton.

Poole, Deborah, and Gerardo Rénique. (1992). *Peru: Time of Fear*. London: Latin America Bureau.

Pottier, Johan. (1997). Towards an Ethnography of Participatory Appraisal and Research. In Grillo and Stirrat, eds., *Discourses of Development*, 203–27.

Pratt, Jeff. (2007). Food Values: The Local and the Authentic. *Critique of Anthropology* 27/3: 285–300.

Pribilsky, Jason. (2010). El Desarrollo y el 'Problema Indígena' en los Andes Durante la Guerra Fría: Indigenismo, Ciencia y Modernización en el Proyecto Perú Cornell en Vicos. In Bolton et al., eds., *50 Años de Antropología Aplicada en el Perú*, 153–92.

PRONASAR. (2006). *Manual de Operaciones Revisado*. Lima: Ministerio de Vivienda, Construcción y Saneamiento/PRONASAR.

Purcell, Trevor. (1998). Indigenous Knowledge and Applied Anthropology: Questions of Definition and Direction. *Human Organization* 57/3: 258–72.

R.L.S. Antonio Raimondi – N° 132. (n.d.). Reseña Logia Antonio Raimondi 132. http://www.antonioraimondi132.org/resena.htm.

Radcliffe, Sarah. (1993). 'People Have to Rise Up – Like the Great Women Fighters': The State and Peasant Women in Peru. In Sarah Radcliffe and Sallie Westwood, eds., *'Viva': Women and Popular Protest in Latin America*, 197–218. London: Routledge.

Ragoné, Helena. (1996). Chasing the Blood Tie: Surrogate Mothers, Adoptive Mothers and Fathers. *American Ethnologist* 23/2: 352–65.

Rahnema, Majid. (1992). Participation. In Wolfgang Sachs, ed., *The Development Dictionary: A Guide to Knowledge as Power*, 116–31. London: Zed.

Rahnema, Majid, with Victoria Bawtree, eds. (1997). *The Post-Development Reader*. Halifax: Fernwood.

Ramirez, Susan. (1996). *The World Turned Upside Down: Cross Cultural Context and Conflict in 16th-Century Peru*. Stanford, CA: Stanford University Press.

Ramos, P., et al. (n.d.). No title. Unpublished m.s., in author's possession.

Rathgeber, Eva. (1990). WID, WAD and GAD: Trends in Research and Practice. *Journal of Developing Area Studies* 24: 489–502.

Ravines, R. (1972). Los Primeros Habitantes. In D. Bonavia et al., *Pueblos y Culturas de la Sierra Central del Perú*, 25–33. Lima: Cerro de Pasco.

Redfield, Robert. (1956). *The Little Community and Peasant Society and Culture*. Chicago, IL: University of Chicago Press.

Remy, María Isabel. (2005a). *Los Múltiples Campos de la Participación Ciudadana en el Perú*. Lima: IEP.

– (2005b). Los Gobiernos Locales en el Perú: Entre el Entusiasmo Democrático y el Deterioro de la Representación Política. In Victor Vich, ed., *El Estado Está de Vuelta: Desigualidad, Diversidad y Democracia*, 111–36. Lima: IEP.

Robles Mendoza, Román. (2002). *Legislación Peruana sobre Comunidades Campesinas*. Lima: Fondo Editorial de la Facultad de Ciencias Sociales, Universidad Nacional Mayor de San Marcos.

Rogers, Barbara. (1980). *The Domestication of Women: Discrimination in Developing Societies*. London: Tavistock.

Rondinelli, Dennis A. (1979). Administration of Integrated Rural Development Policy: The Politics of Agrarian Reform in Developing Countries. *World Politics* 31/3: 389–416.

Rose, Nikolas. (1999). *Powers of Freedom: Reframing Political Thought*. Cambridge: Cambridge University Press.

Roseberry, William. (1989). *Anthropologies and Histories: Essays in Culture, History, and Political Economy*. New Brunswick, NJ: Rutgers University Press.

Ross, Eric. (2010). Reflexiones sobre Vicos: La Antropología, la Guerra Fría y la Idea del Conservadurismo Campesino. In Bolton et al., eds., *50 Años de Antropología Aplicada en el Perú*, 193–236.

Rostow, W.W. (1961). *The Stages of Economic Growth: A Non-Communist Manifesto*. Cambridge: Cambridge University Press.

Rostworowski de Diez Canseco, María. (1988). *Historia del Tahuantinsuyu*. Lima: IEP.

– (2005). Redes Económicas del Estado Inca: El 'Ruego' y la 'Dádiva.' In Victor Vich, ed., *El Estado Está de Vuelta: Desigualdad, Diversidad y Democracia*, 15–47. Lima: IEP.

Rousseau, Stephanie. (2006). Women's Citizenship and Neopopulism: Peru under the Fujimori Regime. *Latin American Politics and Society* 48/1: 117–42.

Rowe, John. (1946). Inca Culture at the Time of the Spanish Conquest. In J. Steward, ed., *Handbook of South American Indians,* vol. 2, *The Andean Civilizations,* 183–330. Washington, DC: Smithsonian Institution.

– (1957). The Incas under Spanish Colonial Institutions. *Hispanic American Historical Review* 37/2: 155–99.

Ruttan, Vernon. (1984). Integrated Rural Development Programs: A Historical Perspective. *World Development* 12/4: 393–401.

Sachs, Jeffrey. (2005). *The End of Poverty: Economic Possibilities for Our Time.* New York: Penguin.

Sachs, Wolfgang, ed. (1992). *The Development Dictionary: A Guide to Knowledge as Power.* London: Zed.

Salas, María. (1994). The Technicians only Believe in Science and Cannot Read the Sky. In I. Scoones and J. Thompson, eds., *Beyond Farmers First: Rural People's Knowledge, Agricultural Research and Extension Practice,* 57–69. London: Intermediate Technology.

Salhuana Cavides, Roger. (2008). Participatory Budgeting in Peru, 2003–2008. Ministry of Economy and Finance, Peru. Presentation at the Africa Regional Seminar on Participatory Budgeting: Strengthening Budget Transparency, Participation, and Independent Oversight, Durban, South Africa, 10–13 March. http://web.worldbank.org/WBSITE/EXTERNAL/WBI/WBIPROGRAMS/CMUDLP/0,,contentMDK:21952519~pagePK:64156158~piPK:64152884~theSitePK:461754,00.html agenda, accessed 28 April 2009.

Sánchez León, Abelardo, ed. (1996). *Los Mundos del Desarrollo: 30 Años de Trabajo con ONGs.* Lima: DESCO.

Sánchez-Páramo, Carolina, et al. (2005). *Opportunities for All: Peru Poverty Assessment.* Washington, DC: World Bank. http://irispublic.worldbank.org/85257559006C22E9/All+Documents/85257559006C22E98525715B004B489C/$File/PeruPovertyAssessment2006.pdf, accessed 6 April 2010.

Sara, Jennifer. (2003). *Giving Communities Choice Is Not Enough!* http://www.wsp.org/english/conference/communities.html, accessed 18 Sept. 2003.

Sardenberg, Cecilia. (2008). Liberal vs. Liberating Empowerment: A Latin American Feminist Perspective on Conceptualising Women's Empowerment. *IDS Bulletin* 39/6: 18–27.

Sayer, Derek. (1994). Everyday Forms of State Formation: Some Dissident Remarks on 'Hegemony.' In Gilbert Joseph and Daniel Nugent, eds., *Everyday Forms of State Formation: Revolution and the Negotiation of Rule in Modern Mexico,* 367–77. Durham, NC: Duke University Press.

Scheper-Hughes, Nancy. (2000). The Global Traffic in Human Organs. *Current Anthropology* 41/2: 1191–224.

Scupin, Raymond. (2006). *Cultural Anthropology: A Global Perspective,* 6th ed. Upper Saddle River, NJ: Pearson, Prentice-Hall.

Seltzer, Geoffrey, and Christine Hastorf. (1990). Climatic Change and Its Effect on Prehispanic Agriculture in the Central Peruvian Andes. *Journal of Field Archaeology* 17/4: 397–414.

Sempat Assadourian, Carlos. (1994). *Transiciones hacia el Sistema Colonial Andino.* Lima: IEP.

Sen, Gita, and Caren Grown. (1987). *Development, Crises and Alternative Visions: Third World Women's Perspectives.* New York: Monthly Review Press.

Sick, Deborah. (1997). Coping with Crisis: Costa Rican Households and the International Coffee Market. *Ethnology* 36/3: 255–75.

Siddharth, Veena. (1995) Gendered Participation: NGOs and the World Bank. *IDS Bulletin* 26/3: 31–8.

Sider, Gerald. (1988). *Culture and Class in Anthropology and History: A Newfoundland Illustration.* Cambridge: Cambridge University Press.

Sillitoe, Paul. (1998). The Development of Indigenous Knowledge: A New Applied Anthropology. *Current Anthropology* 39/2: 223–52.

Silverblatt, Irene. (1987). *Moon, Sun and Witches: Gender Ideologies and Class in Inca and Colonial Peru.* Princeton, NJ: Princeton University Press.

– (1995). Becoming Indian in the Central Andes of Seventeenth Century Peru. In Gyan Prakash, ed., *After Colonialism: Imperial Histories and Post-Colonial Displacements,* 279–98. Princeton, NJ: Princeton University Press.

Slocum, Rachel, Lori Wichhart, Dianne Rocheleau, and Barbara Thomas-Slaytor, eds. (1995). *Power, Process and Participation: Tools for Change.* London: Intermediate Technology.

Smith, Gavin. (1985). Reflections on the Social Relations of Simple Commodity Production. *Journal of Peasant Studies* 13/1: 99–108.

– (1989). *Livelihood and Resistance: Peasants and the Politics of Land in Peru.* Berkeley: University of California Press.

– (2006). When 'The Logic of Capital Is the Real which Lurks in the Background': Programme and Practice in European 'Regional Economies.' *Current Anthropology* 47/4: 621–39.

Smith, Michael. (1991). *Rural Development in the Crossfire.* Ottawa: International Development Research Centre.

Somos Perú. (2000). Los Candidatos y sus Propuestas: Luis Bernardo Guerrero Figueroa. http://www.rcp.net.pe/elecciones/propuestas/somos–peru/lguerrero–semb.htm, accessed 18 April 2002.

Spalding, Karen. (1974). *De Indio a Campesino: Cambios en la Estructura Social del Perú Colonial*. Lima: IEP.

Starn, Orin. (1992). Antropología Andina, 'Andinismo' y Sendero Luminoso. *Allpanchis* 39: 15–71.

– (1994). Rethinking the Politics of Anthropology: The Case of the Andes. *Current Anthropology* 35: 13–38.

– (1995). Maoism in the Andes: The Communist Party of Peru – Shining Path and the Refusal of History. *Journal of Latin American Studies* 27/2: 399–421.

Starn, Orin, Carlos Ivan Degregori, and Robin Kirk, eds. (1995). *The Peru Reader: History, Culture, Politics*. Durham, NC: Duke University Press.

Stein, William W. (2003). *Deconstructing Development Discourse in Peru: A Meta-Ethnography of the Modernity Project at Vicos*. Lanham, MD: University Press of America.

Stern, Steve. (1993). *Peru's Indian Peoples and the Challenge of the Spanish Conquest: Huamanga to 1640*. Madison, WI: University of Wisconsin Press.

–, ed. (1998). *Shining and Other Paths: War and Society in Peru, 1980–1995*. Durham, NC: Duke University Press.

Stirrat, R.L. (2000). Cultures of Consultancy. *Critique of Anthropology* 20/1: 31–46.

Straughan, Baird. (2003). The Secrets of Ancient Tiwanaku Are Benefiting Today's Bolivia. In A. Podolefsky and P. Brown, eds., *Applying Anthropology: An Introductory Reader*, 86–91. Boston, MA: McGraw-Hill.

Streeten, Paul, with Shahid Javed Bukki, Marbub Ul Haq, Norman Hicks, and Frances Stewart. (1981). *First Things First: Meeting Basic Needs in Development Countries*. New York: Oxford University Press for the World Bank.

Streeten, Paul. (1995). *Thinking about Development*. Cambridge: Cambridge University Press.

Stromquist, Nelly. (2002). Education as a Means for Empowering Women. In Jane Parpart, Shirin Rao, and Kathleen Staudt, eds., *Rethinking Empowerment: Gender and Development in a Global/Local World*, 22–38. London: Routledge.

Sweezy, Paul M. (1997). More (or Less) on Globalization. *Monthly Review* 49/4: 1–4.

Tanaka, Martín. (2006). *Palabras Reflexivas del Sociólogo Martín Tanaka Respecto al Tema ONGs: El Acoso Contra ONGs Se Repite con Cada Gobierno*. http://marconaprotesta.wordpress.com/2006/09/13/palabras-reflexivas-del-sociologo-martin-tanaka-respecto-al-tema-ongs/.

Taussig, Michael. (1980). *The Devil and Commodity Fetishism in South America*. Chapel Hill, NC: University of North Carolina Press.

Terry, Geraldine, and Belinda Calaguas. (2003). *Financing the Millennium Development Goals for Water and Sanitation*. London: WaterAid.

Thompson, Donald. (1972). Etnias y Grupos Locales Tardíos. In D. Bonavia et al., *Pueblos y Culturas de la Sierra Central del Perú*, 66–75. Lima: Cerro de Pasco.

Thorp, Rosemary. (1983). The Evolution of Peru's Economy. In Cynthia McClintock and Abraham Lowenthal, eds., *The Peruvian Experiment Reconsidered*, 39–61. Princeton, NJ: Princeton University Press.

– (1991). *Economic Management and Economic Development in Peru and Colombia*. Pittsburgh, PA: University of Pittsburgh Press.

Thurner, Mark. (1995). 'Republicanos' and 'La Comunidad de Peruanos': Unimagined Political Communities in Post Colonial Peru. *Journal of Latin American Studies* 27/2: 291–318.

– (1997). *From Two Republics to One Divided: Contradictions of Postcolonial Nationmaking in Andean Peru*. Durham, NC: Duke University Press.

Toche, Eduardo. (2003). *ONG Enemigos Imaginados*. Lima: DESCO.

Trivelli, Carolina. (1992). Reconocimiento Legal de Comunidades Campesinas: Una Revisión Estadística. *Debate Agrario* 14: 23–37.

Truman, Harry. (1949). *Inaugural Address*. http://www.saidnews.org/history/United_States_Presidents/PDF_Presidents/President_Speeches/Htruman_1st_inaugural.pdf, accessed 6 Jan. 2010.

Tvedt, Terje. (2006). The International Aid System and the Non-Governmental Organisation: A New Research Agenda. *Journal of International Development* 18/5: 677–80.

Tullis, F. Lamond. (1970). *Lord and Peasant in Peru: A Paradigm of Political and Social Change*. Cambridge: Harvard University Press.

UNDP (United Nations Development Program). (n.d.). Millennium Development Goals Frequently Asked Questions. http://www.undp.org/mdg/faqs.html, accessed 12 Aug. 2004.

Urrutia, Jaime. (1992). Comunidades Campesinas y Antropología: Historia de un Amor (Casi). Eterno. *Debate Agrario* 14: 1–16.

– (2001). La Comunidad Campesina Reinventada: El Ejemplo de Cumbico, Cajamarca. *Debate Agrario* 32: 1–12.

Vincent, Susan. (1992). *Crisis and Livelihood Strategy in the Central Peruvian Andes*. Doctoral dissertation, University of Toronto.

– (1999). Género y Desarrollo: Género ≠ Mujer/madre. Paper presented at the Universidad Nacional del Centro, Huancayo, Peru. 6 July.

– (2000). Flexible Families: Capitalist Development and Crisis in Rural Peru. *Journal of Comparative Family Studies* 31/2: 155–70.

– (2003). Preserving Domesticity: Reading Tupperware in Women's Changing Domestic, Social and Economic Roles. *Canadian Review of Sociology and Anthropology* 40/2: 171–96.

– (2005a). Participation, Resistance and Problems with the Local in Peru: Towards a New Political Contract? In Sam Hickey and Giles Mohan, eds., *Participation*, 111–24. London: Zed.

– (2005b). *Cooperación Internacional, Desarrollo y Comunidades Campesinas: ¿Del Asistencialismo al Libre Mercado?* Lima: IEP.

– (2005c). Localizing State Practices in the Translocal Community. Paper presented at CASCA Conference, Merida, Mexico. 5 May.

– (2010). Participatory Budgeting in Peru: Democratization, State Control or Community Autonomy? *Focaal: Journal of Global and Historical Anthropology* 56: 65–77.

Wachtel, Nathan. (1973). Rebeliones y Milenarismo. In J. Ossio, ed., *Ideologia Mesiánica del Mundo Andino*, 105–42. Lima: Prado Pastor.

Wallace, Anthony F.C. (1956). Revitalization Movements: Some Theoretical Considerations for Their Comparative Study. *American Anthropologist* n.s. 58/2: 264–81.

Wallerstein, Immanuel. (1974). *The Modern World-System: Capitalist Agriculture and the Origins of the European World Economy in the Sixteenth Century*. New York: Academic.

Webster, Andrew. (1992). *Introduction to the Sociology of Development*, 2nd ed. Houndsmill: Macmillan.

Webster, Neil, and Lars Engberg-Pedersen, eds. (2002). *In the Name of the Poor: Contesting Political Space for Poverty Reduction*. London: Zed.

Williams, Raymond. (1983). *Keywords: A Vocabulary of Culture and Society*. New York: Oxford University Press.

Wolf, Eric. (1955). Types of Latin American Peasantry: A Preliminary Discussion. *American Anthropologist* 57(3): 452–71.

– (1957). Closed Corporate Communities in Mesoamerica and Java. *Southwestern Journal of Anthropology* 13/1: 1–18.

– (1982). *Europe and the People without History*. Berkeley, CA: University of California Press.

– (1986). The Vicissitudes of the Closed Corporate Community. *American Ethnologist* 13/2: 325–29.

– (1990). Distinguished Lecture: Facing Power – Old Insights, New Questions. *American Anthropologist* 92/3: 586–96.

– (1999). *Envisioning Power: Ideologies of Dominance and Crisis*. Berkeley, CA: University of California Press.

Woolcock, Michael, and Deepa Narayan. (2000). Social Capital: Implications for Development Theory, Research and Policy. *World Bank Research Observer* 15: 225–49.

Youngers, Coletta. (2003*). Violencia Política y Sociedad Civil en el Perú: Historia de la Coordinadora Nacional de Derechos Humanos.* Lima: IEP.

Zaidi, S.A. (1999). NGO Failure and the Need to Bring Back the State. *Journal of International Development* 11: 259–71.

Žižek, Slavoj. (2009). *First as Tragedy, Then as Farce.* London: Verso.

Zolezzi, Mario, ed. (1992). *La Promoción al Desarrollo en el Perú: Balance y Perspectivas.* Lima: DESCO.

Index

accounting: logic of in participatory budgeting, 10, 134, 138, 141–8, 153, 154, 162

Adams, R., 23–4, 43, 46, 47

agriculture: desire of farmers for improvements to, 141; in Integrated Rural Development, 9, 22, 23; in participatory budgeting plan, 151; policy linked to economic crisis, 165; in prehistory, 31–4; in projects in Allpachico, 69, 81–3, 86–8, 90–2, 160; role of women in, 94, 100. *See also* farming, decline of in Allpachico

Agua (NGO), 115, 120–4, 128, 129, 131, 161, 164

alienation, 13, 55, 119, 120, 128, 131, 147

Allpachico: autonomous development by comunidad of, 18, 61, 67–9; description of, 3, 5–6, 163; development projects received by comunidad of, 69–70, 72–92, 120, 121, 164; founding of, 46–7, 59–60; as general community, 5, 6, 7, 10, 18, 154, 157; and the state, 5, 20, 46, 47, 60–1

Ana, 106–7

anthropology and development, 8, 11, 21–8

Antonio, 65, 66, 126

asistencialismo (welfarism), 128, 130

Basic Human Needs Development, 10, 72–76, 94, 111, 135

capitalism: analysis of, 11–18, 158–9, 165–6, 171nn1, 3; compared to Inca accumulation, 35; compared to Spanish feudal extraction, 44; Peruvian, 8, 14, 55, 56–7; promotion of in development, 8, 23, 24, 28, 75, 119, 135, 154, 155, 158. *See also under* crisis

capitalist consumerism, 103, 110, 113, 114, 131, 161, 162

capitalist production, 13, 58, 159–61, 163

capitalist rationality, 44, 159, 166; calculation of value, 8; contradicts expectation of community contribution, 10, 113–14, 117, 128–32, 154; infiltration with development

ANTHROPOLOGICAL HORIZONS

Editor: Michael Lambek, University of Toronto

Published to date: